The Language of Fiction in a World of Pain

University of Pennsylvania Press

NEW CULTURAL STUDIES SERIES

Joan DeJean, Carroll Smith-Rosenberg, and Peter Stallybrass, Editors

Alex Owen. *The Darkened Room: Women, Power and Spiritualism in Late Victorian England.* 1990.

Barbara J. Eckstein. *The Language of Fiction in a World of Pain: Reading Politics as Paradox.* 1990.

The Language of Fiction
in a World of Pain:
Reading Politics as Paradox

BARBARA J. ECKSTEIN

University of Pennsylvania Press / PHILADELPHIA

Copyright © 1990 by the University of Pennsylvania Press
Printed in the United States of America

Library of Congress Cataloging-in-Publication Data

Eckstein, Barbara J.
    The language of fiction in a world of pain: reading politics as
paradox / Barbara J. Eckstein.
        p.   cm. — (New cultural studies series)
    Includes bibliographical references and index.
    ISBN 0-8122-8254-X (cloth). — ISBN 0-8122-1321-1 (pbk.)
    1. Fiction—History and criticism.   2. Feminism and literature.
3. Politics in literature.   4. Politics and literature.   5. Women in
literature.   6. Feminist literary criticism.   I. Title.
II. Series.
    PN3401.E25   1990
    809.3'9358—dc20   90-39345
                                                        CIP

*Permissions are listed after the index and should be considered a continuation of the
copyright page.*

for John, whose kindness abides

Contents

Preface

I began writing this book in 1987. Since that time the leadership has changed in every one of the homelands of the writers I examine: Czechoslovakia, Japan, South Africa, and the United States. Some of these changes came as a surprise; others did not. Whether or not any of these changes in leadership will result in greater justice and less suffering remains to be seen. Whether or not these changes will result in wider awareness of political paradox and less assertion of political polarity also remains to be seen. I hope with a modest, deconstructive hope. If a more romantic hope proves justified, I will be glad my circumspection was unnecessary.

I *am* certain of my gratitude to those who helped me with this manuscript through advice and encouragement: John Cooke, John Gery, Patricia Smith of the University of Pennsylvania Press, Austin M. Wright, and several anonymous readers. I would also like to thank my colleagues in Educators for Social Responsibility for years of provocative conversation and Mackie J. V. Blanton for the loan of his computer.

4 December 1989
New Orleans

She died   a famous woman   denying
her wounds
denying
her wounds   came   from the same source as her power

Adrienne Rich, "Power"

Chapter I

Power and Wounds

Literature and Politics

A survey of contemporary attitudes about the relationship of literature and politics is a walk in a mine field. Opinions are so many and so deeply planted that I am bound to overlook one even as I am standing on it. So I go forward gingerly but not fearfully because my metaphor reminds me of the distance between the risks of literature and the risks of politics even as I bind them together. I am a white woman from the central United States. I have never witnessed the explosion of a mine.

I begin with the most basic questions. Are literature and the study of it political? Should they be? Assumptions run both ways. Those who assume that the study of what is called literature is not sufficiently political are often marxists. Take, for example, Terry Eagleton: "[Criticism] engages at no significant point with any substantive social interest, and as a form of discourse is almost entirely self-validating and self-perpetuating."[1] Or Frank Lentricchia:

> We have let our beliefs and our discourse be invaded by the eviscerating notion that politics is something that somehow goes on somewhere else, in the "outside" world, as the saying goes, and that the work of culture that goes on "inside" the university is somehow apolitical—and that this is a good thing.[2]

And yet marxists are not necessarily content with the work of other marxists. Again it is Terry Eagleton who, despite praise for Fredric Jameson, argues that in *The Political Unconscious* Jameson still leaves the outside world to the politicians and writes only for literary critics.[3] Edward Said agrees with this assessment (though notes the paradox of Eagleton's chiding Jameson even as he identifies with the same marxist school of literary interpretation) and adds,

> Unlike France, high culture in America is assumed to be above politics as a matter of unanimous convention. And unlike England, the intellectual center here is filled not by European imports (although they play a considerable role) but by an unquestioned ethic of objectivity and realism, based essentially on an epistemology of separation and difference.[4]

I am in sympathy with such statements, and yet the more of them that I find, the more I wonder about this inside/outside split. Who assumes high culture is only "inside," above politics? In *Criticism and Social Change,* Lentricchia accuses Paul de Man. But Lentricchia is not entirely successful in demonstrating that Kenneth Burke's form of deconstruction, praised as political (that is, politically correct), is distinctly different from de Man's deconstruction, criticized as antipolitical (that is, politically incorrect). Who is responsible for divorcing literature from politics, if indeed they are divorced?

In the United States conventional notions about the estranged relationship of literature and politics run to two extremes. On the one hand is the belief that literature and, especially, literary theory are nihilistic or struggling with nihilism and that this is responsible for the split between literature and politics. For example, in *Atrocity and Amnesia: The Political Novel Since 1945,* Robert Boyers admires the political novel but expresses disdain for "la nouvelle critique." By this he means most all theory written since the sixties, but deconstruction in particular. He assumes all deconstructionists resist not only meaning but also ethics. In contrast, he praises Irving Howe's 1957 text *Politics and the Novel* (now revised). Boyers defines politics by the public actions of nation-states and the political novel by its subject: it has "something to do with ideas about community, collective action, and the distribution of power." Firm beliefs allowing for firm authority are the basis of Boyers's literary and political values. "To be serious about politics is after all to believe that there is such a thing as legitimate authority, which owes its legitimacy to binding truths on which it can take its stand."[5]

The popularity of the term "postmodern" seems to exacerbate the animosity that those, like Boyers, feel for deconstruction; postmodern suggests that contemporary culture is somehow after the fact, even after the fact of life. Postmodern fiction or theory seems by its very name to be nihilistic. In contrast, those who want theory and fiction of certain political values admire writers, such as Milan Kundera or Nadine Gordimer, whose governments have provided solid targets for resistance at which these writers are perceived to be taking steady aim.

Accusations that deconstruction is antipolitical or apolitical seem to be aimed at statements such as Paul de Man's that

> we end up therefore, in the case of rhetorical grammatization of semiology, just as in the grammatical rhetorization of illocutionary phrases, in the same state of suspended ignorance. . . . The resulting pathos is an anxiety (or bliss, depending on one's momentary mood or individual temperament) of ignorance, not an anxiety of reference.[6]

Or they are aimed at statements such as J. Hillis Miller's that "this thread is like the filament of ink which flows from the pen of the writer, keeping him in the web but suspending him also over the chasm, the blank page that thin line hides."[7] However, in defense of the social responsibility inherent in deconstruction, Christopher Norris chooses different passages from de Man, such as:

> What we call ideology is precisely the confusion of linguistics with natural reality, of reference with phenomenalism. It follows that, more than any other mode of inquiry, including economics, the linguistics of literariness is a powerful and indispensable tool in the unmasking of ideological aberrations, as well as a determining factor in accounting for their occurrence.[8]

In *Marxism and Deconstruction,* Michael Ryan asserts that this social theory and this philosophy both conclude that "philosophy cannot be apolitical and that politics often rests upon philosophic or conceptual presuppositions." He also forcefully argues that

> the deconstructive critique of absolutist concepts in the theory of meaning can be said to have a political-institutional corollary, which is the continuous revolutionary displacement of power toward radical egalitarianism and the plural defusion of all forms of macro- and microdomination. In many ways deconstruction is the development in philosophy which most closely parallels such events in recent critical marxism as solidarity, autonomy, and socialist feminism.[9]

Defense of the politics of deconstruction notwithstanding, the debate between socialists or marxists and deconstructionists is only one of the battles about the relationship of literature and politics.

The other conventional notion about the relationship of literature and politics is held by the descendents of the New Critics. These bearers of what Said calls "objectivity and realism" maintain the separation of art and politics which Said and the marxists abhor. This still-dominant tradition implies, sometimes asserts, that political art or political interpretation results in propaganda, and propaganda is always a pejorative term. The reticence of these humanists to address politics suggests that they associate propaganda with Nazi or Stalinist programmed art in particular and manipulative political rhetoric in general. For them politics *is* propaganda. It lacks "negative capability." It lacks subtlety. It addresses a popular audience. It is what art must not be.

Criticizing deconstruction and in the process defining himself as "old-fashioned," M. H. Abrams seeks confirmation of his objective interpretation when he says, "Such criticism has nothing whatever to do with our common experience of the uniqueness, the rich variety, and the passionate human concerns in works of literature, philosophy, or criticism."[10] Abrams defines, by omission, the purview of New Critical humanists: "our common experience" (not theirs) and "works" of culture (but not of politics). Abrams opposes what he labels the "graphocentric model" of deconstruction and the nihilism he sees resulting from it, but he never suggests that this narrow graphocentricity, as he sees it, is objectionable because it is politically irresponsible. The suggestion is instead that deconstruction is cold or abstract or amoral.

Ironically, some "objectivists and realists" seem ready to connect the alleged nihilism of deconstruction—particularly as practiced by Paul de Man—with the ambiguous, early, anti-Semitic writing of de Man.[11] The fact that fascism is not the absence of but rather a preponderance of absolute moralistic and political belief makes it a particularly odd fellow of deconstruction and nihilism. But apparently what Sander Gilman says about stereotypes, which use a few facts and many myths to create analogies joining together blacks, Jews, and women as inferior others,[12] is here true of a wholly different set of disparate others. Deconstructionist, nihilist, and Nazi are illogically brought together to play the part of the inhumane other threatening the humanists' study of literature.

Humanists also eschew marxism and other left-leaning polemics—or any explicit articulation of politics—as antithetical to the humane purposes of art. As the board of a state Endowment for the Humanities recently told me, the study of the humanities does not include the study of politics. Opposition to apartheid notwithstanding, even Nadine Gordimer wants it understood, "I'm a writer. I'm not a polemicist; I'm not a politician; I'm not a propagandist."[13]

Are literature and the study of it political? Should they be? While some answer "no, but they should be" and others answer "no, and they shouldn't be," yet others answer "yes." The latter assume that literature is, by its nature as a cultural phenomenon, always political. Most often it is feminists who make this assumption. For example, in her introduction to *The New Feminist Criticism,* Elaine Showalter writes of Sandra Gilbert: "She argues that feminist criticism cannot limit itself to literature by women, for every text can be seen as determined by aesthetic and political assumptions about gender that might be called 'sexual poetics.'"[14] In her introduction to *Writing and Sexual Difference,* Elizabeth Abel extends this assertion about literary texts by averring that textual politics need not exclude larger political contexts.[15] With some reservations, Terry Eagleton concurs, "The women's movement has reformulated in a historic move the relations between public and 'intimate' spheres."[16] If it functions as it is described, feminist interpretation makes salient the politics inherent in any text, fictional (literary) or not.

To the question of whether literature should be political, both marxists and feminists would answer yes. Both concern themselves with voiced authority in relation to silent histories. And yet the two define and pursue politics differently. The pluralities within marxism and within feminism and the intercourse between them are richly cultivated fields.[17] I will not glean them here, however, because it is politics in contemporary fiction, and not marxism or feminism per se, that is my subject. I have begun with these two movements because, at this juncture in the twentieth century, they have asked the questions most relevant to the study of politics in fiction. But individuals who do not describe themselves as distinctly marxist or feminist, such as Henry Louis Gates, Jr., Sander Gilman, and Edward Said, ask equally provocative political questions finding their locus in "race" or ethnicity rather than class or gender.

I need not now assume, as Said did a half-dozen years ago, that "high culture in America is . . . above politics as a matter of unanimous convention." Although within the United States academy, in the classroom and in print, many scholars maintain the conventional separation of art and politics which Said decries, I need not imagine that I am alone in my conviction that fiction is political and interpretation a necessarily political act. Nor need I assume that this conviction in itself aligns me unequivocally with any one political ideology. My task, as I have defined it, is not to prove that fiction and interpretation are political texts, that politics is intellectually worthy of consideration, or that one political ideology is the measure of any text's worth. Rather it is to stipulate a definition of politics, from "literary" and "political" sources, and to present a method for reading politics in contemporary fiction. Finally, it is to offer a definition of good political fiction.

Politics and Desire

In *Criticism and Social Change,* Frank Lentricchia defines politics as literature. Politics is a war of representations between conservatives (status quo) and radicals (change), and literature is those representations. (In this definition of politics, there are no liberals; liberals are only uncomfortable conservatives.) Lentricchia's theory embraces political rhetoric, drawing it into the literary world. As did Kenneth Burke, Lentricchia even includes within his embrace the term "propaganda." While maintaining a distrust of nihilistic deconstruction, Lentricchia seeks to reconcile and then erase the estrangement between literature and politics. Literature, he argues, must first of all see itself as more than only imaginative writing. In all its manifestations literature must own up to its responsibility to create desire through its representations, its rhetoric. Both Burke and Lentricchia conclude that rhetoric may pursue and produce cultural ends they would not want. Nevertheless, they insist, tropes must be used for social change; literature, that is, rhetoric, is more effective political work than pamphleteering. Even though the "epistemological claims of representation" may be undercut by deconstruction—understood as the source of nihilism—"the real work of representation [is] its work of power." The politics, the representations, one desires should be a synecdoche for the larger cultural whole so that one's politics is naturally irresistible. In this definition of politics, the proposed method for change is marxian, and the goal is "the formation of genuine community. Marxism as a kind of rhetoric, a reading of the past and present, invites us to shape a certain future: an invitation to practice, not epistemology."[18]

Václav Havel, George Konrád, and Christa Wolf, three writers living in what, until very recently, were communist bureaucratic states (Czechoslovakia, Hungary, and East Germany, respectively), all share Lentricchia's attraction to a genuine community but not his will-to-power politics. Havel speaks of ad hoc communities which spring up spontaneously but do not seek an accumulation of power.[19] And in describing community, Konrád writes, "We speak of circles of friends in which the free and equal relations of autonomous individuals are more valuable than the alleged effectiveness of the organs of power."[20] Similarly, Wolf thinks of her friends around the dinner table as a little utopian community and imagines many such utopias in a troubled world.[21] Even Wolf, who is a proclaimed socialist and a publicly acclaimed novelist in East Germany, steps gingerly around ideologies of collective community. Havel and Konrád actively eschew such collectivism. Within Lentricchia's own argument the path to the genuine community bound by rhetoric is strewn with disclaimers and loopholes: rhetoric cannot predict its results; rhetoric can be used with various goals in mind. One concludes that even a modest desire for a modest community requires skepticism.

Though all literature is political rhetoric, its agenda vary greatly. And the desires it creates, whether consciously or not, vary as much. Prescribing the subject for the political novel as Boyers does (it has "something to do with community") or prescribing the goal for all literature as Lentricchia does ("the formation of genuine community") will not enhance readers' understanding of what politics is and how to read it. If I describe rather than prescribe politics, I can say that politics is the use of language, with or without violence, to produce power. As politics is usually practiced, language is used to produce the power of what asserts itself as not-other over what is asserted as other. Politics is of the state and of the self.

Unlike Lentricchia, who writes of a binary opposition between stasis (conservatives) and change (radicals), Czech playwright—and president—Václav Havel notes an internal division. Havel asserts that, in a post-totalitarian state (that is, a communist, totalitarian bureaucracy), the conflict between the aims of life (plurality, independence, freedom to work in the area of one's training) and the system has not been one between two separate communities: the dividing line runs through each individual. Each, in differing degrees, is a supporter and victim of the system.[22] Hungarian novelist George Konrád, Havel, and Havel's colleagues have not aspired and do not aspire to power in opposition to a diabolical will, and yet they continue to seek change, a movement away from bureaucratic systems which paralyze government and clients. Even when Peter Uhl, an essayist in Havel's Charter 77 text, *The Power of the Powerless,* suggests the possible necessity of violent revolt, he defines "politics as an effort to emancipate the oppressed and manipulated and do[es] not confuse politics with a desire for power."[23] Konrád distances himself even farther from a will to power (that is, state power) in *Antipolitics.* He contends that the power of the state (what he calls politics) is irreconcilable with the power of the spirit (antipolitics). "Antipolitics is the political activity of those who don't want to be politicians and who refuse to share in power."[24] And yet Konrád too seeks social change. Despite their important differences, Lentricchia, Havel, Konrád, and Wolf all see the need for literature to participate in the process of change for a more secure and just world, as they define it. Change is the nexus of literature and politics.

Of course, one way or another change will occur. To define United States conservatives as maintaining the status quo and United States radicals as advocating change—as is conventionally done and as Lentricchia does—is to ignore the full array of possible change and the arguments for and against it. Environmental activists, whose activities are perceived as radical, devote their energies to preserving wilderness areas while United States supporters of the Nicaraguan resistance, whose ideas are perceived as conservative, have devoted their energies to changing the government of Nicaragua. Change is central to politics and yet change does not clearly divide one ideology from another.

Radicalism and Change

Three dangerous issues persist into the late twentieth century. Change will in some way work on all of them. They are the nuclear weapons race (the recalcitrant bureaucracy provoking both Wolf's *Cassandra* and Konrád's *Antipolitics*); the violence and economic inequity perpetuated by myths about "race," gender, class, ethnicity, or any other; and severe ecological mismanagement. How is change likely to occur at the end of the twentieth century? From what quarter is it likely to come? How does the politics of change manifest itself in contemporary fiction? To analyze the efficacy of any single movement for change and its possible influence in the culture at large requires a more precise definition, than any I have so far considered, of the supposed vehicle for political change: radicalism. Seweryn Bialer, a scholar of comparative communism and revolutionary change, offers such a definition in *Sources of Contemporary Radicalism*.[25]

Bialer's method is to present common conceptions of radicalism and to examine the validity of such assumptions. He considers first the assumption that radicalism is fundamentally militant, an assumption that perceives radicalism as more focused on means than ends. Bialer replies that militancy is not a necessary and sufficient condition of radicalism and that militancy and violence have much more often been the means of nation-states than of radical movements. He also responds to the assumption that radicalism is a desire for change in core inequities of a system. Bialer counters that this definition implies one right radicalism, namely marxism, and does not even address the plurality of marxism. In addition, the marxist stress on the

> primacy of the economic roots of all inequities negates or ignores the importance of the self-consciousness of the various radical impulses. . . . It ignores or at least minimizes the fact that what are perceived as core inequities may and do differ drastically from different vantage points in society.[26]

Finally, this definition limits radicalism to the left's quest for freedom from injustice and inequality when, in fact, successful radical movements in the twentieth century have brought about inequities at least equal to those they replaced. Also, Bialer reminds us, some of the twentieth century's most successful radical movements have come from the far right.

Bialer defines radicalism as having three attributes: (1) radicalism has an openness in choosing its methods and does not confine itself to existing political structure, (2) radicalism has a commitment to structural change of the existing order, and (3) radicalism projects goals into the future and has a "coherent vision of a better order."[27] Though Bialer's purview is primarily industrial democratic states, while Havel and Konrád have concerned themselves with communist totalitarian states, all three analysts focus on the growing bureaucracy of the state as the major change in state-client relationships in the late twentieth century. Havel and Konrád suggest and Bialer asserts that marxian theory is unprepared to deal with this contemporary reality. With characteristic appreciation of paradox, Havel spoke late in 1989 of Marx: "And what about Marx's words? Did they serve to illuminate an entire hidden plane of social mechanisms, or were they just the inconspicuous germ of all the subsequent appalling gulags. I don't know: most likely they were both at once."[28]

Bialer notes that the character of intellectuals in contemporary industrialized democracies differs from the intelligentsia of the past. Thus, to anticipate an intelligentsia as the principal carrier of new discontent may well be inappropriate. Traditionally, as in nineteenth-century Russia, the intelligentsia is estranged from the ruling elite because it aspires to advance society as a whole, not just its own material interests. But when writing in 1977 of radicalism in the late twentieth century, Bialer saw part of the intellectual elite serving the political elite and part of the intellectual elite estranged from it. The influence of intellectuals through government consultation, the expanded educational establishment, the revolution in communications, and the international nature of discontent together present a very different context for radical intellectuals from that of seventy or a hundred years ago. Bialer finds present-day radical intellectuals isolated from organized, lower-class radicalism and, in their alienation, contributing to a "wide-spread feeling of cultural discontinuity," "a state of chaos, uncertainty, and drift."[29]

Bialer penetrates a number of conventional assumptions about radicalism and offers in their place a working description of radicalism in a contemporary context. What he does not do, in this introduction to *Sources of*

Contemporary Radicalism, is consider contemporary radicalism in the context of the nuclear weapons competition, a condition that may well contribute to "a state of chaos, uncertainty, and drift." Both Konrád's *Antipolitics* (1984) and Wolf's *Cassandra* (1984) are explicitly motivated by anger at and anxiety about the superpowers' nuclear arms race. Bialer's 1986 book, *The Soviet Paradox,* does include a consideration of the arms race and the precarious conditions of the nuclear age, particularly those pertaining to the military and ideological competition between the United States and the Soviet Union. Perhaps he explains his reasons for excluding nuclear issues from the earlier survey of contemporary radicalism when he asserts, *"in the 1970s no policy towards the Soviet Union would have worked.* American paralysis denied credibility to any coherent policy."[30]

Bialer also does not mention feminism in his assessment of radicalism. Responding to these omissions, I would like to examine both the antinuclear movement and, to a greater extent, the feminist movement in light of Bialer's definition of radicalism. Both nuclearism and feminism are fundamental conditions of late twentieth-century life and art. They speak to the relationship of literature and politics and the place of change in that relationship. One might as fruitfully examine the radicalism of the right—various sects of religious fundamentalism, for example. It too participates in the struggle to control change and the relationship between literature and politics. The important task is to reexamine assumptions about radicalism and change.

Bialer's first criterion for radicalism is that it does not confine itself to existing political structure. But like the United States civil rights movement, the antinuclear movement in the United States has participants who, for the most part, choose to act within the established laws.[31] And yet no laws exist that oppose nuclear proliferation as federal civil rights laws opposed state segregation laws. Daniel Berrigan observes that if there were a nuclear holocaust, the whole thing would be legal.[32] Neither the allocation bills passing through Congress nor the free market laws of supply, demand, and competition, as they are manipulated by defense contractors and the nuclear industry, serve the antinuclear movement.[33] International agreements limiting testing and system deployments, such as the Limited Test Ban Treaty or the Antiballistic Missile Treaty, are the only kinds of laws that do serve the antinuclear movement. It has every reason to be a radical movement which chooses methods outside the existing political structure, and a few individuals, like Father Berrigan, do.

Most participants in the United States antinuclear movement have not been radical apparently because the majority's vision of the future is one of a capitalist democracy changed only in having less dependence on a nuclear defense and far fewer nuclear warheads. Commitments to structural change and the kind of coherent vision that Bialer describes appear absent. Critics, left and right, of the United States antinuclear movement fault it for lacking a coherent vision. Its apparently confused or "conservative" goal should, however, be evaluated in its context. The bureaucracy of which Bialer speaks is the opponent of the movement, and that bureaucracy of government, military, and industry is broad and deep. Direct action (lying on railroad tracks over which missile parts are transported, sitting on test sites, breaking into weapons plants) is of some spiritual significance to some small group within the movement but, for lack of numbers or of media attention, has not provided spiritual and/or political leadership for the populace. Many who have persisted in their commitment to nuclear disarmament have found themselves faced with the inertia, if not the power, of their bureaucratic opponent and the inadequacy of their own vision.

Even individuals who oppose the arms race most often separate nuclear politics (a national security decision) from culture (including literature). So, for example, when Terrence Des Pres or those individuals represented in the *Nuke-Rebuke* anthology of poems do speak of political poetry, they mean only that which directly addresses military decisions made by the government;[34] they do not include poems about the paradox of uncertain survival and certain annihilation, poems like Thom Gunn's "The Annihilation of Nothing" or John Ashbery's "Absence of a Noble Presence."[35] They do not assume that the inertia of bureaucracy and pervasiveness of nuclearism cuts through each individual (the state and all its clients, as Havel presents it). Nor do they assume that politics is culture and culture is politics.

Psychiatrist Robert Jay Lifton defines nuclearism as a cultural condition. Particularly in the book *Indefensible Weapons,* which he wrote with political scientist Richard Falk, Lifton explores nuclearism. Lifton speaks of the fundamental absurdity that life goes on as usual even as we hold in our minds the understanding, if not the imagery, of annihilation. And he speaks of the "sense of mystery," "the sense of [nuclear weapons] possessing more-than-natural (supernatural) destructive power. This sense of mystery is bound up with the weapons' relationship to the *infinite*." In addition, Lifton describes the paradox of depending on nuclear weapons for security while fearing the instability they create. Lifton describes his overall concern as "our mental relationship to the instrument we have created and our altered relationship to life and death resulting from its presence among us."[36] Lifton does not address reductionists, who wonder if the arms race has raised the teenage suicide rate or increased our hedonistic tendencies—though these things may be true. Nuclearism is a condition, a web of paradox, of all our lives; we defend against and write about its absurdities as our individual characters allow. Other eras have had their cultural paradoxes. This is one of ours.

For state and military planners, as well as every other client of the state, nuclearism is a paradox. After an exhaustive analysis of military strategy and of the developments in nuclear weaponry, Lawrence Freedman concludes that "nuclear strategy" is an oxymoron. Strategy is a series of steps, a plan. But the use of even smaller "tactical" nuclear weapons so thoroughly destroys a target that it prohibits the subsequent use of soldiers or conventional machinery to claim that territory. The whole purpose of battle, territorial gain, and war, political gain, cannot be strategically achieved.

> At the end of 35 years of attempts at constructing nuclear strategies one is forced to the conclusion that . . . if strategic thought in the future is to consist of no more than permutations of old concepts in response to new military capabilities . . . then it may have reached a dead end. For the position we have reached is one where stability depends on something that is more the antithesis of strategy than its apotheosis—on threats that things will get out of hand, that we might act irrationally.[37]

In *The Fate of the Earth,* Jonathan Schell's eloquent compilation of some of the best thinking about nuclearism, he writes of second death, the death of death.[38] In our cultural consciousness is the recognition that the cycle of life-death-mourning-birth (the cycle which permits Walt Whitman to present "Death, death, death, death, death" as the key to life) can be annihilated. Extinction would be the end of grief and ideas, life and art. Literature—always, somehow, about life and death—must contend with a desire and loss different in kind, not just in degree. Authors and readers must not only acknowledge that literature creates desire, as Lentricchia insists, but also that it now does so in the contemporary paradoxical context that is nuclearism.

Nuclearism, imbedded in our bureaucracy and consciousness, is a difficult opponent for a movement, even one that wants to be radical, let alone

one that does not. Those in the movement who apply a marxian analysis to the arms race see the problem as inequitable distribution of wealth and sow their energy in domestic social movements. Certainly a substantial amount of money is now spent on nuclear technology even though it was originally perceived to be a military and energy bargain. Nevertheless, the cries for redistribution of wealth and social reform have very little effect domestically or internationally on the nuclear bureaucracy and consciousness. They present no radical challenge to the existing order.

Those in the peace movement who seek a more concrete opponent turn their protest to the United States' involvement in the affairs of foreign nation-states, most recently Nicaragua, El Salvador, and Panama. This protest keeps politics in its place, government and the military, and focuses its opposition on those opponents. Without drawing conclusions about the justice of the protest or about its chances for success, I am, however, willing to suggest that the movement is not, by Bialer's definition, fundamentally radical. If the United States did not intrude itself into the affairs of Central American nations, this would certainly be a major change in policy. But would it require the sort of structural change in the existing order which Bialer describes? The much more massive movement protesting United States' involvement in Vietnam included some extreme behavior and yet even its effects on the United States political structure and cultural consciousness were not sustained, perhaps because at "the heart of the [sixties] counter-culture was not commitment but withdrawal."[39]

Radical behavior, that is, behavior most able to instigate and control change, is not necessarily the most exotic or militant behavior. Rather, effective radical behavior is thorough in its analysis of the system that it wishes to change. Radical individuals see beneath a system's power and into the assumptions supporting its structure. If a radical movement particularly aspires to elicit change in support of social justice and economic equity, then it must also move beyond a certain and unbending designation of its opponents and extend its analysis to include its own ongoing participation in the system it proposes to undermine. Radical individuals must consider internal difference.

The most radical and humane possibilities for the antinuclear, or peace, movement are those which perceive and address paradox and uncertainty, those which try to present a social, psychological, historical, and rhetorical analysis of the whole condition, and those which propose action based on that analysis. The psychohistorical analysis of Lifton, the philosophical analysis of Schell, and the military analysis of Freedman are all radical in their implications. Those who study connections between nuclearism and gender politics offer another radical possibility. For example, Brian Easlea, a science historian and nuclear physicist, has researched both the history of science and the feminist analysis of rhetoric. In his *Fathering the Unthinkable,* he argues that the gender division of labor, evident in science and in child-rearing, has made possible an isolated, male-dominated nuclear science whose rhetoric and technology seek to master nature. From Francis Bacon to René Descartes to the Manhattan project, a prevalent line of scientific development has sought dominance of a nature it described with female metaphors.[40] The goal of such a study is not narrowly to lay blame but broadly to radicalize assumptions about history, science, rhetoric, and culture.

As Bialer states, and Havel and Konrád concur, that opposition which is most militant is not necessarily most radical or most likely to result in structural change, particularly in large bureaucracies, particularly in the nuclear age.[41] Furthermore, they question the ability of marxism to answer the present need for change perceived by radicals in "first-" and "third-world" nation-states. Feminists Adrienne Rich and Dorothy Dinnerstein also doubt that marxist economic theory of bourgeois and proletarian classes is an adequate explanation of the world's primary relationships.[42]

At this moment in history, it is feminism that most fully incorporates the attributes of radicalism which Bialer delineates. Having largely extricated itself from association with the 1960s old New Left, feminism has unearthed its historical roots from sources far deeper than the nineteenth-century suffrage movement. Feminism has found its ideological base in all theories which describe the highly political structure of what is conventionally understood to be outside politics. The work of Michel Foucault, for example, participates in what I am calling feminism. Whether writing of prisons or madness or sex, Foucault shows how political structures have controlled private as well as public life. In *The History of Sexuality,* for example, he argues that excessive discourse about sex and the family has thoroughly manipulated and institutionalized these "private" areas of life, not suppressed them.[43] In just such a way, feminism does not confine its analysis to what is conventionally understood as existing political structures. To confront the institutions of sexuality, motherhood, and the family as political constructs and the production of desire as a political activity is a radical change in the conception of society.

Feminism has a commitment to structural change of the existing order. Rich quotes several women who assert this.

> Elizabeth Oakes-Smith, an early-nineteenth-century suffragist, writer, and preacher, had demanded in 1852: "Do we really understand that we aim at nothing less than an entire subversion of the present state of society, a dissolution of the whole existing social compact?" By 1970, Shulamith Firestone was responding: "Rather than concentrating the female principle into a 'private' retreat . . . we want to rediffuse it—for the first time creating society from the bottom up." And Mary Daly continued, in 1973: "Only radical feminism can act as the 'final cause', because of all revolutionary causes it alone *opens up human consciousness* adequately to the desire for non-hierarchal, nonoppressive society revealing sexism as the basic *model* and source of oppression. (emphasis mine)[44]

To those who think of feminism solely as the liberation of middle-class housewives from their homes or as the license to be sexually promiscuous, the idea that sexism, and not racism or classism, is the source of oppression is absurd. In a private conversation with me, in the spring of 1987, Nadine Gordimer responded to a question about the women's movement by saying she thought men suffered as much as women. To her sexism is not the source of oppression of all kinds. It is true that the young black man in Soweto suffers more violently than the white housewife in Durban. No one could honestly deny that. But it is the structural causes of everyone's suffering which must be analyzed—not only the comparative degrees of violence which must be measured—if we intend subsequent change to alleviate suffering.

Though some in the women's movement began by setting up a binary opposition between men and women, the movement's best philosophers saw a system of patriarchy which allowed for, even encouraged, oppression of all sorts. This is what requires analysis and radical action. In explaining her statement to Rich, Daly writes

> ["Final cause"] is motivating purpose, an insight which elicits seeking, movement. It is "first in the order of intention," opening the subject to action. . . . So to say the Women's Movement is the final cause is to mean it sets many-dimensional movements in motion, e.g. liberation of children, of the aged, of the racially oppressed. To say this is to see a priority for the women's movement as catalyst, as *the* necessary catalyst—hardly to see it as a self-enclosed system.[45]

Feminism's goal, its vision for the future, is a political order in which relationships between mother and child, woman and man, and thus, employee and employer, African and Afrikaner have all been self-consciously revealed as political and radically altered to diminish oppression. Feminism is open in its methods, being sometimes Freudian, sometimes marxian, sometimes utopian, but most often deconstructing—looking at the tain of the mirror, the underside, the inside of political structures housed in private homes and public buildings. As Elizabeth Abel says of the essays in *Writing and Sexual Difference,* feminism provides "a different and enabling mythology,"[46] for example, Nina Baym's and Annette Kolodny's de/reconstructing of the United States literary canon or Christa Wolf's rewriting of the Trojan War epic from Cassandra's point of view. Feminism is radical.

For many this is hardly a recommendation. But whether governments or clients, readers or writers embrace or resist feminism as an ideology of change, they must contend with it, as they must contend with nuclearism. Because, at its best, radical feminism is thorough in its analysis of systems of power and in its analysis of women's own participation in those systems of power, it deserves careful consideration as a dominant, humane vision. Under thorough feminist analysis sexism can be the model of oppression, as Mary Daly claims. The feminist perception of politics as pervasive while appearing to be absent is a useful vision from which to begin constructing a method for reading politics in contemporary fiction.

When feminist theories confront contemporary fiction, both theory and fiction are challenged. For example, Milan Kundera's *The Book of Laughter and Forgetting* is a novel critics usually describe as political. Critics do not speak of Kundera's novel as feminist, and in fact, its presentation of female characters and sexual practices is often troubling to women. In the afterword to the novel, however, Kundera does argue, as a feminist would, for a political interpretation of private life. He says that "the metaphysics of man is the same in the private sphere as in the public one. . . . Politics unmasks the metaphysics of private life, private life unmasks the metaphysics of politics."[47] His text's analysis of the private/public nexus in nation-state politics is a conventional but powerful politics literary feminists rarely address so directly. Kundera's text is only one reminder that if sexism is to be useful as a *model* of oppression and feminism useful as a *model* of humane radicalism, then feminism must face the challenges to its focus on gender concerns.

Feminism and Opposition

Other Central Europeans, Havel and Konrád, significantly contribute to and challenge feminism and its ideas of politics. In that both Havel and Konrád resist bureaucracy through social means and not by seeking the same kind of power the state usually holds, they share a perspective with many feminists. For this reason, Havel and Konrád are important voices in an essentially feminist dialogue defining politics. Konrád writes (in 1984),

> The anachronistic pattern of great-power spheres of influence [pursued primarily by the United States and the Soviet Union] has less and less place in European political thinking. It is beginning to be as old-fashioned as the cult of the patriarchal family or the right of a master craftsman to cuff his apprentices.

But Konrád defines politics as other when he asserts that

> politics cannot be explained in any context or medium but its own. . . . Any approach to politics is bound to fail if it strays far from the standpoint of that political genius Machiavelli, who explained power by saying that power wills itself. . . . Any philosophy of history will miss its mark if it tries to explain the riddle of political power in terms of economic interest, biological instinct, or religious enthusiasm.

He further separates power from the intellectual life to which he is devoted by adding, "To have power, one must want power, and to think, one must want thought; you can't want both." If this were true, we could never expect intelligent political leadership—influenced by the women's movement, the antinuclear movement, the anti-apartheid movement, the Charter 77 movement, or any other human rights movement. Nor could we more modestly hope for change wrought by thoughtful people who pursue and acquire power.

Konrád averts stagnation and despair by using the term "antipolitics" to describe "the political activity of those who don't want to be politicians and who refuse to share in power." "Antipolitics is the ethos of civil society, and civil society is the antithesis of military society."[48] What may be only a semantic difference (Konrád's use of "antipolitics" where feminists would use "politics") is something more. For Konrád unabashedly addresses an international intelligentsia—an intelligentsia Bialer believes no longer exists—whom he calls upon to oppose "the aggressive imbeciles" of East and West state powers with antipolitics. In contrast, academic feminists are increasingly uncomfortable with any exclusion of workers or people of color or "third-world" women as subjects or audience. They fear what Bialer asserts, that intellectual radicals are removed from any mass radical movement. Konrád's antipolitical politics does address an audience to whom, and even for whom, he can speak. He is himself a central-European intellectual. Can feminists say the same of their proposed audience? And yet feminists do seek the voices of the silent. Can Konrád say the same?

Konrád and Havel also present a challenge for feminism on the issue of censorship. Konrád, Havel, and Kundera all describe life in nation-states which politicized (and proposed to radicalize) all facets of public and private life. Whatever the original intentions of the states' programs, the result has been a substantial suppression of ideas and information in the Soviet Union and central-eastern Europe. Thus, Havel speaks of a "post-totalitarian system" whose bureaucracy, blanketing all aspects of life, has ossified all aspects of life.[49] Both Havel and Konrád associate political power with the power of censorship. Anticensorship and individual rights have been central to both men's arguments for greater justice in their native countries. "Centralized Party rule and censorship are inseparable," writes Konrád.[50]

In contrast, not only do Western radicals call for community rights over individual rights, but a substantial contingent of feminists is willing to sacrifice individual rights in order to censor what degrades women.[51] Whatever the difference in Soviet bloc and Western state systems, the urge to suppress information that one does not like for initially utopian ends is sufficiently similar to warrant consideration. Though, fundamentally, feminism means to politicize, radicalize, private life by making us aware that private institutions are already politically determined, this program of self-consciousness includes some will to power that would control information.

If feminism is to be a model radical movement it must also address challenges from the movement against racism. Any definition of politics must consider the political uses of "race." Though feminism may argue sexism as "final cause" and perceive itself the radical ideology most likely to produce structural change and diminish oppression of all sorts, it cannot ignore the recalcitrant tropes of racism. Indeed, because feminists perceive their ideology as a catalyst and a model, they must study the tropes of racism. Henry Louis Gates, Jr., for example, asserts that

> race . . . pretends to be an objective term of classification, when in fact it is a dangerous trope. . . . Race has become a trope of ultimate irreducible difference between cultures, linguistic groups, or adherents of specific belief systems

which—more often than not—also have fundamentally opposed economic interests. Race is the ultimate trope of difference because it is so very arbitrary in its application. The biological criteria used to determine "difference" in sex simply do not hold when applied to "race."[52]

Anthony Appiah supports Gates's biological contentions.

Contemporary biologists are not agreed on the question of whether there are any human races. . . . Every reputable biologist will agree that human genetic variability between the populations of Africa or Europe or Asia is not much greater than that within those populations. . . . differences between peoples in language, moral affections, aesthetic attitudes, or political ideology . . . are not biologically determined to any significant degree.[53]

"Race" is a sociohistorical phenomenon created usually for economic reasons. "Race" is a trope. The creation of a difference and the assignment of what Appiah calls a "badge of insult" to possessors of certain skin color, hair texture, or bone structure was and is a largely linguistic activity enforced with violence. Racism, like sexism, engages in political control of the bodies of others.

Gates pinpoints the so-called Age of Reason, dominated by Descartes, as the source of a rationalization for racism.

[The Enlightenment] used the absence and presence of reason to delimit and circumscribe the very humanity of the cultures and people of color which Europeans had been "discovering" since the Renaissance. The urge toward the systemization of all human knowledge (by which we characterize the Enlightenment) led directly to the relegation of black people to a lower place in the great chain of being.[54]

Similarly, Michel Foucault notes in *The History of Sexuality* that in the eighteenth century people became "population" requiring reproductive management, that is, control of their physical, economic, and political behavior. Then he adds, "In time these new measures would become anchorage points for the different varieties of racism of the nineteenth and twentieth centuries."[55] In his feminist analysis of the history of science, Brian Easlea also indicts Descartes and the Age of Reason.[56] For Descartes declared nature to be lifeless matter, a machine to be controlled by the mind of man. Susan Bordo confirms, in a study of his *Meditations,* that Descartes proposed thorough separation of the mind from the body, that manifestation of all which is unclean, impure, and uncertain.[57] Finally, Adrienne Rich in *Of Woman Born* indicts the Age of Reason by describing the seventeenth through nineteenth centuries as a period when male surgeons were entering the field of obstetrics for reasons of profit and scientific experimentation. (Rich writes about the use of forceps specifically.) Surgeons brought not only "objective science" but also hands infected by other, diseased patients into the labor room. For nearly two centuries, in the Age of Reason, an epidemic of "childbed fever" killed many thousands of women in Europe. For two centuries, Rich argues, influential surgeons suppressed studies showing surgeons' unsanitary hands were responsible for the epidemic.[58] Reason, defined in the Cartesian and post-Cartesian world as the means to objectivity and certain knowledge, presents a major challenge not only to feminists but also to anyone who studies designations of difference. Reason is the challenge that brings together those studies of difference which question its authority.

Reason and Certainty

The Age of Reason is the Age of Certainty: certainty that people of color belong on a lower rung of the evolutionary ladder; that sex and reproduction must be managed; that nature is unfeeling data; that science can only fight disease but cannot cause it. Though every era has produced mystics, iconoclasts, or radicals who oppose the conventional definition of reason, reason and its certainties continue to dominate systems of interpretation and power. As Gates and Foucault explain and Easlea and Rich imply, certainty requires a mythology and an extensive discourse to promote that mythology. Politics, again, is a text. Certainty is power.

Power conventionally derives from certain separation of self and other. And yet in the case of "race," for example, the arbitrary difference between self and other challenges racism's certainty. In a study of Zora Neale Hurston, Barbara Johnson writes,

> Difference is a misreading of sameness, but it must be represented in order to be erased. . . . The difference between difference and sameness can barely be said. . . . What Hurston rigorously shows is that questions of difference and identity are always a function of a specific interlocutionary situation—and the answers, matters of strategy rather than truth.[59]

Resistance to the power of certain difference and separation requires that difference be acknowledged so that sameness can be asserted. It requires looking carefully at each "specific interlocutionary situation" to see difference and sameness as both the same and different.

Though "race" may be the most arbitrary, and therefore most paradoxical, of differences, sexual discourse is similarly paradoxical, as described by Foucault. He asserts silence and talk about sex are not a certain dichotomy.

> There is no binary division to be made between what one says and what one does not say [about sex]; we must try to determine the different ways of not saying such things, how those who can and those who cannot speak of them are distributed, which type of discourse is authorized, or which form of discretion is required in either case.[60]

Apparent repression of and talk about sex are both functions of particular rhetorical situations. Foucault, in fact, argues that excessive discourse about sex has become interpreted as repression and silence. Traditionally, those who have spoken in public about private life have maintained their power to speak by assertion of binary division between discreet and indiscreet behavior, indeed, between men and women. But the certainty of this rhetorical strategy dissolves when examined. It is a paradox.

A study of power and politics must be a study of paradox. Feminism, or any ideology practicing thorough and radical analysis of texts, faces the paradox of asserted differences of all sorts. Similarly, a study of any difference contributes to the disrobing of certainty. If sexism is the "final cause," the model of private-political oppression, racism is the ultimate, arbitrary trope, the model of created difference. Feminism provides a radical vision; studies of "race," a politics of difference. As Foucault's argument shows, neither is self-enclosed.

The relationship between the "third world" and the "first world" which is often but not necessarily a "racial" relationship, is another area of difference creating a challenge for the radical vision of feminism or any other radical movement.[61] In speaking of Europe and Africa, Gates has already been quoted as saying that the "first world" created difference separating itself from the "third world" and yet demands of the Africans "reason" so that they might be understood by the Europeans. In addition, Reed Way Dasenbrock argues that to resist such domination, yet write meaningfully, "third-world" writers who use English, or other "first-world" languages, are selectively unintelligible so that "first-world" readers cannot simply absorb another culture. Unintelligibility has meaning.[62]

More often than not the "third world" is present only in its absence. For example, Bialer limits his analysis of contemporary radicalism to a consideration of industrial democracies. Delimiting his subject makes Bialer's analysis clear. Konrád addresses a European audience of intellectuals. Thus, he focuses on a particular goal. And yet such clarity and focus remove whole cultures, classes, or societies from our field of vision. The meaning of lives not in the text evaporates, entering our consciousness unseen, unheard, but somehow felt. Rich asserts that our oppression and suppression of other cultures are "murderous of the spiritual integrity of all of us."[63] Gayatri Spivak is especially consistent in reminding the women's movement and the intellectual community in general that peoples of the "third world" and their texts exist in defiance of patriarchy, racism, and reason. In summarizing Spivak's introduction to and translation of "Draupadi," a fictional text by the Bengali woman novelist Mahasveta Devi, Elizabeth Abel reminds the "first-world" reader of her culpability.

> Draupadi's shattered body [once raped and tortured] is itself a text that silences both her male interrogator and his allies in exegesis: us. As a well-educated pluralist aesthete, the literate army officer is our intellectual representative within the text; like his, our interpretive strategies should be shaken by Draupadi. As Western readers, female and male, we are blind to the radical difference of Third-World sexual politics.[64]

The politics of "first-world" intellectuals, a politics of defining language, and the politics of "third-world" texts, a politics of the body defined, is a difference challenging any theory of literature, any theory of politics.

The relationship of the body and the mind arises from every corner as central to designations of difference and definitions of politics. This relationship—often a tyranny of language over the body—requires from students of language or politics an unblinking examination. Elaine Scarry's analysis of interrogation and pain in the practice of torture, in *The Body in Pain,* is one such steady gaze.[65]

Whether those who seek radical and humane change perceive feminism as their model and whether those who study politics and literature perceive feminism as their theory, both must see the cultural creation of difference as their subject. In *Difference and Pathology,* Sander Gilman explains why.

> The deep structure of our own sense of self and the world is built upon the illusionary image of the world divided into two camps, "us" and "them." . . . Difference is that which threatens order and control; it is the polar opposite to our group.

Gilman describes the designation of other, what he calls stereotyping, as an inevitable, even necessary, developmental process. Its barbaric manifestations, however, must be made visible. For "like many other innate and ungovernable human needs, the need to stereotype has acquired increased catastrophic potential at a pace roughly in step with technological advances in our ability to harm one another."[66] In each of his essays Gilman demonstrates that stereotyping operates by superimposing one threatening other on top of another. A little fact and a lot of myth, Gilman argues, have made black, Jew, and woman analogous others dangerous in their perverse sexuality and downright madness. All that is other is not-reason; it is madness and disease. Gilman's research challenges feminism to study the stereotyping of woman in explicit conjunction with analogous stereotyping done in the name of reason.

Certainty and Difference

Stereotypes of difference, which are bipolar, are the basis and the practice of will-to-power politics. Beginning with this premise, I add to it the assumption that any attempt to understand, perhaps even diffuse and redistribute, this power is well advised to start with this premise. If one takes seriously the obvious binary oppositions of politics as it is usually practiced, one can discover, as Gilman has, how these polarities are made but also how—at least rhetorically—they are undone. Inherent in difference is sameness. And when the certain designation of the other proves applicable to the self, uncertainty intrudes upon the definition of the self. What was difference, manageable through dialectic, becomes paradox, vulnerable to dialogue. Paradox, that is, the conjunction of opposing poles, is the psychic and political condition we humans create for ourselves as we work to define the self.

A consideration of cultural difference and political power leads me back to deconstruction because, despite the political accusations leveled against it, its acceptance of uncertainty and its methods of reading absence are well suited to a study of paradox. Deconstruction discloses what Gayatri Spivak calls "complicities,"[67] whereas a will to knowledge, desire for certainty, creates only more oppositions, the binary mythology of politics as it is usually understood. In *The Critical Difference* Barbara Johnson describes well the process of deconstructing binary opposition, though she does not speak of politics per se. "The 'deconstruction' of a binary opposition is thus not an annihilation of all values or differences; it is an attempt to follow the subtle, powerful effects of differences already at work within the illusion of a binary opposition." Johnson directs our attention away from the illusion of differences between and redirects it toward the differences within entities: a strategy crucial to an analysis of politics. "The differences *between* entities . . . are shown to be based on a repression of differences *within* entities, ways in which an entity differs from itself."[68]

The politics of nation-states, nuclearism, gender, "race," sex, and interpretation all demand an examination of the differences within if they are to disclose the sources of their power. Whether reading the history of nuclear strategy or of childbirth, I see again and again the central paradox of a desire for certainty leading to greater insecurity. Whether or not this was the central condition of being in other eras, it is in ours. In "Psychoanalysis and the Polis," Julia Kristeva writes of an interpreter's desire for meaning met instead by all she cannot know. Kristeva calls this condition "delirium." Though I would not choose to associate the limits of human knowledge with madness, I accept her description of the interpreter's position as a paradox of desire (will) and "delirium."[69] Adrienne Rich puts the difference within in feminist terms.

> The rejection of the dualism, of the positive-negative polarities between which most of our intellectual training has taken place, has been an undercurrent of feminist thought. And, rejecting them, we reaffirm the existence of all those who have through the centuries been negatively defined: not only women, but the "untouchable," the "unmanly," the "nonwhite," the "illiterate": the "invisible." Which forces us to confront the problem of the essential dichotomy: power/powerless.

In order to confront dualism, we reject its "fact," and its method.

This includes the "fact" of the essential power/powerless dichotomy created by the language of will to power. "The language of patriarchal power," Rich writes, "insists on a dichotomy: for one person to have power, others—or another—must be powerless."[70] That the key differences lie within the powerful and within the powerless is a condition certainty cannot abide. Thus, for example, once people designate any individual or nation-state as their enemy, they must not imagine that any negotiation which proposes something good for the enemy could also be good for them or that something bad for the enemy could also be bad for them.

The valorization of uncertainty, the exploration of internal difference, I intend to be descriptive as much of contemporary politics and culture as of my interpretive method. The possibilities for infinite regression within the practice of what is called deconstruction are aptly criticized by Lentricchia, Spivak, Abrams, and others; I will not repeat those warnings here. Rather I applaud deconstruction's resistance to totalitarian assignments of meaning (in which I too am always implicated). As a philosophy it cannot promise to instill in its practitioners humane language or behavior, but it can promote a questioning and self-consciousness less likely to result in certain, inhumane force and interpretation.

Because Jacques Derrida is the name most often invoked in current discussions of deconstruction, I want to make some attempt to place my use of "difference" within the context of Derrida's work. But I do this with the understanding, first, that the choice of Derrida as a starting place for deconstructive analysis is arbitrary and, second, that a thorough explanation of what Derrida might mean by "*différence*" and "*différance*" would require a far longer and more complex discourse than I intend to engage in here. I offer only an array of what I hope are relevant comments made by Derrida in *Writing and Difference* and by Alan Bass, the translator of *Writing and Difference*. (I have already quoted from Spivak and Johnson, two other translators of Derrida.)

In speaking of translation and of the foundation of difference between signifier and signified—that is, the delusion and necessity of both difference and certainty—Bass writes,

> Derrida states that the history of metaphysics has never ceased to impose upon semiology (the science of signs) the search for a "transcendental signified," that is, a concept independent of language. However, even if the inherited opposition between signifier and signified can be shown to be programmed by the metaphysical desire for a transcendental, other-worldly meaning (that is often derived from the theological model of the presence of God), this does not mean that the opposition between signifier and signified can simply be abandoned as an historical delusion. Derrida states: "That this opposition or difference cannot be radical and absolute does not prevent it from functioning."[71]

That there is a perceived opposition between meaning and articulation, that meaning may exist without language, is a perception derived from the belief that there exists certain meaning that God knows which is beyond human articulation. Both the certainty (e.g., of a god's knowledge) and the opposition (i.e., between ideal meaning and fallible articulation) function (in translations, for example) whether or not they are "true."

What interests me most about this statement is neither its metaphysical nor its linguistic contents but its psychosocial implications. Oppositions derived from certainty function whether true difference exists or not. Gilman documents this process extensively. Thus, to deconstruct an opposition one must first acknowledge the function of the opposition and underlying certainty. Robert Lifton addresses the function of one such certainty in his analysis of what he calls "nuclear fundamentalism."

> Faced with the loss of fundamental structures [because of nuclear explosions] one has depended on in the past—of a reliable spiritual or physical universe—one important response can be an exaggerated restatement of those threatened "fundamentals" that can readily lapse into the narrowist [sic] of fundamentalisms.[72]

Both scientists' and laymen's awe of the infinite power (and beauty) of the splitting atom has resulted in a created opposition between the signifier (technology created by human knowledge and will) and the signified (a power so great it grapples with death itself). Belief in the transcendent meaning of nuclear explosion has even attributed to it Armageddon, the certain annihilation promised in Revelation. That the bomb's meaning functions as though it is different, separate, from its technology is evident. Some implications of this perception of difference are acquiescence to the certainty of annihilation and the assumption that this technology (and other technology) transcend human will, human articulation.

Bass also explains that Derrida uses "*différance*" to mean both difference and deferral at once. Derrida connects the concept of *différance* to the words "totalitarian" (associated with structuralism) and "solicitation" (derived from the Latin *sollus,* all, and *ciere,* to move or shake).

> Derrida submits the violent, totalitarian structural project to the counter-violence of *solicitation.* . . . Every totality, he shows, can be *totally shaken,* that is, can be shown to be founded on that which it excludes, that which would be in *excess* for a reductive analysis of any kind.[73]

The importance of such a process for interpreters of politics and poetics in the areas of gender, "race," sex, nuclearism, and the "third world" is enormous. Though I use the English word "difference," I aspire to this interpretive process which shakes the totalitarian structure whatever it might be.

My sense of my self may well be included as a totalitarian structure. (Indeed, self-consciousness seems a paltry answer to the accusations leveled against the "first-world" interpreter by Abel and Spivak.) Derrida describes the interpreter's task this way.

> To grasp the operation of creative imagination at the greatest possible prox-
> imity to it, one must turn oneself toward the invisible interior of poetic
> freedom. One must be separated from oneself in order to be reunited with the
> blind origin of the work in its darkness.[74]

Or as Barbara Johnson describes it: "The one imperative a reading must
obey is that it follow, with rigor, what puts in question the kind of reading
it thought it was going to be."[75] I might say that, by necessity, every
inscription of word on paper delimits meaning, thus making it clearer
though more false. Furthermore, the very process sets me up as an authority even if my intention is to debunk authority. If I intend an authentic
voice, the best I can do is to accept responsibility for the authority (the
deciding of the undecidable) which language confers. That readers will
not necessarily take her seriously is a writer's bane and comfort.

Authenticity and Complicity

The *Oxford English Dictionary* defines authenticity as "the quality of being
entitled to acceptance; as being authoritative or duly authorized; as being
in accordance with fact, as being true in substance." That which is authentic has a sense of being both "authoritative" and "original." When, in
Sincerity and *Authenticity,* Lionel Trilling speaks of the self and its capacity
for authenticity, he adheres to this accepted definition in that the self he
posits is "autonomous in being," integrated, whole. "It is through our
conscious certitude of our personal selfhood that we reach our knowledge
of others."[76] Authenticity is reached when there is no within (the self) and
without, when the self is one, for example, with its grief. Trilling offers as a
model of this authentic self Wordsworth's common man, Michael. In
contrast to Trilling, I see the self as always becoming, never being. One's
changing perceptions of the other provide the changing definitions of the
self (not-other). One is in a continuous dialogue with what is different
and what is the same. The self becoming through dialogue is not a self of
"conscious certitude," as Trilling argues; it is never authoritative beyond
question. Neither is it original in the sense that it could ever separate from
the history, the process, that made it. And yet this self is entitled to
acceptance.

Trilling asserts "that authenticity is implicitly a polemical concept,
fulfilling its nature by dealing aggressively with received and habitual
opinion, aesthetic opinion in the first instance, social and political opinion

in the next."[77] In support of his assertion that authenticity is aggressive, Trilling provides the Greek ancestry of the word "authentic": *Authenteo* meant "to have full power over," and "to commit a murder"; *Authentes,* "not only a master and a doer, but also a perpetrator, a murderer, even a self-murderer, a suicide." Trilling sees this violence in the modern definition of "authenticity," and also accepts this violence as necessary to stir the world from its nonbeing.[78]

I agree that authenticity is, if not polemical, rhetorical and that it is radical, even "intending offense," as Trilling chooses to describe it. And yet what is most radical about contemporary authenticity is its assertion of values, methods, and a vision that do not adhere to the convention of violence with "full power over" others. This radical authenticity intends to stir the world but does not assume its audience exists in nonbeing, some state of unacceptable otherness. It assumes instead what Adrienne Rich says of Marie Curie: "her wounds came from the same source as her power."[79] There is authenticity in a self whose goal is not power over the other.

This authenticity arises from a recognition of internal difference. Like Trilling, I pursue justifications for my definitions in poetry. But while he finds authenticity in Wordsworth's character Michael, I find it in the illusive persona within Emily Dickinson's voice. Metaphor and syntactical oddity prove the most literal statement of private and political paradox that I can offer. Dickinson writes,

> We can find no scar,
> But internal difference,
> Where the Meanings, are—
>
> None may teach it—Any—

She does warn that in that certain time of day when we can recognize this "internal difference" we also feel "the Seal Despair." And yet

> When it comes, the Landscape listens—
> Shadows—hold their breath

These are the moments when, if we also are attentive, we can learn something of our divided selves, although such insight is difficult to sustain.

When it goes, 'tis like the Distance
On the look of Death—[80]

When recognition of internal difference leaves, taking meaning with it, we are left with the perception and the delusion that death is distant. Disease, pain, mortality—all that is strange and other—appear equally distant and different while we, the self, appear certainly near. But "a certain slant of light," a laceration in us as it is in the afternoon, can remind us again how paradoxical is any distance, even that between life and death. Within the wound is internal difference.

Whatever authenticity I can achieve here depends upon disclosure of the self-contradictions which rule my interpretation. I offer some biography hoping to disclose more than I am able to describe. My history is of assimilation into the United States enterprise and of discomfort with the culture that willingly absorbs me. The discomfort furthest from home was easiest for me to name. So first, I became aware that the United States' treatment of "third-world" nations made me uneasy. My recognition that I participated in racist foundations of power came more slowly; that I embraced sexist foundations of power, even more slowly. But most slowly (at least to date) has come recognition that assimilation has taken from me my own roots in otherness: the narratives of immigrant relatives, knowledge of their language, the identity of a dark great grandmother in an aging photograph. My past is neither unique nor representative, but it propels my work with its discomfort and its questions.

Rich asserts that to recover one's history (an identity of some authenticity) requires resistance to "two powerful pressures in present-day American culture. . . . One is the imperative to assimilate; the other, the idea that one can be socially 'twice-born.' "[81] Though Rich uses examples of Christian fundamentalism and escape to the frontier as prevalent forms of second birth in the United States, my impulse has been neither of these. I have instead aspired to be reborn free of guilt for the racism that pervades the domestic and foreign, personal and public affairs of the United States. This deleterious guilt is a white badge of insult analogous to the black badge of insult Appiah says blacks have been forced to wear ever since they encountered whites. It is the kind of self-hatred which, Rich states, commonly accompanies a desire to be twice-born.[82]

I have seen my desire for second birth in the words and behavior of other middle-class whites (women and men), especially those living in large United States cities whose majority populations are blacks or Hispanics or Asian-Americans. These whites yearn, as I do, for a large "colored" audience who will not only believe the sincerity of our desire for humane social and political change but will embrace our plans for achieving these changes. We want to be forgiven without being humiliated. One particular experience I had made me aware of the blindness of my desire, a blindness for which this book tries to compensate.

A few years ago I had a plan to bring together a group of lecturers (white academics) who could speak about the economic, environmental, cultural, and social impact of the nuclear weapons industry on inner-city poor people (almost exclusively black), and to take these lecturers to the recreation halls adjacent to large public housing projects. In order to obtain the help and approval of a black activist, I presented this idea to him. He responded by calling me and the idea racist. He then advised me to take my lectures to my own people (middle-class whites), among whom he said the problem lies, and not to lower-class blacks, who already know in experience what I wanted to tell them.

Though I have retained some doubts about this man's authority to speak for all those he claimed to represent (I wonder, for example, how his female colleagues would have responded to me), no one has ever said to me anything more important. His remarks forced me to claim as my people white middle-class United States citizens and also a particular white middle-class family who lived in a particular white middle-class town in northeastern Ohio. However sincere my desire to communicate honestly with people of color in my city and outside it, I could not be an authentic representative or interpreter of my "race," gender, and class, or of any particular political ideology, until I accepted the conditions of my first birth. I indulge in this anecdote because it presents an example of internal difference, difference within the self. I suggest that this internal difference is the place to look for an understanding of politics and a method for reading it in contemporary fictional texts.

In an essay entitled "Victorians and Africans," Patrick Brantlinger points to the significance of the moment when white confronts white. It is a description I identify with, a moment whose significance I pursue in this book.

> Nothing points more uncannily to the processes of projection and displacement of guilt for the slave trade, guilt for empire, guilt for one's own savage and shadowy impulses than those moments when white man confronts white man in the depths of the jungle.[83]

Though the guilt for slavery is deferred (*différant*) and I am not a man, the confrontation of white and white (characters, writers, and critics—interpreters all) in the "jungle" is a source of identity and racial understanding for me.

The word "guilt" is appropriate as Brantlinger uses it, but it often elicits such anger, squeamishness, or self-satisfaction that it is immediately submitted "to the processes of projection and displacement" Brantlinger describes. Because of this projection and a host of other connotations of guilt, I choose to focus on two other words: "compassion" and "complicity" (a quality, as I have mentioned, that Spivak believes is inherent to deconstruction). When one meets one's own kind in the jungle of stereotypical others one has made, one needs a capacity for compassion in its most literal form. The *Oxford English Dictionary* gives the definition of compassion, from the fourteenth to the seventeenth centuries, as a literal "suffering together with another," but by the eighteenth century—the Age of Reason—this definition has given way to the other definition: "a feeling or emotion, when a person is moved by the suffering or distress of another, and by the desire to relieve it; pity that inclines one to spare or succor." The distance between the self and other is greater in the latter definition than in the earlier one. This distance allows charity, which rarely penetrates the source of the other's suffering, to replace identity, which recognizes that the self is like the other. Charity never has to acknowledge that the other suffers and therefore needs help, indeed, because of that individual's designation as other (black, madwoman, Palestinian, Jew). Suffering together with another does have necessary limits. Physical pain, for example, cannot literally be shared. And yet, a compassion which examines internal difference and identity with the other fosters an authentic, however uncertain, existence. Pity or charity, on the other hand, can maintain the other safely in her place.

According to the *OED* "complicity" is related to "complicate" and "accomplice," the roots of which (*com* + *plic-*) mean "fold together." In contemporary definitions complicity means both "being an accomplice" and the "state of being complex or involved." It is a far better word than "guilt" to describe the effect when one confronts one's own kind in the "jungle" of otherness. It is also a better word to describe the effect of contemporary political fiction—at least that written by "first-world" authors. Complicity implies that self and other are complicated, folded together. If evil befalls the other, the self is not simply guilty, to blame, but is rather complicit in a network of personal, social, political, even aesthetic conditions which perpetuate the stereotypes and which, in turn, rationalize the suffering. The self is an accomplice in this complexity. But in the web of complicity the self also suffers.

The image of a spider's web is an analogue common to J. Hillis Miller's descriptions of deconstructive criticism. The way his use of the web is the same and different from mine may serve to clarify my use of deconstruction and my understanding of complicity. Miller derives his analogue of the spider's web from Ruskin's *Fors Clavigera,* from which Miller quotes: "So that this thread of Ariadne's implied that even victory over the monster [spider] would be vain, unless you could disentangle yourself from his web also." Miller perceives the method of the deconstructing critic—what he calls the "uncanny" critic—to be a "labyrinthine attempt to escape from the labyrinth of words," a web. But he argues that escape, or disentanglement, is ultimately impossible, and thus, victory over the spider and its web (the artistic text the critic interprets) is vain. "One can never escape from the labyrinth because the activity of escaping makes more labyrinth." Instead, the reader of a deconstructing text reaches an impasse, or aporia, and "the bottom drops out." Below is an abyss (a focal word in Miller's use and description of deconstruction). Assuming one can begin (and end) not with a transcendent signified but only with the written text, marks on paper, Miller writes,

> This thread is like a filament of ink which flows from the pen of the writer, keeping him in the web but suspending him over the chasm, the blank page that thin line hides. In one version of Ariadne's story she is said to have hanged herself with her thread in despair after being abandoned by Theseus.[84]

Miller's writer is suspended from his web over the chasm of the blank page—the yawning nothingness he assumes in place of transcendental meaning. But it is striking how transcendental is the nothingness Miller's image evokes despite some disclaimers to the contrary. Nothingness in itself—if indeed it can be said to be in itself—is as absolute as God. When Miller echoes the imagery of Jonathan Edwards's "Sinners in the Hands of an Angry God," the metaphysical qualities of Miller's analogue are particularly striking. Look at Edwards's language: "it is easy for us to cut or singe a slender thread that any thing hangs by"; or, "the pit hath opened its mouth under them"; or, "the God . . . holds you over the pit of hell, much as one holds a spider or some loathsome insect over the fire."[85] Both men's language displays a will to power through the use of a transcendent threat. In Miller's analogue the web is not entanglement in responsibility for the condition of this world but instead solitary entanglement in a despair about the existence of some other, transcendent world—an absent safety net. Victory is vain because victory (power over) is sought.

If the spider who weaves Miller's deconstructive web is Edwards's, the spider who weaves my web of complicity may be Whitman's. Whitman's spider is a democrat.

> It launch'd forth filament, filament, filament, out of itself,
> Ever unreeling them, ever tirelessly speeding them
>
> .   .   .   .   .   .
>
> Till the gossamer thread [it] fling[s] catch somewhere.[86]

The effect is an accumulation of disparate others, complicit in one another's sorrow and success. There is no transcendent signified; there is no nothing. We are bracketed in this life. I assume neither that the significance of language is confined to black marks on blank pages nor that it has fixed referents, the signified, in the world outside the blank page. But it has political, social, cultural relationships—relationships marked by difference and sameness. In deconstructing distinctions between difference and sameness, self and other, a text or interpretation weaves a web of complicity entangling its author and its readers. As Miller says, we cannot escape—but then we need not be in despair over the existence of an abyss. If we cannot escape, we cannot fall.

Any literature of any era can be read as political, that is, as rhetoric promoting certain desires of the self in relation to others. But I stipulate a particular political fiction by a normative definition: complicity is the measure of its effectiveness as Aristotle measures tragedy by pity and fear. Good political fiction produces the effect of complicity. Robert Boyers's definition of the political novel by its subject, which he describes as community, is both too restrictive and too vague. It is more useful to describe a form called political fiction which addresses the binary oppositions evident in public politics and in so doing also makes evident the binary oppositions of personal politics. Declaring the difference between self and other is the common practice of power in both the personal and the public realm. But political fiction discloses that these binary oppositions and this practice of power exist as paradoxes. The internal difference within entities complicates, even contradicts, the difference between entities. And the reader, who has a desire to choose a side or to remain aloof from the conflict altogether, is drawn into a web of complicity in which her desires are exposed as contributing to the political conflict and suffering that the fiction addresses. Her dependence on the sophistication of literary language is itself implicated in a political dilemma that uses such language to define and suppress the other.

This genre of political fiction cannot be measured by its ability to elicit action in the world. Even the relationship between the most polemical art and the actions of its audience is very difficult to determine. But if I define contemporary political fiction as that which exposes paradox inherent in political binary opposition, then it can be described by the effect of complicity. This fiction posits no heroes larger than life whose tragic fall the reader pities and fears. Neither is it satire which looks down upon society's victims trapped in hopeless conditions. In this political fiction the victim, the other, asserts some selfhood which may not give her hope but does identify her with the reader. The reader cannot be aloof or immune to her own internal difference. Instead, along the way, she is caught in the web of complicity paradox has woven.

Stanley Fish asserts that in reading meaning occurs along the way and not after the text is finished (as, Fish says, the formalists would have it).[87] Such is the case with the effect of complicity. It occurs gradually rather than epiphanically and cannot be purged. Contemporary political fiction removes the distance between the character and the reader, the fictional world and the reader's world, the distance necessary to purge the haunting effects of the fiction. The reader remains complicit.

Complicity and Democracy

To assert the value of complicity and uncertainty is to assert the value of democracy. This is not an advertisement for the West but a statement about the present world in which political fiction is written and read. Despite the various ways the word "democracy" is used, it is after all a process requiring patience with uncertainty. Citizens of the contemporary world suffer without democracy and suffer with it.

In analyzing the possibilities for democracy—in this case, in Latin America particularly—Albert O. Hirschman summarizes his argument this way:

If a democratic regime is to have any chance at all of surviving, its citizens must accept Przeworski's uncertainty about outcomes, they must acquire a measure of patience. To become consolidated, the regime needs in addition some admixture of Manin's uncertainty, the awareness on the part of citizens that they are, and ought to be, somewhat tentative about what are the correct solutions to current problems in advance of any democratic debate.[88]

When Walt Whitman asks himself the rhetorical question, "Do I contradict myself?" and answers, "Very well, then, I contradict myself," he proclaims his devotion to democratic method over personal certainty.

If many in the United States today are far less pleased with democratic method than was Whitman, it is because we associate it with adversarial democracy in which parties bitterly oppose one another (whether their ideologies are actually different or not), and the minority (sometimes a very large minority) does not get what it wants. As citizens observe it, this democratic method does not enhance the moral character of government, politicians, or citizens. Disillusioned by adversarial democracy, some citizens create their own small polities on the model of what Jane J. Mansbridge calls "unitary democracy."[89]

Analysis of the internal differences within democracy creates one final context for an examination of political paradox in contemporary fiction. In *Beyond Adversary Democracy* Mansbridge describes the differences between and within adversary and unitary democracy: in an adversary democracy there are conflicting interests which are settled by a majority vote; in a unitary democracy there are strong common interests which are pursued through consensus decisions. Unitary democracy, the kind of democracy originally described by Aristotle, "extends to the level of a polity the social relations of friendship. . . . [Friendship] becomes a 'natural' or 'organic' basis for democracy, just as the family is the natural metaphor for legitimating a monarchy."[90]

It is some sort of unitary democracy Wolf, Havel, Konrád, and even Lentricchia imply when they describe their modest (Wolf) or far-flung (Lentricchia) desires for "genuine community." Mansbridge shows that unitary democracy, valorized by some as ideal, dismissed by others as naive or totalitarian, is necessarily neither. Rather, the advantages and pitfalls of unitary democracy enlighten the usual understanding of familiar adversary democracy.

An advantage of unitary democracy is that each individual has more power in the group (polity) and can express her position to others face-to-

face. In an adversary democracy each individual's power is equally protected by the one-person one-vote rule, but under majority rule that equal
power will not protect equally the interests, say, of a permanent minority.
Also, the protection intended by secret ballot, as well as the equity intended by representative government, denies someone the opportunity to
argue a case one-on-one with someone else, an argument that might result
in personal compromise or even agreement. And yet an individual, who
has more power in a unitary democracy, a smaller group, does not have
more power in relation to the larger world.

While the problem with adversary democracy is that it sees everything
in terms of binary oppositions (conflicting interests) and so cannot imagine common interests and may not accept agreements when they occur,
the problem with unitary democracy is that, as the group grows, appeals
to unity and consensus can "obscure conflict to the benefit of those
who launch the appeal."[91] Adversary democracy is particularly dangerous
when it defines its enemies (e.g., communism) with certainty and therefore precludes ever perceiving common interests (e.g., nuclear arms control) with those "enemies." Agreement is perceived as antithetical to
democracy. Unitary democracy is particularly dangerous when its pursuit
of common interests becomes certainty about common good. Then disagreement is perceived as antithetical to democracy. Indeed, both agreement and disagreement, sameness and difference, must be a part of democracy, and thus, one must anticipate, in both private and public life, a
flexible strategy which employs either the adversary or the unitary model
depending on whether interests in the group differ or converge. Either
one is patient, with a "wild patience," as Adrienne Rich describes it,[92]
patient for a lifetime, or one acknowledges that it is not the equality and
uncertainty of democracy one desires. Then the individual must acknowledge and accept the consequences and responsibilities for more autocratic
forms of rule.

Correspondence between the strategies of adversary and unitary democracy is a crucial context for my analysis of politics in fiction. This
correspondence is fundamental to politics of sameness and difference
whether the subject is gender or "race," nuclearism or the "third world."
Democracy challenges our tolerance for uncertainty. It is the victim of
certainty and impatience. By advocating patience and uncertainty, I do
not mean to suggest that in a democracy decisions are never made,
political action never taken. Rather, both unitary and adversary demo-

cratic polities are fora for discussion and forms for change, which will occur one way or another. Indeed, one cannot say that democratic action, be it by majority vote or consensus, will always or never result in the greater good of everyone concerned. But democratic strategies, as described by Mansbridge and Hirschman, Konrád and Havel are integral to my understanding of the uncertainties in contemporary societies and the manifestations of those uncertainties in selected contemporary fiction from around the world.

Contemporary Political Fiction

The works of fiction I have chosen to discuss in the pages that follow are contemporary examples of that genre I have described as political fiction. They are products of an era struggling with democracy and challenged by the nuclear weapons race, the continued stereotyping of the other for purposes of political manipulation, and ecological mismanagement. The political paradoxes inherent in these conflicts are the milieu of this fiction. It addresses a broad range of binary oppositions from East/West to mother/child to body/voice. But in each of these texts, binary oppositions give way to internal difference and are exposed in the process as paradoxes. The effect is the entanglement of the reader in a web of complicity. Some of this fiction is representational or even historical (texts by Gordimer, Paley, and Ibuse). Some of it is linguistically self-reflexive or metafictional (texts by Kundera, Coetzee, and Hawkes). The deconstruction of political oppositions and assertion of paradox are not restricted to one set of fictional illusions or another.

Except one, the texts I have chosen to write about here are, however, limited to those by authors of the "first world," or white world. Using "white" as a generic term for those who live with substantial comfort in the developed world, I want to study how white author confronts white reader in the world of contemporary cultural and political conditions. One could study the undoing of political oppositions in texts by authors of color, but the relationship between those authors and the reader of color or the white reader would be in some ways different. Thus, the choices available to those authors are different. I want to study texts primarily by those who wear the badge of whiteness, that is, those who bear the responsibility for the dominant definitions of self and other.

The one significant exception to this criterion of whiteness is the Japanese author Ibuse Masuji and his novel *Black Rain*.[93] I include this novel in the last chapter as a transition to the next step: applying my proposed method of reading politics in fiction to the rhetorical condition of a "racially" and culturally different text confronting a white reader. I compare the effects of Ibuse's novel to the effects of a "white" novel which treats the same subject, nuclear annihilation, in a very different way.

One could apply the methods of deconstructing political oppositions to texts which themselves seem to assert no internal difference and elicit no complicity. One could then conclude something about the political self-consciousness of the fiction and the way its unconscious politics works on the reader.[94] I have chosen instead to analyze texts which are some of the most intriguing examples of the genre of political fiction that I have described. Each of these texts becomes a model for the method, proposed here, of reading politics. Each, however, also defies designation as a paradigm. As deconstruction teaches, the theory can never be adequate to its examples.

Milan Kundera's treatment of the themes of laughter (both cynical and utopian) and forgetting (both active suppression and passive memory loss), in *The Book of Laughter and Forgetting,* have won him considerable respect in the West. He has become an unofficial spokesperson for the relationship of personal life, loss, and desire (including the creation of art), to public life, loss, and desire (including freedom of public expression). Because of its deft mingling of personal and public, client and state, Kundera's *Book of Laughter and Forgetting* has also found its way into women's studies courses. And yet, his treatment of sex in this and other works has left many women readers confused if not dismayed. For this reason, in using *The Book* as a model teaching how to read political differences within, I concentrate on the placement of sex and motherhood along the private/public axis. *The Book*'s internal difference lies here. Specifically, the section called "Mother" seems least integrated into the whole of the novel and its two major themes of laughter and forgetting. What and how "Mother" contributes to the novel's insights about the paradox of politics are my central concerns.

Like Kundera, J. M. Coetzee exploits his context, that is, his South African citizenship, to deconstruct difference. Because South Africa has been a synecdoche for racism, Coetzee can rely on the reader's assumptions about "racial" difference. He is free, as his subjects are not, to explore the sameness in this difference and thus expose the reader's complicity in the enforcement of difference. This is the method I want to examine in *Life and Times of Michael K*. Colonialism, which made racism and made it a commodity, is the subject of *Waiting for the Barbarians*, the other Coetzee novel I consider. In this earlier novel the dichotomy of the "first world" and the "third world" is deconstructed by providing a narrative etymology for "civilization" and "barbarity," as *Michael K* provides the etymologies of "charity" and "theft." In both Coetzee novels the relationship of the "third-world" body to the "first-world" voice is central.

The last two chapters function as comparisons between authors from other nations and authors from the United States: Grace Paley and Nadine Gordimer, Ibuse Masuji and John Hawkes. I choose to juxtapose selected stories from the various decades of Paley's career to selected stories from the various decades of Gordimer's because both women's stories are about how change happens in the self and in the state. Their stories of change differ, however, in that Paley's exist in an ethos of assimilation while Gordimer's exist in an ethos of separation. The fiction displays the paradoxes inherent in these two state mandates.

Finally, I choose to write about John Hawkes's novel *Travesty* because its psychopathic monologue knits and simultaneously unravels the tension between (and thus, within) certainty and uncertainty, security and insecurity. Its destructive narrator demands apocalypse; the novel's self-conscious form asks for deconstruction of destruction. Furthermore, *Travesty*'s psychic and aesthetic destruction warps when compared to Ibuse's pristine description of massive destruction in *Black Rain*. The irradiated Hiroshima bombscape casts an eerie glow over the aesthetics of destruction Hawkes's narrator defines. *Black Rain* illuminates *Travesty* as a novel of the nuclear age. In addition, the paradoxes that permeate the fiction discussed earlier are evident here in these two novels: sex and the state, action and passivity, commitment and freedom (to love or kill, as Konrád defines it), reason and madness, family and community. As a culmination to analyses of political paradox in the fiction of Kundera, Coetzee, Gordimer, and Paley, a comparison of these novels by Hawkes and Ibuse exposes the differences within the final polarity: life and death.

Now perhaps more than ever, politics is discourse. As history moves toward the millennium, we, who are a part of that history, would be well served, I submit, by attempts to measure the degree to which individuals and nation-states achieve and maintain power through tropes of difference. To the extent that difference can be marketed as dichotomy, a will to power succeeds in defining inferiority, "race," madness, desire, weakness, and insecurity. But if one learns to recognize and read differences within the binary oppositions of political power, that power is threatened. Though the hungry may not then eat, however much we may wish it, the power of difference may be diminished.

The tropes of difference are in all literature, in the broad sense that Lentricchia defines literature: in advertising, politicians' speeches, and historical texts. They are also in literature, as it is narrowly defined. Some of this literature transforms those dichotomies into paradox and shows the reader how to do the same. It is this process I mean to describe, but not only to enhance appreciation for these few pieces of fine fiction. I also want to demonstrate the necessity, despite the complexity, of reading politics as paradox without undue cynicism or credulity. This requires an understanding of how change can and does happen now rather than how it used to happen or seems to happen. (What was once radical action may not be radical any more.) The circumstances of this age demand determined patience, forthright uncertainty, and a desire for justice as authentic as vigilant self-consciousness allows. We cannot afford to deny our wounds come from the same source as our power.

If it was treason it was so well handled that it
Became unimaginable. . . .

No it was something not very subtle then and yet again

You've got to remember we don't see that much.

John Ashbery, "The Absence of a Noble Presence"

Chapter II

Sex, Motherhood, and the State: Milan Kundera's *Book of Laughter and Forgetting*

> The main task is to distinguish allies from enemies; to recognize reactionary and
> progressive forces . . . We ask: is this work for us or against us? Does it harm or
> help us? Is the writer on this side of the front or that? This is the principal
> question: everything else must give way to that . . . We ask: On which side of
> the barricade does he stand?

In 1949 the Czechoslovakian Minister of Education asked these questions at a conference of the Writers Union.[1] Although the minister put his
remarks in the form of questions, it is clear he is certain of the difference
between "work for us and work against us." The two are mutually exclusive.

Norman Podhoretz seeks the same certainty. In his "Open Letter to
Milan Kundera," he pleads with the novelist not to allow his warning
against communism in the East-West struggle, manifested in *The Book of
Laughter and Forgetting,* to be misinterpreted by liberal Western intellectuals. "I beg you to stop giving aid and encouragement to the cultural
powers who are using some of your own words to prevent your work
from helping to alert a demoralized West to the dangers it faces from a
self-imposed Yalta of its own."[2] Kundera must make it clear on which side
of the barricade he stands.

Even an admiring analysis of Kundera's novel gives way to the principal
question: on which side of the barricade does he stand? In David Lodge's
analysis of *The Book of Laughter and Forgetting,* the barricade is the English
Channel. Kundera's novel becomes an occasion for attacking Roland
Barthes and Michel Foucault's ideas on "the death of the author."[3] Lodge
subjects Barthes's writerly/readerly distinction to reduction rendering
Barthes, his so-called followers, and all practitioners of poststructuralism
or deconstruction the unreasonable enemies on the opposite side. Meanwhile, Lodge begs the question, is Kundera on this side of the border or
that? He is on "our" side.

Terry Eagleton also fires a couple of shots, albeit muted shots, across the
Channel. In an essay for *Salmagundi,* Eagleton's right hand analyzes
Kundera's work with insight into the effects of ideology on everyday life
in the East and in the West. At the same time his left (Left) hand is quietly
sorting out enemies and allies. The enemies are deconstruction and the
West's avant-garde. The allies are Kundera, of course, and those (men?)
who appreciate the "laid-back companionability" and sexual humor in
Kundera's fiction.[4]

Masters of the deconstructed dichotomy cannot themselves always resist the charms of mutual exclusion, the binary opposition. In her analysis of Derrida's reading ("The Purveyor of Truth," "*Le Facteur de la Vérité*") of Lacan's reading ("Seminar on The Purloined Letter") of Poe's story, Barbara Johnson points to an aggressive competition between the two French theorists. It is a

> rivalry over something neither man will credit the other with possessing. . . . If it thus becomes impossible to determine "who started it" (or even whether "it" was started by either one of them), it is also impossible to know who is ahead or even whose "turn" it is.[5]

In *Atrocity and Amnesia* Robert Boyers admits an "aversion to *la nouvelle critique*" regardless of whether it is written by Derrida or Lacan. Boyers identifies instead with the New Critics and socialists of the fifties and sixties and sets himself in opposition to theorists of the seventies and eighties, all of whom he describes as "deny[ing] that there can be a valid ethical criticism."[6] Not distinguishing among structural, deconstructive, feminist, psychoanalytic, or any other theories, Boyers implies that all contemporary literary theory defines "politics [as] an epiphenomenal instancing of desire."[7] Thus, he concludes that political seriousness and contemporary literary theory of any kind are on opposite sides of the barricade. Theory is against "us."

Certainty about those who are for us and those "ag'in" us is a well-known attribute of political behavior. That it does not confine itself to politics of the state, if well-known, is less well-remembered. And if one hesitates to remind others of this well-known, little-remembered attribute, it is for good reason: she is sure to display it herself. Certainty, which lures us all, demanding an answer to the question, is this for us or against us, violates the integrity of a work and of a self. For as Barbara Johnson asserts, the

> story of the self's difference from others inevitably becomes the story of its own unbridgeable difference from itself. Difference is not engendered in the space between identities; it is what makes all totalization of the identity of a self or the meaning of a text impossible.[8]

Deconstruction, applied not as a theory of destruction or of infinite regression, undermines (literally, mines under) a "claim to unequivocal domination of one mode of signifying over another."[9] Exposing the internal difference of a particular text or self, deconstruction also unveils the political and ethical efficacy of uncertainty. But it recognizes, as

Gayatri Spivak argues, that its own discourse can never be adequate to its example.[10]

Even an author's discourse cannot be adequate to that author's novel. The proliferation of interviews with contemporary writers—and there are many with Milan Kundera—does arouse readers' attraction to certain truth. And yet respect for writers and their art demands that we not defer, unreservedly, to their discourse outside that art. In Kundera's case that discourse is eminently quotable—and I confess, I will quote it. But not without some trepidation. In the West the Chosen quickly become celebrities; celebrities easily become commodities. And their work is reduced to advertisements of the self. But then, Kundera very likely knows this; he speaks eloquently about reduction and certainty.

In an interview with Alain Finkielkraut, Kundera asserts,

> Life is constantly chipped away by these *reductive forces* [i.e., summary, simplification, certainty, getting a fix on x], and the work of the novelist is a Don Quixote–like effort to defend man from reduction, to recreate the small imaginary world that has the freshness of an unexpected question.[11]

A dialogue among different value systems is the form of the novel Kundera describes. It is a form conducive to an analysis of internal difference and to a reconciliation of deconstruction and political seriousness.

Kundera's belief in dialogue precedes this interview in the 1980s. It was a belief practiced in June 1967, for example, when Kundera was chosen to read the Writers Union's prepared statement on censorship at the Writers Congress. The rift between official Party representatives and the Writers Union, created largely by the issue of censorship, widened to a chasm at the Writers Congress. Kundera read the expected statement, and it surprised no one. But following its reading Kundera "made it clear that he understood [the statement] rather as a starting point for free discussion." The ensuing dialogue offended the Party leaders, who left the room.[12] Dialogue rehabilitated the diversity of interpretations bludgeoned by the totalization of meaning.

This rehabilitation and other earlier attempts to liberalize the Czech Communist Party in the post-Stalinist sixties did come to an abrupt end. The uneasiness of Czech Party officials in 1967 and then the certain authority of Russian tanks in 1968 saw to that. Milan Kundera, Václav Havel, Antonin Liehm, Josef Škvorecký, and many others attest to the dire consequences for Czech culture. Liehm uses the word *Ausrottung,* extermination.[13] Until very recently there was little evidence to claim political success for dialogue in Czechoslovakia. Memory must retain a place for all such human and cultural atrocities.

So the sentence "dialogue rehabilitated the diversity of interpretations bludgeoned by the totalization of meaning" cannot in honesty ascend to the realm of Babel where there are no state politics and no serious consequences for action. And yet I want to argue that concern for the serious consequences of political action and the analysis of a self or a text's internal difference are not mutually exclusive. To the contrary, understanding of political action depends on such analysis. So rather than praise the heroism of past Czech victims (rhetoric probably more gratifying to me than to Kundera), I intend to analyze the dialogue within Kundera's fiction. How does it explore the internal difference within apparent oppositions? How does this method "recreate the small imaginary world that has the freshness of an unexpected question"? And if the unexpected question valorizes authenticity over authority, how can authenticity be sought amidst all the intimate and advertised political maneuverings of everyday life?

Authenticity is a claim to be heard arising from a text's or an individual's self-consciousness about its own or her own internal difference. It is not a claim of originality, that is, of privileged origin. It is not a claim of power over others; it is not a claim of authority. It *is* a claim of responsibility for the power one does have.

Kundera's most carefully wrought presentation of authenticity is in his fiction. But a quotation from an interview provides a sense of the task Kundera sets for himself. With a vigilance like that of Adrienne Rich, Kundera asserts, "Every evil comes from the moment when a false word is accepted."[14] He gives as an example the word "Soviets," which has ignored the nations that have been "Russified." A similar example is the word "Americans," which usurps the identity and often the sovereignty of the many nations in the Western Hemisphere. The term "Soviet-American relations" muddles the world-effecting significance of the relationship by suggesting that "Soviets" and "Americans" speak for nations, even continents, they do not represent.

A canvass of statements both by Kundera and about his work offers some insights into the challenge of authenticity and Kundera's own vulnerability to certain dichotomy. Most fundamental to comments by and about Kundera are his opposition to lyricism and his adherence to irony.

One manifestation of this position is deep skepticism about the valorization of feeling. For example, in explaining his refusal to write a stage adaptation of Dostoevsky's *The Idiot,* Kundera writes,

> What irritated me about Dostoevsky was the *climate* of his novels: a universe where everything turns into feeling; in other words, where feelings are promoted to the rank of value and of truth.[15]

The novelist expressed a related position in a 1976 interview: there is an "infinite distance between feelings and existence. . . . To grasp this . . . is the art of irony."[16]

The binary opposition of lyricism and irony (associated for Kundera with poetry and novels, respectively) appears repeatedly without equivocation in interviews. It reappears in its most pronounced fictional form in the novel *Life Is Elsewhere.* Unlike the method in *The Joke, The Farewell Party,* most especially *The Book of Laughter and Forgetting,* and *The Unbearable Lightness of Being,* the method of *Life Is Elsewhere* is more one of an attack on lyricism than its undoing. The poet Jaromil and his mother are as often dupes of the author's ire as of the exigencies in their own characters or the metaphysics of their fictional condition. Certainty about the evils of lyricism (including, for example, the poetry of Keats, the confidence of youth, and the loyalties of motherhood) devalues its polar opposite, irony. Just as there is a distance between feeling and truth (a great distance within the self), there is a distance between ironic attack and authenticity.

Irony's attacks on the evils of character and culture best serve authenticity when, as in Kundera's *The Book of Laughter and Forgetting,* the difference within the enemy and the ally complicates the difference between enemy and ally. Irony further serves authenticity by questioning the totality of the author's control of and the reader's understanding of the text. But authenticity, like humility, is a paradox: it demands the self-undoing of characters, author, and reader while it prohibits any declaration of the value of such undoing. When, for example, François Ricard declares Kundera's "subversion" is radical because it "forces me to question the very means by which I thought myself able to be free of the political comedies and jokes of the world,"[17] I admire Ricard's self-consciousness. And yet I think of when I have made similar statements and how they are accompanied by a creeping sense of superiority which renders self-consciousness so delicious. For while I am confronting my bogus political and literary beliefs, I am also tacitly assuming there are others, in the text or outside it, who still hold these beliefs as genuine; in other words, they are fooled. Ricard may be less inclined toward self-congratulation than I. My experience of myself as a reader tells me, however, that truly to surprise a reader's sense of self is a challenge to the authenticity of the novelist's irony. It requires a web of implications tangled as a net in which the reader discovers her complicity, or rather, complicity discovers the reader.

Contemporary writers and critics—those in the United States perhaps most of all—love newness: "make it new," "the shock of the new," "newness of the new." The philosophy of the new pursues authenticity not through the examination of internal difference and complicity but through the renunciation of social and aesthetic conventions. Like other apparent enemies of authenticity—here defined as originality—conventions are not total, coherent entities baring their old breasts for the onslaught of the new. They are replete with mysteries, ambiguities, internal differences. In his afterword to Carlos Fuentes's *Terra Nostra,* Kundera speaks to the assault of the new novel on the novel's conventions. "Paradox: renunciation is immediately visible . . . what is new, what constitutes a discovery, is much harder to discern."[18] That which is most extreme is not necessarily that which can most totally describe and assault its enemy. The face of radical change might pass unrecognized in a world where so many faces purport to be new.

The Book of Laughter and Forgetting is a model study of the internal difference of a self, of a text. The novel provides persuasive evidence for Roland Barthes's theory of rereading: "[rereading] alone saves the text from repetition (those who fail to reread are obliged to read the same story everywhere)."[19] The new discovery, so hard to discern, lies somewhere in the undoing of a self, a text, an authority encountered again and again. For Barthes the reading of each different text tells the same story the reader already knows. But in rereading there is the possibility for the reader honestly to undo her self with the "freshness of the unexpected question."

Rereading complicates one's initial impression that *The Book of Laughter and Forgetting* is a collection of mostly unrelated stories connected by the themes of laughter and forgetting. As the novel itself explains its form, it is a theme and variations. One notes early on, as Lars Kleberg has done, that laughter and forgetting are not a pair like war and peace or the red and the black.[20] Not a dichotomy, laughter and forgetting have a relationship complicated by each term's internal difference. The form of *The Book,* which means to differ from itself, is the ever-fleeting object enticing the rereader.

The Book rewards a search for the totality of its form by spinning out connections of history to fiction to theory and of one story to another to another. At the center of this web of memory is the photograph of Czech Party officials with which the novel begins. In writing of photography John Berger asserts that memory works radially and not linearly like an argument. To serve history authentically, Berger further argues, a photograph must be presented in a context that permits diverse approaches to it. "A radial system has to be constructed around the photograph so that it may be seen in terms which are simultaneously personal, political, economic, dramatic, everyday and historic."[21] Kundera creates such a radial system and diverse approach. *The Book*'s details and diversity defy totalizing theory even as they return the reader to the initial image in the photograph. Even the dichotomy of theory and image, however, is undone by internal difference, the form of *The Book.* As Goethe suggests, "There is a delicate form of the empirical which identifies itself so intimately with its object that it thereby becomes theory."[22] History and art and theory, laughter and forgetting: each differs from itself and identifies with the others even as self and other remain separate inviolable entities.

Part 1 of *The Book,* "Lost Letters," begins with a historical example of a kind of forgetting we might literally call erasure. On a cold February day in 1948, communist leader Gottwald and his comrades, among them Clementis, stand on a balcony and are photographed. Gottwald wears a hat loaned him by the "solicitous Clementis." When in 1952 Clementis is hanged for treason, he is also airbrushed, erased, from the photographs taken on that February day in 1948. "All that remains of Clementis is the cap on Gottwald's head."[23] This is an example of a state's ability to produce negation, forgetting.

The example acts as a warning against collective amnesia which passively accepts actively produced forgetting. Forgetting, in this example, is less a natural result of time and hardening arteries than a constructed artifice of power and control. The erasure practiced by the Czech communist leadership is as absolute as death. It has real consequences unlike the slight-of-hand Derrideans call erasure. In that form of erasure, a term is "disappeared" but reappears with a difference from itself. The difference between the one form of erasure and the other is absolute. Or so it seems.

The photograph, "put out [in] hundreds of thousands of copies" by "the Party propaganda section" (3), was itself a constructed artifice: the Party erased Clementis, replacing him with a brick wall. The Party also unwittingly reproduced and distributed Clementis's cap. The cap remained as a sign for those who could read it. Kundera read it and wrote *The Book*, another constructed artifice, which interprets the sign. *The Book* warns of passive forgetting, active forgetting, and the sign which undoes the power of any artifice to control the totality of forgetting. In *The Book* the absence of Clementis's noble presence is a presence declaring his noble absence. The erasure of Clementis, so skillfully accomplished by Party public relations and photographic technicians, becomes as visible as the erasure by Branwell Brontë of himself from his famous painting of his sisters. *The Book* announces, through Clementis's absence, the presence of Clementis and the process that forgot him. Each form of erasure, the political and the deconstructive, shows the other its difference from itself and its identity with the other.

In *The Book* the history of Clementis becomes The Word which is followed by a parable of lost letters. Mirek, the protagonist of "Lost Letters," is introduced by his assertion in 1971 "that the struggle of man against power is the struggle of memory against forgetting" (3). The point here seems quite clear, for memory, unlike laughter, is the opposite of forgetting. If the individual remembers the abuses of power, he resists that power's ability to overwhelm him. One's political survival and social conscience depend on this memory—of Auschwitz and Birmingham, Hiroshima and Budapest, Soweto and My Lai, San Salvador and Prague.

And yet memory, like forgetting, is a creation anticipating a moment to which it is assigned. One then recreates that memory, that moment, in a thousand other moments dangling in time. In *The Book* (written more than a decade before the important events of 1989), Kundera carefully notes the dates of the moments in which Czech memory has appeared and then reappeared transformed: 1948, 1952, and 1971. Liberation from the Nazis, Stalinism, and the aftermath of the Prague Spring create and recreate memory of power. Mirek's idea of memory that polarizes man and power proves to be a more equivocal lesson to draw from The Word about Clementis than it first appeared. For in 1971 Mirek tries to recreate his memory of 1948 and 1952 without acknowledging that both man (namely himself) and power, as well as memory and forgetting, are filled with paradox. The irony that undoes Mirek reflects back on the earnestness with which the author tells and reader reads the story of Clementis: The Word.

The second sentence of Mirek's story is a paradox: "That [Mirek's philosophy of man and power, memory and forgetting] is his attempt to justify what his friends call carelessness: keeping a careful diary" (3). Mirek has recorded the proceedings of all meetings with his friends about "the current situation," and they are afraid that he and they will be arrested. Mirek's insistence that they are not violating the constitution and must not act guilty rings with the same nobility reverberating through his defiance of power by remembering. And yet Kundera is not interested in sustaining our attraction to Mirek's ideas through a deeply developed sympathy for his courageous character.

Within two paragraphs Mirek has shifted his position to that of his more practical friends. He decides not only to "put the incriminating papers in a safe place" (4), but to reclaim other incriminating papers of his youth. "Keeping a careful diary" is not a new trait for Mirek. Twenty-five years earlier, in 1946, Mirek wrote long and voluminous letters to his lover Zdena, a woman older than he and devoted to the Party. By 1971, however, his memories of Zdena had all become "caricatures," and he "was particularly gratified to note that he had completely forgotten their copulations" (5). Mirek wants the letters back in order to destroy them. Memory of private affairs does not have the same value as memory of political debate.

The story of Mirek's journey to retrieve the letters from Zdena is interrupted by sections of authorial comment explaining the nature of history and the history of Czech intellectuals in particular. While Mirek drives in pursuit of the lost letters, followed by the secret police in pursuit of his political diary, the author tells the reader of the young, intelligent Czechs. As "the body of Clementis swung back and forth like a bell," these young radicals began to doubt their belief in the communist idyll. They tried to call back their deed. "If I were to write a novel about that generation of talented radical thinkers, I would call it *Stalking a Lost Deed*," Kundera tells us (9). Meanwhile Mirek, a fictional representative of these former young radicals, is trying to call back a personal deed, and Kundera, a former young communist himself, is writing a novel called *The Book of Laughter and Forgetting*. *The Book* calls back the absent Clementis and the complicity of state and citizen, author and reader in Clementis's erasure.

Kundera encourages the analogy between Mirek and the author—this "I" who calls himself Milan Kundera and speaks of the history of Czechoslovakia and the writing of *The Book*. He compares his character Mirek to a novelist deprived of his right to cross out Zdena, the beginning of his "novel." "Zdena's existence deprived Mirek of his prerogative as an author" (11). This prerogative to which Mirek aspires is the power of the author to forget a character or scene. Like the state, the author's power is defined by his ability to forget. Rather than uphold his principle asserting his manhood and memory in defiance of power and forgetting, Mirek seeks the power to forget. His ironic failure to achieve the power to forget reflects on his author's power to forget.

Though Mirek fails to forget, he is successfully forgotten, erased by the state with the other "names of the people who rose up against their own youth" in 1968 (14). Even as shadow, Mirek is, in 1971, still rising up against his youth—his youth as Zdena's lover. Because Zdena and her ugliness are a blemish on Mirek's picture of his life, he defines her as opposite. He even assumes she has been given authority by the Party to negotiate with him. He is citizen and man; she is state and power. But he is also forgetting (or wants to be), and she is memory. He denies the power Zdena's love gives him and squanders the power his political diaries, if hidden, could retain because he does not recognize his internal difference or Zdena's.

Because Mirek and Zdena relinquish their power, the only players left to claim authority are the author and the state. The author intrudes his authority petulantly when Mirek's "impulse is to . . . break loose from that memory" of Zdena's face peeking out from behind a flower box. The author asserts, "this time I won't let myself be cheated, I'll call the memory back" (21). He does call it back to assert that Mirek once loved Zdena when his young face was as blemished as hers. The author reads the sign of the flower-lined window, but his power appears short-lived. Mirek drives away having retouched the photograph, removing Zdena.

Like the author's power, the state's power is both possible and limited because of Mirek's blindness to his internal difference. While Mirek is failing to retrieve his lost letters from Zdena, his careful political diary is being confiscated by the state. He, his son, and "ten or so of their friends" are sent to prison. Nevertheless, Mirek insists that "he has been irresistibly attracted by the idea of prison all year. . . . Mirek is going to stretch out full length over [the state's] idyll, like a blemish. And stay there, like

Clementis's cap on Gottwald's head" (24). These words reflect back to the beginning of Part 1 proclaiming the humanity, even the power, of memory and the hope it inspires. There are, however, a number of mitigating circumstances dividing Mirek from himself, the text from itself.

The "Zdena problem," as Mirek calls it—a phrase reminiscent of the "Jewish problem" or the "Negro problem"—is never resolved. The author insists on her presence; Mirek, on her absence. Because the lost love letters remain lost, and the author himself earlier compares Zdena to Clementis, it would seem the shadow of her large nose is as much a presence in her absence as Clementis's cap on Gottwald's head. She is the blemish on Mirek's personal idyll not only because of the youth he wishes to recant but because of his own values he chooses selectively to erase.

Also, Mirek's irresistible attraction to the idea of prison is comparable to an earlier attraction he now wishes to deny. Mirek's attraction to Zdena was also genuine and nobly connected to another higher cause, the formation of the new Czech communist state. Compared to his youth, weakness, poverty, and acne, Zdena's greater age and supposed Party connections were a higher power enhancing his attraction. But Mirek's later renunciation of his weakness, his love, Zdena's ugliness, and the communist idyll have not made him so new a man as he imagines. Ironically, he still perceives himself as a blemish, though now this strikes him as strength rather than weakness. But his adherence to self-deception is, as Peter Kussi argues, a Sartrean "bad faith."[24] This attraction to prison—announced conveniently after the fact of the arrests—is not so different from but rather is the same as his earlier attraction.

The statement that "Mirek is going to stretch out full length over their idyll . . . like Clementis's cap" (24) would seem to suggest the author approves of Mirek's attraction to prison. In fact, the structure of the sentence, as translated, makes ambivalent the origin of this decision to "stretch out." Does the author believe that Mirek is the same as Clementis's cap, a sign resisting erasure? The final words of Part 1—"Mirek was sentenced to six years, his son to two years, and ten or so of their friends to terms of from one to six years" (24)—cast a shadow of their own.

By denying the vulnerability of his youth and relinquishing his power to influence Zdena, Mirek carelessly exposes his friends and son as well as himself to the power of the state. He avoids his responsibility for their arrest, his complicity, by asserting himself as an unambiguous opponent of the state. But in this and all his self-assertions, Mirek prohibits these others—presumably his loved ones—from making their own choices. As Václav Havel explains, the conflict is not between the individual's aims of life and the state system: the dividing line runs through each individual. Each is a supporter and victim of the state.[25] Mirek's story appears to move with rhetorical vigor toward its conclusion reaffirming the moral of the Clementis story. And yet the text differs from itself as Mirek does from himself. The method of *The Book* undoes the totality of self and text thereby valorizing neither appearances nor some hidden reality. In the absence of a noble presence the method recognizes the absence and the presence and that "we don't see that much."

The lost letters Mirek sought, in remaining lost to him, are secure in Zdena's possession while the lost letters Mirek possessed, in being found by the police, are lost to Mirek and perhaps to all subsequent generations. But there is one way in which both sets of letters are lost. The reader knows the contents of neither. We know one set is love letters and the other is political notes, but the words of both are hidden from us. As Barbara Johnson says of Poe's "Purloined Letter," it is

> [not] the contents of the letter, but the position of the letter within the group which decides what each person will do next. . . . the letter does not function as a unit of meaning (a *signified*) but as that which produces certain effects (a *signifier*). . . . the letter acts like a signifier to the extent that its function in the story does not require that its meaning be revealed.[26]

Both as epistles and as graphemes, letters in "Lost Letters" assert their significance not through the revelation of totalizing meaning but through their "position within the group" (including fictional characters, historical characters, the author, and the reader). They decide what each member of the group "will do next" as a participant in the process that is *The Book*. In the presentation of this process, *The Book* asserts a theory about how language functions as it also asserts a theory about how power functions.

The question of lost letters is taken up again in Part 4, also entitled "Lost Letters." Here too, the contents of the lost letters are lost to the reader. Tamina, the author of these letters, is, in many ways, different from Mirek, even a foil for Mirek, but this difference finally enhances the ways in which lost letters render the characters the same. They are different in that though they both want to reclaim lost love letters—in Tamina's case, a journal—her motivation is to remember the details of her relationship with a now-deceased husband, not to erase the relationship.

Even if she can get back her journals, Tamina fears that she will find gaps in them like those in her memory. She had only begun the journal at her husband's request and did not always faithfully make entries. "She loved him too much to admit that what she thought of as unforgettable could ever be forgotten" (84). Mirek, on the other hand, sought to preserve memory of feeling and idea by writing everything down. Though Mirek does not quite qualify as a graphomaniac, defined by Kundera as one who writes "to have a public of unknown readers" (91–92), he does write of his life to enhance its value. Yet both characters are subjected to a network of relationships because of lost letters whose contents they can either not remember or not control.

Tamina lost her notebooks when she and her husband left Czechoslovakia because the state persecuted him and his friends betrayed him. The notebooks were left in Prague; Tamina is alone in a village in the West. It is politics, not love, that prohibits the return of the notebooks to Tamina. She needs the help of someone from the West. But neither her friends in the West nor her relatives in Prague prove to be as loyal or sympathetic as Mirek's son and friends. Circumstances force upon Tamina more desperate and solitary measures. For example, although Tamina has not enjoyed sex with any man since her husband's death, she sleeps with the student Hugo who promises to retrieve her notebooks. (Hugo later reneges on his promise.) Mirek has also lost his spouse, but the death of his beautiful wife only enhances his sexual activities by rendering him a "pathetic" widower. Yet Mirek does not seduce Zdena to win back his letters, withheld from him by Zdena's "love," not state politics. Both Tamina and Mirek fail to reclaim their lost letters. She sacrifices the silence she desires and her habitual, celibate devotion to her dead husband so that she can better remember their love. She tries to sacrifice her image of herself to preserve her image of her husband but fails. Mirek tries to destroy his image of his former lover to preserve his image of himself, but he fails.

Tamina and Mirek also differ in their roles as political beings. Mirek believes that as a prisoner he will be an unforgettable blemish on the state's idyll. Tamina announces no political ambitions. The author does declare "[Tamina] knew [Czechoslovakia] inside out, and I can tell you—everything she said was true" (95). And yet Tamina is an émigré because of her *husband's* situation in Czechoslovakia. She left her native country because of him and she cannot return to it for fear of betraying him, as their friends had done. Her love for and memory of her husband are her sole expressed criteria for decision-making. Political conditions seem only to exist as an obstacle to her love. Ironically, she lets Hugo assume her notebooks are about politics to convince him of their significance. Yet both Mirek and Tamina suffer the political consequences of having written lost letters regardless of their content. What matters is the letters' absence and presence in the group.

When first introducing Tamina, Kundera interjects a personal, passionate note: "my heroine belongs to me and me alone (and means more to me than anyone ever has)" (79). He speaks of her with consistent sympathy even as love for her husband and her obsession about the notebooks drive her to failure. He understands that she is the frustrated émigré told but never asked about her native land. Indeed, "Tamina had long since realized that if she wanted to make her life comprehensible to people [in the West] she had to simplify it" (94).

While Mirek is demonstrably self-deceived, Tamina does not "cheat" the author. And for his part, Kundera only interrupts her story to reaffirm her. Tamina is the "human being" for whom "the eyes of a single outsider are enough to destroy the worth of her personal diaries" (105). Discounting Tamina's authorship of the diaries, the author tells us that the opposite of Tamina, the human being, is the writer—Kundera offers his own characters, Goethe, and himself as examples.

> If a single individual *fails* to set eyes on [the writer's] lines, that individual calls his . . . entire existence into question. . . . A person who writes books is either all (a single universe for himself and everyone else) or nothing. And since *all* will never be given to anyone, every one of us who writes books is *nothing*. Ignored, jealous, deeply wounded, we wish the death of our fellow man. In that respect we are all alike: Banaka, Bibi, Goethe, and I. . . . Once the writer in every individual comes to life (and that time is not far off), we are in for an age of universal deafness and lack of understanding. (105–6)

The more *The Book*'s author writes of himself, the more he differs from himself. For example, he means totally to possess his heroine creating from letters a character who is "a universe for himself." But the more he defines her significance, the more she is lost letters revealing his internal difference. When he tries to assign Tamina a fixed meaning, he despairs of all writing. *The Book* is, however, testimony that letters are the cause of the relationship between the characters of history and those of fiction, between the author and the reader, and the cause of the relationship of the author with himself, the reader with herself.

Like Mirek, Tamina is a means to show the text and the author-ity of the text differing within themselves. The impulse for certainty (all or nothing), so understandable, deceptive, quixotic, and destructive, propels Tamina as it does Mirek and their author. While Mirek survives by defining his failure and shifting circumstances as meaningful (all), Tamina suffers the loss of what she thought she would never forget by the same impulse for certainty (nothing). And when Tamina later drowns trying to live, she cheats her author as Mirek has done. Both leave the author behind. Tamina's intimate body human and Mirek's public body politic are parts of the same metaphysics of uncertainty which humbles actors in the world of love and power.

Tamina is the love letter whose identity her author works to control as though it were his own. His relationship to her reveals internal differences in *The Book* which draw him and the reader into a net of complicity flung out from the image of the dead Clementis. When Tamina appears in Part 6, "The Angels," the author again speaks explicitly about her role.

> This entire book is a novel in the form of variations. . . . It is a novel about Tamina, and whenever Tamina is absent, it is a novel for Tamina. She is its main character and main audience, and all the other stories are variations on her story and come together in her life as in a mirror. (165)

The presence of the mature Tamina in Part 6 among the undifferentiated selves of the angelic children is of considerable interest, particularly as it is juxtaposed to the death of the author's father.[27] Appreciation of the ironies of this presence in Part 6 depends upon examination of Tamina's absence in Part 2, "Mother," in which Tamina's effect is felt in her absence.

"Mother" seems the oddest of the novel's seven parts, a digressive improvisation. Its use of sex (at least for this woman reader and others I have talked to) seems gratuitous titillation. "Mother" is intriguing for these reasons and others. The situation of motherhood plays a significant role in Kundera's attack on lyricism in *Life Is Elsewhere*. The mother of the poet exits the novel no less scathed than Jaromil, her poet-son. Tereza's mother in *The Unbearable Lightness of Being* is a coarse woman whose cruelty scars her daughter's life. In the comic *Farewell Party,* motherhood is manipulated by pregnant Ruzena, who wants the devotion of a famous trumpeter she slept with once, and is duped by Dr. Skreta, who artificially inseminates his unsuspecting patients with his own sperm. On the other hand, within *The Book* the author writes an extended, loving account of his father's final days.

Analyzing "Mother" as a variation on *The Book*'s theme and as a manifestation of the absent Tamina, I have in mind the prominent role of motherhood in Kundera's fiction and the prominent placement of the author's father in Part 6 with Tamina and the children. I also have in mind Adrienne Rich's *Of Woman Born* and Dorothy Dinnerstein's *The Mermaid and the Minotaur*. Feminist questions open *The Book,* revealing how it differs from itself.

Symmetry might pair Part 2, "Mother," with Part 5, "Litost." Indeed, the relationship in "Litost" of the poet-student and the older, provincial butcher's wife bears more than a slight resemblance to that of mother and son. If, however, the introduction of Tamina in Part 4 is the core of the novel and the other sections extend in opposite directions from her, then this symmetry pairs "Mother" with Part 6, "The Angels." Any attempt to create symmetry of seven parts probably deserves a laughing response. But there are reasons other than symmetry to see Parts 2 and 6 as mirror images—folding together reflection and opposition, saming and othering.

"The Angels" is about the author's dying father and about Tamina, big as a mother or an Amazon, on an island of children. "Mother" is about Karel's aging mother, Eva (the tall lover of Karel), and his wife, Marketa. Together Mother and Eva remind Karel of Nora, another tall, imposing woman, whom Karel once saw nude when he was a child. In the story of the author's father, no wife and mother appear. In the story of "Mother," the only husband and father is Karel, the son. In both "The Angels" and "Mother," the role of the son is prominent. The transmission of culture depends on the father-son relationship, as it is conventionally practiced; in "the Angels" the father's aphasia, as disease and metaphor, both interrupts and enhances this transmission. Communion with sexual partners and with nature depends on the mother-son relationship, as it is conventionally practiced, and in "Mother" the mother's memory—selective though it be—enhances but also interrupts this communion.

"Mother" asks the question Dinnerstein asks: Why do people go on consenting to intolerable gender arrangements?[28] Marketa and Karel, typical of many Kundera couples, love one another but suffer in their relationship because he is promiscuous and she is jealous, or at least they have the habits of promiscuity and jealousy learned in the early days of their relationship. They need "someone to set them free" (38) from this binary opposition. This someone is Eva. Like Eve, Eva is born of man's desire. One day Karel unexpectedly receives sensual photographs of a

strange young woman; soon she is doing a striptease for him and mastur-
bating in his friend's apartment. The "birth" of Karel's Eva usurps the
woman's procreative role as does the "birth" of Adam's Eve.[29]

Prior to the advent of Eva, Marketa had suggested that she, Karel, and
one of Karel's mistresses make love together to alleviate what is intolerable
about their marriage. The possibility excites Karel, but he finds the experience grueling because he believes the women act only as rivals. The author
explains,

> If he could have believed that Marketa requested their little orgies out of pure
> sensuality . . . he would certainly have enjoyed them. But since it had been
> established early in the game that *he* was worse, all he could see in her debauch-
> ery was a painful denial of self and a noble attempt at meeting his polygamous
> lapses halfway. . . . When he saw her in the arms of another woman, he felt like
> falling to his knees and begging her forgiveness. (40)

The author here posits the possibility that Marketa finds pleasure in the
sensual enjoyment of another woman, but the sight of this pleasure makes
Karel want to fall to his knees. The scene presents a challenge—almost a
paradigmatic challenge—to binary opposition as it is so forcefully defined
by sexual mores: husband versus wife; woman versus woman. Because
Karel does not recognize how he might participate in the undoing of
binary opposition when he witnesses it, he wants instead to beg his wife's
forgiveness, thereby returning her attention to the conventional tension
between husband and wife.

Dinnerstein's analysis of gender arrangements is based on the fact that,
in the overwhelming number of cases, women are the primary caretakers
of infants and on the hypothesis that in the prerational stage of infant
sexuality, girls as well as boys find a deep sensual satisfaction in their
proximity to the mother's body, a satisfaction they try to recreate the rest
of their lives.[30] For women this desire is usually, by cultural necessity,
translated into heterosexual relations. But in sexual relations with Karel's
mistresses, Marketa has an opportunity to have the mother's body and a
heterosexual relationship. To Marketa, Eva is not of Karel's rib at all. In
fact, Marketa and Eva secretly agree to meet without Karel but with Eva's
new husband instead.

Juxtaposed to Eva's weekend visit at the home of Karel and Marketa is
the visit of Karel's widowed mother. Mother once seemed a hostile figure
from whom Marketa and Karel wanted to flee. But now, shrunken to child
size, she produces in her son and daughter-in-law a "surge of indulgence,

tolerance" (27). Convention assumes mothers are powerful, but their place in children's sexual desires and their often sole responsibility for children's well-being creates instead a myth of power. Fear of what might be real about maternal power has exaggerated the power and turned fiercely against it. In this dichotomous thinking mothers are powerful and all that is not-mother (child, man) is powerless. Therefore, we who are not-mother will work to transform and imprison maternal power so that we may be free.[31] Marketa and Karel "free" themselves first by getting away from Mother and later by transforming her into a pathetic child smaller than their adult figures. Neither act frees them from their unhappy gender arrangement. If I follow Dinnerstein's argument, then I conclude that imbedded in Marketa and Karel is the unacknowledged memory of the mother's body, the source of their sensual pleasure and internal difference.

"Mother" poses an analogy between sexual paradox and the other political and linguistic paradoxes evident in *The Book*. All three radiate from the paradox of memory. While Mother sits in her absent grandson's room trying to remember her past, her son, Eva, and Marketa prepare for love-making in the living room. But "[Karel] was not looking forward to the evening's adventure. . . . he was tired and not particularly in the mood" (39). When Mother remembers what she had forgotten earlier in the evening, she goes to the living room to tell the three lovers. She also tells them that Eva reminds her of her old friend Nora. Because Mother's interruption catches the scantily clad women off guard, it pleases Karel. But he is even more pleased when the mention of Nora reminds him of himself as a child looking up the long legs of Nora to a naked backside. This image, awakened by Mother's fading memory, inflames Karel's flagging desire. After Mother's exit he leaps on Eva and begins making love. It is

> the leap of a little boy hurtling his way from childhood to manhood. And as he moved on her . . . he felt he was describing the movement from . . . a boy staring powerless at an enormous female body to a man gripping that body and taming it. (47)

Karel's aged, child-size mother brings back for him the infant's pre-memory desire for the mother's body which Karel remembers as a boy's awe of statuesque Nora. He remembers being powerless and now imagines being powerful. But because of a belief in the dichotomous myth in which power cannot be shared, Karel cannot leap into authentic adult-hood—though he can leap into that manhood which is conventionally defined as conqueror. Instead, it seems he will repeat again and again the same leap as Barthes's reader who pursues the same story in different texts. The more different mistresses he has, the more his leap will be the same.

The effects of the mother-child (i.e., sole caretaker–dependent) rela-tionship on adult (in this case, especially male) sensuality is further com-plicated by the role of the Amazon myth in this story and in "The Angels." According to myth, the function of Amazon warrior-women is to oppose monogamy and motherhood and man. Eva declares herself unaffected by the jealousies that plague monogamy and acts as a mistress. Nora proves an impossible woman with whom Mother had an unreconciled falling out. Neither Eva nor Nora contends with the quotidian conflicts of monogamy or motherhood so disturbing to Marketa (also a mother) and Mother. But these Amazons are also not clear opponents of wife, mother, or man. Eva complicates the dichotomy of husband and wife by being the lover of both. And Nora, or memory of Nora, penetrates Karel's isolation from the women bringing him back into the sexual nexus. At the same time, however, this memory prompts Karel's bogus leap into manhood and exposes the rift in his sexuality.

In "Mother" the Amazons Eva and Nora are the absence of Tamina. In "The Angels" Tamina is present—tall and beautiful like Eva and Nora. Though painfully monogamous, Tamina is also not a mother. On the island among the children, she most especially seems an Amazon. On the allegorical island she learns the evils of innocence without memory (the insidious euphoria of a totalitarian idyll). But her experiences there also raise questions about the myths of Amazons and mothers, the insidious idylls of womanhood that lie beneath conscious memory. The author's protagonist is pointedly a woman among children, not a Gulliver among the Lilliputians. The children treat her size and strength as warrior com-modities to be leashed and used in their relentless competition of "inno-cent" games. She is like a helpless babysitter with none of the mother's power to discipline: implied in her helplessness is the fact that she is not their mother; she is not anybody's mother. Despite this fact, the children work to harness her mature sexuality as if she were a mother. With fierce determination the children first stroke, then prod and poke the body of Tamina: adoration as humiliation. At first Tamina feels privileged but quickly feels abused. She tries to escape the island of perpetual childhood where sexuality never matures and a woman need not be a mother to be throttled by the myths and countermyths of motherhood. Tamina's presence among "The Angels" and her absence in "Mother" demonstrate that totalitarian childhood (sexual, psychological, and political) abuses the complexities of adult life.

In Part 3 the author tells a story about Milan Kundera which again raises the question about man's desire to possess the other. By expressing his vulnerability to totalitarian impulses, Kundera turns the reader around to face her own. Having acted pseudonymously as a horoscope writer, the author learns the authorities have uncovered his ruse. Now the young woman editor who came to him with the job will be in trouble for fraternizing with persona non grata Milan Kundera. When she (called only R) and he meet secretly to discuss their dilemma, her bowels are reacting to fear. Though the author had always had an "innocent, asexual" fondness for R, the sheer physicality exposed by her unruly bowels arouses in the author "a violent desire to rape her."

> To throw myself on her and take possession of her with all her intolerably exciting contradictions. . . . It was contradictions like those, I felt, that made up her true essence. . . . I felt like leaping on her and tearing it out of her. I felt like engulfing her—her shit and her ineffable soul. (75)

The author recognizes how "scandalous" this desire is, yet he swears the desire to rape his friend remains with him.

The reader might dismiss Karel's arousal as silly, but the author's is undeniably complex and frightening. Karel wants to control a certain memory whose unchanging image he can depend on. He acknowledges no contradictions. The author is motivated to rape by his awareness of contradictions. And yet the difference between the character and author is in a fundamental way the same: both want to "tame," to "engulf" in a "leap," another, to make that other self be whole, undivided, unchanging, so that he too may be undivided. The author does not want to know, as he does know, that his presence is a political liability for his friends. Only his absence can now be friendship.

The leap to contain what is uncertain and changing is an act in defiance of mortality. It is a corporeal act in defiance of the corpus. The leap is personal and political, physical and metaphysical. As Rich and Dinnerstein argue, the myths of culture have made women the battleground on which this duel with death takes place.[32] Death is the one totality we can count on and the one we cannot accept. Motherhood—thus, woman—suffers from its proximity to the beginning of life which is also its end.

In her afterword to *Of Woman Born,* Adrienne Rich writes,

> In arguing that we have by no means yet explored or understood our biological grounding, the miracle and paradox of the female body and its spiritual and political meanings, I am really asking whether women cannot begin, at last, to *think through the body.*[33]

She looks for a mode of thinking that does not divide mind from body, nature from culture, a kind of thinking based not on dichotomies but on paradox. In Part 7, "The Border," Kundera also returns to the significance of the body. Juxtaposed to the imminent death and then the funeral of Passer, a man loved by many friends, are various forms of sexual liberation debated and practiced by these friends: orgies, nude beaches, braless women, technically proficient sex, and reasonable sex. On the one extreme (the orgies), the mature sexual body is all; on the other extreme (the nude beaches), it is nothing. Or so it seems.

Barbara's commands to her orgy participants truncate any sensual feeling they are experiencing making them interchangeable bodies with no distinguishing marks. Barbara's will is all, not the bodies she rules. At the nude beach bodies are presumably freed by being ignored. And yet the author personifies their genitals in his novel's last sentence. While the characters discuss the demise of Western civilization, "their naked genitals star[e] dully, sadly, listlessly at the yellow sand" (228). They are alive, but human will again insists on controlling them by ignoring them—as the communists do the cap on Gottwald's head. None of the forms of liberation practiced by the characters and satirized by their author is the "thinking through the body" Rich describes.

"The Border" has only one character whose will serves his body: Passer, the dying man who works to stay alive, as the author's father worked, in his dying days, to remember. Passer's work is only temporarily rewarded, but it is nonetheless authentic acknowledgment of the body in life and in death. All other liberation of the body does not set it free. Of course, Passer must fail, but he does assert his corporeal self even at his funeral when his coffin, aided by the wind, mysteriously attracts the hat of a mourner. The other mourners try to ignore this unexpected (comic) event just as the people at the beach ignore their genitals staring at the sand. Little do they suspect the connections between the hat on Passer's coffin and the cap on Gottwald's head, between those sad "faces" on the beach and the decline of Western civilization.

An émigré lives, as the author has, always on the border, neither in his country nor out. But so do we all in our analogous, mortal state. The politics of *The Book* are the politics of the body, of gender, of sex, motherhood, and the state. The totality of death and uncertainty of life are the parameters within which human beings must be lovers, mothers, and citizens. If we mean to pursue authenticity in our roles as any of these, then we need to imagine how we differ from ourselves, how the dividing line runs through each individual. *The Book of Laughter and Forgetting* defies totalizing interpretation and asserts instead a politics, a history, a theory, a fiction, a sexuality—in short, a metaphysics of internal difference. *The Book* is not The Word on East-West relations or any other manifestation of power, but neither are its letters lost. It is authentic.

The method of *The Book* is a model for democratic citizenship which depends on unexpected questions asked of author-ity. Uncertainty insists on these questions. Deconstruction provokes them. But deconstructive analysis need not prohibit action or leadership as so many seem to fear. In his open letter to Milan Kundera, Robert Boyers writes, "To be serious about politics is after all to believe that there is such a thing as legitimate authority, which owes its legitimacy to binding truths on which it can take its stand."[34] Boyers and I seem to agree that *The Book* is a political novel and probably would agree on various appropriate political actions for citizens who want to assert democracy. And yet his fear is of uncertainty; mine, of certainty.

I could claim Kundera as an ally standing on my side of the barricade by quoting the afterword to *The Book:*

> It seems to me that all over the world people nowadays prefer to judge rather than to understand, to answer rather than ask, so that the voice of the novel can hardly be heard over the noisy foolishness of human certainties. (237)

But the greater value for the novel and for politics lies in asking how Boyers differs from himself, I from myself, *The Book* from itself.

Feminism is a case in point. In Part 3, "The Angels," the author refers to the French feminist Annie Leclerc and associates her joy in the female body with the idyllic (destructive) laughter of the angels. In addition, the author presents the passionless sexuality of Edwige as well as the willful orgies of Barbara in "The Border" as examples of "liberated" womanhood. So it is not surprising that Boyers assumes that "the angels in your novel also include the 'liberated' French and Americans who in the name of feminism or some other advanced ideology promote a progressivism as mindless as that celebrated by the Communist faithful."[35] I, on the other hand, assume that "Mother" and Tamina, the whole novel really, are well-served by questions derived from Rich and Dinnerstein's feminist thinking through the body.[36] And I call this analysis political. I see in the novel significant examples of mother-child relationships crucial to an analysis of totalitarian power and humanitarian change. Who is blinded by ideology? Boyers? Me? Kundera?

> You've got to remember we don't see that much.
> We see a portion of eaves dripping in the pastel book
> And are aware that everything doesn't count equally—
> There is dreaminess and infection in the sum.[37]

We move   but our words stand
become responsible
for more than we intended

and this is verbal privilege

>   Adrienne Rich, "North American Time"

>   from the center of my body
a voice bursts   against these methods

>   Adrienne Rich, #12 of "Contradictions"

Chapter III
The Body, the Word, and the State

Torture and Interrogation: J. M. Coetzee's
Waiting for the Barbarians

In "The Presence of Absence" Lance Olsen gives a Derridean reading of J. M. Coetzee's *Waiting for the Barbarians*.[1] Calling upon Derrida's definition of a metaphysics of presence, Olsen asserts as his thesis that absence is at the center of Coetzee's language. This "metaphysics of presence [is] a [misguided] metaphysics that longs for the 'truth' behind every sign, . . . a stable 'meaning.'" According to this theory, writing is, by nature, antithetical to this metaphysics. It creates absence.[2] Olsen describes the torturer from the Third Bureau, Colonel Joll, as a misreader who deals in the metaphysics of presence while he describes the old, colonial magistrate as one who believes meaning and truth "float free." In his argument Olsen defends Coetzee's novel as a postmodern fiction misunderstood by its prescriptive reviewers who seek a specific historical setting in the novel (and thus, they imply, a clearer political context).[3]

I too would defend this South African novel's temporally and geographically enjambed setting as I would Olsen's thesis about the struggle between presence and absence, certainty and uncertainty. And yet, I do not share Olsen's conclusions. For example, in arguing that the novel (all writing) produces gaps, or absence, Olsen refers to the wood slips, a sort of ancient hieroglyphics unearthed by the magistrate whose avocation is archaeology. Though Joll assumes the magistrate knows the meaning of the wood slips, in fact the magistrate has no idea how to decipher them. Of this situation Olsen writes, "As Derrida would have it, those wood slips form an absence which may be supplemented in an endless number of ways, *cut off from responsibility,* from authority, an emblem of orphaned language, nothing more than a productive mechanism" (my emphasis).[4] Leaving aside how "Derrida would have it," I am struck by the words "cut off from responsibility." Granted that these wood slips and all linguistic "truth" in the novel are gaps open to various interpretations and thus without an ultimate authority, I reject the leap from no authority (or no certainty) to no responsibility. In the passage quoted above I cannot be sure whether Olsen refers to the responsibility of the writers or readers of the wood slips, but in either case, I believe he is wrong. Neither inside nor outside the context of this novel is responsibility contingent upon authority or certainty.

The other of Olsen's conclusions with which I disagree is that "in postmodern fiction," such as Coetzee's novel, we arrive at "a frustration, a despair before the arbitrariness of language and its essential defectiveness for depicting the world."[5] Of this particular novel and what Olsen calls the "brutal flatness" of its language, he writes, "We are in a monologue with nowhere to go, nothing to say, no one to say it to, a web of linguistic misfirings that disintegrate before anyone has heard, a field of blankness and a desolation that there has to be such blankness."[6] Placing *Waiting for the Barbarians* in a category of fiction called postmodern, Olsen describes only the ways in which the language of the novel is about language. He does not mention the salient, sentient fact that the novel is also about physical torture, the body in pain. The body in pain has everything to do with the language of the novel.

I focus on Olsen's essay because I can easily imagine that his conclusions feed the fear of uncertainty and the hostility toward deconstruction found in, say, Robert Boyers's *Atrocity and Amnesia: The Political Novel Since 1945.* Boyers writes that he finds nothing in criticism written after the mid-sixties that facilitates his discussion of the political novel. In fact, his book sets itself squarely against deconstruction. Furthermore, Boyers asserts, "To be serious about politics is after all to believe that there is such a thing as legitimate authority, which owes its legitimacy to binding truths on which it can take its stand."[7] I can also imagine Olsen's conclusions would cause a politically conscious writer such as Irving Howe to return to his desire for a historical setting in *Waiting for the Barbarians:* "one possible loss [in the novel] is bite and pain, the urgency that a specified historical place and time may provide," Howe writes in his review of the novel.[8] Olsen's conclusions could even reinforce the belief expressed in *Olive Schreiner and After* by South African critic Rowland Smith: Nadine Gordimer's novels are artistically, morally, and politically superior to Coetzee's because her approach is direct and historical while his is "oblique."[9] Many who express a commitment to political concerns have grave doubts about deconstruction and about novels such as this whose language deconstructs itself. Olsen's aesthetic defense of the novel reads as condemnation for those who concern themselves with the plight of South Africa in particular or politics and the political novel in general. For he suggests that the wood slips are a paradigm of the novel. It too is "cut off from responsibility."

Like Boyers, my intent is to be serious about politics and the political novel (and South Africa). But like Olsen (and Derrida), I question the metaphysics of presence which pursues *the* truth, the "binding truths" in which Boyers believes. The method of deconstruction which questions certainty, scrutinizes authority, examines paradox, and undoes the rigidity of binary oppositions can serve serious political concern and analysis of politics in texts. When a critic practicing a deconstructive method leaps to conclusions of irresponsibility and despair, it is not because those conclusions are inherent in the method. And certainly irresponsibility is not inherent to *Waiting for the Barbarians*. If its ending is desolate, it is so with a particular and moral-centered skepticism and not just with a "blankness" of "linguistic misfirings."

Waiting for the Barbarians is about language and about the body in pain. The relationship between the two, so crucial to the novel, is discussed by Elaine Scarry in her controversial book *The Body in Pain: The Making and Unmaking of the World*. Because scenes of physical torture are the central, heightened drama and the principal dilemma of Coetzee's novel, the insights of Scarry and others who have studied historical and contemporary torture practices are particularly useful in reading it.

The *Oxford English Dictionary* distinguishes between two kinds of torture. The first is "the infliction of excruciating pain . . . by cruel tyrants, savages, brigands etc. from a delight in watching the agony of a victim, in hatred or revenge, or as a means of extortion"; the second, referred to as judicial torture, is "inflicted by a judicial or quasi-judicial authority for the purpose of forcing an accused or suspected person to confess, or an unwilling witness to give evidence or information." Alan Sheridan, the translator of Michel Foucault's *Discipline and Punish,* also refers to the public mutilation and execution of convicted criminals as torture.

Foucault focuses on judicial torture, whether in secretive interrogation or public mutilation, in pre-eighteenth-century Europe, while Scarry focuses on the relationship of pain and interrogation, what Foucault calls *"la question,"* without separating torturers who are savages from those who are judicial authorities. The thinking of both Foucault and Scarry about torture is relevant to Coetzee's *Waiting for the Barbarians,* but if Scarry's less historical analysis is somewhat more pertinent, it is because the novel's colonial conditions and its author's postcolonial South African context employ an ambiguous amalgamation of the various European definitions of torture. Despite the extreme cruelty in seventeenth- and eighteenth-century European torture and despite extreme class differences among the people of Europe, Foucault, in his description of torture and mutilating executions, can still speak of the criminal's moral dignity and the spectators' identification with the criminal. He even describes the struggle between the criminal and the executioner as a kind of duel.[10] But in the context of Coetzee's novel and in South Africa, both crucibles of colonial ideologies, no such dignity, identity, or equality is granted indigenous peoples as objects of torture. (Moreover, the transformation of eighteenth-century European attitudes toward torture, from public acceptance to moral indignation, the change central to Foucault's argument, did not simultaneously or similarly occur in the colonies.) In all the heterogeneous nation-states occupying the colonized continents (Africa or the Americas, Asia or Australia), the distinction between judicial and nonjudicial torture has been ambiguous and the distance between tortured and torturer paradoxically great and short. Contemporary South Africa is a recalcitrant, perverse apotheosis but of the colonial ambiguity and racial ideology which is the history of much of the contemporary world. Coetzee has good reason to write of torturous colonialism and not name it South Africa.

Central to Scarry's definition of torture is the idea that interrogation (language) and physical threat and abuse (the body in pain) function both against one another and together in the torture process. An understanding of this relationship between language and the body in pain must begin with some ideas about the rhetorical situation of any intense pain, not only that caused by torturers. Scarry writes, "for the person in pain, so incontestably and unnegotiably present is it that 'having pain' may come to be thought of as the most vibrant example of what it is to 'have certainty,' while for the other person it is so elusive that 'hearing about pain' may exist as the primary model of what it is 'to have doubt.'"[11] Scarry suggests here that at least one kind of certainty exists where we would least like to pursue it, in the intense pain of our own bodies. Our human impulse, one may easily observe, is to associate certainty with security, not with the worst insecurity and vulnerability. Reason, verbal expression, technological skill, moral conviction, religious belief: these are the places we decide certainty and security reside. Human will pushes certainty as far from pain and death as it can. And so the body in pain is often not credited, cannot be credited, unless the observer admits this could happen to him; his body can "betray" him just as violently.

In a lengthy review Peter Singer objects to Scarry's assumption: "there is no generally accepted philosophical basis for saying that physical pain is more 'real' than ordinary material objects like cell bars."[12] Though it is not my intention necessarily to defend the manner or even the conclusions of Scarry's book, the arguments she offers and the questions those arguments provoke are so germane to a reading of Coetzee's novel in particular and colonial (and postcolonial) politics in general as to require some careful consideration here. Is pain, especially intense pain, more real than empirically observed cell bars? Keeping this question distinct from that which asks which is the more objectionable punishment, I turn to three philosophers for a discussion of the original question about the body and knowledge: Hannah Arendt, Jean-Paul Sartre, and Susan Bordo. A fourth philosopher, Theodor Adorno, serves as commentator on the other three.

Arendt distinguishes between two kinds of truth in an essay entitled "Truth and Politics." First, rational, or philosophical, truths are described as those produced by the mind in solitude and perceived by the many as opinion in the marketplace (the world of politics). Second, factual truth is "seen and witnessed with the eyes of the body, and not the eyes of the mind . . . it is established by witnesses and depends upon testimony; it exists only to the extent it is spoken about."[13] To which—if either—of these categories does the experience of intense pain belong? Not a philosophic truth, it is, nonetheless, produced in part by the mind and experienced alone if not in solitude. Medical measurements notwithstanding, can any witness say for certain that another individual is or is not experiencing pain? And yet the experience of pain is factual truth for the person in pain. It is witnessed not with the *eyes,* the optic nerves, of the body but with other nerves of the body as capable (or incapable) of establishing factual truth. But because pain does not relate to other people and cannot depend upon their testimony, its factual nature can be perceived as illusion or opinion by those who witness it and those who hear tell of it. In other words, they can doubt it.

An individual in pain cannot doubt it. That person can doubt the degree to which pain is caused by actual physical damage but not the existence of pain itself. Deriving information from Melzack and Wall's *The Challenge of Pain,* Edward Peters explains, in *Torture,* that pain always has physical and psychological dimensions and that these dimensions are dependent upon the unique history of an individual, including that person's fears and hopes for the future.[14] Given this complex context for pain, I am not arguing that one feels severe chest pain and knows for a fact that one is experiencing heart failure; rather, one feels severe chest pain and knows for a fact it is pain. According to Arendt's definitions the imprisonment of an individual behind cell bars is a factual truth when verified by witnesses, but physical pain is no less real though more subject to doubt. Matter shows the insufficiency of the philosopher's method, Adorno argues, a method driven by society's compulsive need for solid truth and philosopher's compulsive need for a totalizing system.[15]

Sartre insists upon a distinction between the body-for-others and the body as being-for-itself in *Being and Nothingness*. The body-for-others is an object which may be known in its observable, anatomical detail by others and, in part, by oneself in as much as one can see or touch parts of one's body or, say, x-ray film of one's body.[16] But the body as being-for-itself "is the *neglected,* the *'passed by in silence.'* And yet the body is what this consciousness *is;* it is not even anything except body. The rest is nothingness and silence."[17] Pain—though not intense pain—Sartre uses as one example of how other the body as being-in-itself is to others. He describes pain as existing not among the objects of the world or even in the body-as-object-for-others. Pain is not in time or space; it makes its own time. It is an example of a particular kind of facticity: "Pain-consciousness is an internal negation of the world; but at the same time it exists its pain—*i.e.,* itself—as a wrenching away from self. . . . It belongs to the category of indefinables and indescribables which are what they are."[18] Pain is a part of the peculiar facticity of the body as being-for-itself which is distinct from the factual truths Arendt defines. This facticity is not more real than other object-truths (for example, cell bars); rather it is differently real and incommunicably real. Sympathy for pain is an affective image, Sartre asserts, in "absence of the quality of being *lived.*"[19]

By stating that the body *is* consciousness of being-for-itself, Sartre includes the body in his conceptual system. But to the extent that Sartre declares that matter is method, he is subject to Adorno's criticism:

> Existentialism raises the inevitable, the sheer existence of men, to the status of a mentality which the individual is to choose, without his choice being determined by any reason, and without there really being another choice.[20]

What keeps Sartre from a totalizing system which transforms matter into abstraction is his discussion of pain. Pain is fact in defiance of definition.

Susan Bordo considers the relationship of the body to doubt in her study of Descartes's anxiety and certainty as expressed in the *Meditations.* Bordo is careful to confine her observations to the seventeenth-century context in which Descartes was living and thinking, but she suggests—as many have done[21]—that our subsequent, dominant ideas about knowledge are those of a decidedly Cartesian nature. Adorno corroborates Bordo's suggestion by asserting that since Descartes there has been "a mania of systems" which quantify all experience in the manner of science without recognizing quantity as a quality. Adorno defines these post-Cartesian systems as "the belly [the rage of the predator to control] turned mind."[22]

To whatever extent one is convinced of Descartes's continuing influence, Bordo's observations are relevant here. Bordo argues that as a response to the "perspectivism" precipitated by Copernican and other contemporary discoveries, Descartes proposed a process of purification and transcendence for the mind. The purification of thought, its separation from all perspective and all emotional attachment, was the role of the philosopher Descartes stipulated.[23] The possibility of a pure, a certain, realm necessitates the existence of an impure realm responsible for messy experience. Bordo writes, "In the history of philosophy, the role of the unclean and the impure has been played, variously, by material reality, practical activity, change, the emotions, 'subjectivity,' and most often—as for Descartes—by the body."[24] Descartes asserts that the body is a prison from which the mind must be liberated, that one cannot allow the body to mystify the mind. He proposes that one can totally separate the functions of one's mind from one's body, even from the brain. Even disease, Descartes argues, cannot prevent an arsenal of rational truth from keeping the mind separated from the body.[25] In a Cartesian world knowledge depends upon not merely doubting but dismissing the signals of the body. And certainty depends upon separation from pain and death. The gap between the fact of pain for the body (as being-for-itself) and the doubt or actual rejection of pain (seeing the body as object, even impurity) is an appropriate place to begin examining the relationship of language and the body in pain.

Neither Boyers's desire for certain "authority, which owes its legitimacy to binding truths," nor Olsen's desire for certain blankness, which is its own kind of relief from uncertainty, includes *the body* in the body politic or the body of literature. Conscious of the body, Foucault describes "the 'body politic,' as a set of material elements and techniques that serve as weapons, relays, communication routes and supports for the power and knowledge relations that invest human bodies and subjugate them by turning them into objects of knowledge."[26] Authority derived from the power of language and will—even that derived from "factual truth" verified by the testimony of witnesses—can obscure whatever knowledge may be obtained from each individual body and its pains. Some writers, for example, Adrienne Rich, Milan Kundera, and, I think, J. M. Coetzee, place the body at the center of their political and literary thinking. When in *Of Woman Born* Rich advocates that women think through the body, she recognizes the facts in opposition to the myths of the female body.[27] When in *The Book of Laughter and Forgetting,* Milan Kundera satirizes fads of sexual liberation, he recognizes the sentience of the body in opposition to all myths of liberation.[28] Coetzee pursues the relationship of torturer to prisoner, language to the body in pain, and finds politics where language and the body meet.

Again, with qualification, Scarry is useful. She begins her discussion of torture with the premise that interrogation is an integral part of torture. She argues that this is so not because the torturer actually wants information he believes the prisoner has, but because he wants "to deconstruct the prisoner's voice."[29] (Scarry uses the word "deconstruct" in reference to a violent context where "dismantle" or "destroy" would be more appropriate because the torturer analyzes the prisoner's voice only in so far as that "analysis" renders the voice powerless, even silent). Peter's legal history of torture in Western Europe might suggest that, indeed, torture was a part of interrogation and not the other way around. But in either case, an answer to this chicken and egg question proves less interesting than another question this controversy implicitly raises: Does torture elicit the truth? Scarry argues that, at bottom, torturers do not even intend to elicit the truth. On the other hand, one could infer that because torture has been defined throughout history as a practice to elicit truth, it has done and does in fact do so. This question of torturers' ability to elicit factual truth (outside the body) by creating pain in the body is key for Coetzee's novel and the relationship of pain to language to certainty.

Peters has compiled legal definitions of torture from the third to the twentieth century. They provide a fascinating context for a discussion of beliefs about torture and truth. From the third century: "By *quaestio* [torture] we are to understand the torment and suffering of the body in order to elicit the truth." From the thirteenth: "Torture is the inquiry after truth by means of torment." From the seventeenth: "Torture is interrogation by torment of the body . . . for the purpose of eliciting the truth about the said crime." From the twentieth: "When we speak of judicial torture we are referring to the use of physical coercion by officers of the state in order to gather evidence . . . [or] to extract information"; "torture means any act by which severe pain or suffering, whether physical or mental, is intentionally inflicted by or at the instigation of a public official on a person for such purposes as obtaining from him or a third person information or confession"; "by *torture* I mean the infliction of physically founded suffering or the threat immediately to inflict it, where such infliction or threat is intended to elicit . . . matter of intelligence or forensic proof and the motive is one of military, civil, or ecclesiastical interest."[30]

In this selection of definitions, torture and interrogation are wedded for the expressed intention of eliciting confession or information. The earlier definitions assume information acquired through torment is true; the more recent definitions assume neither truth nor falsehood. In earlier centuries and in this one, however, those who have defended torture as a political or moral necessity to serve one's country or protect citizens' lives from some threat base their argument on the premise that torture elicits the truth.[31] In his discussion of judicial torture, Foucault emphasizes that because

> the establishment of truth was the absolute right and the exclusive power of the sovereign and his judges . . . the only way in which the truth [and the sovereign] might exert all its power, was for the criminal to accept responsibility for his own crime. . . . The criminal who confessed came to play the role of living truth.[32]

One cannot assume—as Scarry seems to—that torture has never elicited factual truth. But neither can one assume that because torture has been legally defined as eliciting truth, that it ever consistently or reliably did so. Nor can one assume that the expressed intention for torture of eliciting truth, information, confession, is a solitary or uncomplicated intention. Though Foucault argues that the regulated ordeal of past judicial torture "was not the unrestrained torture of modern interrogations,"[33] Peters writes that in the *ancien régime,* when torture was used in criminal cases, the methods used to produce pain created physical effects that made the reliability of the evidence procured approximate and uncertain. And yet the "legal anthropology" of the *ancien régime* was that intractable criminals require pain to tell the truth. In the late twentieth century, technology has much better control over the physical effects of pain and so has, as Peters notes, "invariable success"; however, this era's torturers define success not by the acquisition of information but rather by the reduction of the victim to powerlessness.[34]

In either anthropology reliable truth is not the result of torture. Amnesty International concludes from their case studies of the 1980s that, indeed, twentieth-century torture technology does not necessarily elicit the truth: "Whether the suspects under interrogation possess the sought-for information or not, once made hostile by assaults they may give false information either to mislead their interrogators or because they are eager to stop the pain. Under great mental stress, they may suffer hallucinations that distort the truth, even to themselves."[35] To undermine any assumption that torture elicits truth and, therefore, could be justified, Amnesty International recommended to a United Nations draft Convention Against Torture and Other Cruel, Inhuman or Degrading Treatment or Punishment that "all statements obtained by any such ill-treatment should be excluded from evidence in any trial."[36] I return to Scarry's argument with the understanding that the historically consistent justification for torture (judicial and nonjudicial) has been the need for truth (be it confession or factual information) and that this justification is unfounded.

Scarry concerns herself with the relationship of the prisoner's severe pain to the unmaking of his voice. She asserts that the prisoner's conscious presence in the world is unmade by intense pain, a reality anterior to language. She further asserts that the world, the self, the voice are lost through intense pain as the prisoner's self shrinks to the size of his body. The reality of this pain implicitly confers reality upon the power of the torturer, and the prisoner's shrinking self concedes more "territory" to the torturer.[37] (In the colonial world this territory is literal on both national and personal grounds.) The torturer, who may have been tortured himself in training to torture,[38] may know better than those who have been neither victim nor torturer the reality of intense pain and the sense of powerlessness it creates.

It is weapons that transform pain into power. Scarry notes, however, that the processes of torture practiced around the world have made weapons of all domestic accoutrements in which the prisoner might have found comfort and security: the room (its door, its walls); the furniture (a bathtub, for example); the prisoner's own body (holding one posture for hours or days, for example); and the prisoner's voice (his "confession") are all made into weapons, the enemy of the prisoner. A cruel irony of this brutality is that the "confession" places the onus of "betrayal" on the prisoner, who may well have nothing to confess and may have lost a sense of the world outside his pained body to which his "confession" refers. Largely ignorant of intense pain, the world disdains "confession," thus, in part, rationalizing torture.[39]

Scarry argues that it is interrogation, the question, which makes the prisoner's pain invisible to the torturer while the prisoner's pain erases the torturer's question and the world it refers to from the mind of the prisoner. Though this argument transforms instances of torture into an overriding archetype, it does describe the rhetorical situation of torture in which pain and interrogation participate together. Beneath the rationalization of interrogation, what may well allow the torturer to tolerate or even ignore the prisoner's pain—despite, or even because of, the fact that he himself may have experienced torture—is an indoctrination in otherness, an atmosphere of otherness. This is the Cartesian otherness of the body separated unequivocally from the mind, the soul, and the sources of "truth." (The torturer separated from his body may not even credit his own pain.) It is also the cultural otherness made especially apparent to Europeans, for example, during the centuries of overseas exploration and colonization. Bordo writes, "The recognition of cultural difference . . . is nothing less than the discovery of the *Other*. . . . The consciousness of 'Otherness,' as Mead, Lacan, and Merleau-Ponty have emphasized, makes possible the consciousness of self."[40]

For purposes of power over the other, the operating principle of torture, the other must be not only separate from the self, but, of course, also insignificant, impure, evil. Socially created definitions of race are useful for this purpose. In *The Nazi Doctors,* Robert Lifton notes that the German state was a "biocracy" which maintained its authority in the name of just such a "biological principle," and this "rational," "scientific" principle created an atmosphere in Auschwitz of such profound otherness that genocide was possible—even for those under oath to heal.[41] The logic of the atmosphere of torture is that to gain power—or seem to—the torturer needs the question and the "confession" (his language defining self and other) together with the body in pain. Scarry characterizes the situation this way:

> The goal of the torturer is to make the one, the body, emphatically and crushingly *present* by destroying it, and to make the other, the voice, *absent* by destroying it. It is in part this combination that makes torture, like any experi-

ence of great physical pain, mimetic of death; for in death the body is emphatically present while that more elusive part represented by the voice is so alarmingly absent that heavens are created to explain its whereabouts.[42]

Waiting for the Barbarians examines the differences between, and differences within, body and voice. In another century this duality would have been called body and soul. For those who believe in the heavens, or more modestly, in some spiritual possibilities in human beings, it might still be called body and soul. Coetzee's protagonist, the magistrate, struggles with the vulnerability of the human body and the power of the defining voice. Never really capable of the total separation from the body and purification of the mind Descartes recommends, the magistrate is subject to his own excessive, somatic vulnerability and his own willful, conscious questioning. The political responsibleness and spiritual seriousness of the novel lie in its ability to deconstruct the binary opposition of body and voice, even body and soul, demonstrating how significant is their integration. They are inseparable on this side of the heavens. This central binary opposition, body and voice, contains many others in the novel, such as civilization and barbarity, civil society and military rule; all prove to have important differences within that undo them as opposing entities.

As the title suggests, the most salient binary opposition in the novel is that of barbarity and civilization. In the novel each is defined both by sentience (body) and by consciousness (language). The Empire's representative, Colonel Joll, defines "barbarians" as all indigenous peoples on the frontier regardless of differences in habitat, custom, and sophistication. A leader of the Third Bureau—a Gestapo-like policing army with broad "discretionary powers"—Joll ignores evidence of the cultural differences among the indigenous peoples and instead uses torture to generate "evidence" against them, thus, reducing them to bodies in pain and "proving" they are indeed barbarians, that is, secretive, violent, unsophisticated people who threaten the security of the colonial fort community, the outpost of civilization.

Like the torture practiced by his cohorts in our geographic and temporal world (from Chile to Pakistan; from history's beginning to this minute), Joll's process of torture is an inversion of the trial. In a trial evidence may lead to punishment, but punishment is not used to produce "evidence." Scarry argues that torture is the inversion of both justice (law) and health (medicine). In that "medicine and law . . . are the institutional elaborations of body and state," torture undoes both.[43] I have already argued the disjunction of torture and any reliably truthful confession despite past and present justifications of state-supported torture. Torture is an inversion of justice. One can make an equally strong case for torture as an inversion of health (medicine).

Lifton perceives the Nazi doctors' participation in genocide as a direct result of the justifying power of such an inversion. Nazi ideology and rhetoric proposed killing as healing. The dominant metaphor was of the German state as a sick body plagued by the disease of Jewry. It was most especially the responsibility of doctors to heal the body of the state.[44] One might object that genocide is not torture, that interrogation is not a part of genocide, specifically that practiced by the Nazis. But in fact "the truth" was the justification for genocide of the Jews: the "truth" of the metaphor that the Jews were a disease destroying the body of the German state. This "truth" was so powerful and pervasive it was not necessary to rediscover it by "questioning" each individual Jew before he or she was abused and killed.[45]

Peters and Amnesty International note that doctors or other medical personnel participate in much twentieth-century torture.[46] Peters also tells us that those genuine healers who later offer physical and psychological succor to torture victims, such as the Danish Torture Rehabilitation Center, must be careful to avoid investigation or therapy that resembles the torture because of "the perversion of clinical behaviour by the original circumstances of torture."[47] Colonel Joll and his soldiers, through the inflication of burns, cuts, beatings (with a hammer, a *domestic* tool of construction), degradation, and the ever-present question invert the practices of medicine and law, destroying the world, the civilization, of his prisoners. Pain and his voice make them barbarians, people who live only on the level of sentience.

Joll also destroys the civilization of at least some justice and health existing inside the fort before his arrival. This civilization is largely maintained and articulated by the magistrate who finds in it comfort and peace he is loathe to give up. The magistrate knows as much about the various indigenous peoples and about the local terrain and seasons as most good colonial viceroys. He even unearths evidence, such as the wood slips, of former indigenous civilizations. But he cannot decipher the written language on the wood slips and does not even know the languages of the living indigenous peoples. So for him their civilization lives almost exclusively within his ability consciously to articulate it while their language and their sentient selves, their eating and sanitary habits, are clearly outside his self. When he does admit into his consciousness the reality of their bodies' pain, caused by Joll's torturers, he loses the comfort and peace of his civilization to Joll's power which grows with his victims' pain. From this point forward in the novel, the magistrate struggles both to accept and to resist what Peters declares about torture in the twentieth century and in the past: "for all the new information, the general source of torture has not changed; it is still civil society that tortures or authorizes torture or is indifferent to those wielding it on civil society's behalf."[48] The magistrate continues to hold out hope for his belief that the civilian is innocent of what the military man does.

Even after the magistrate sees that Joll and his interrogators have tortured a boy with hundreds of small cuts and beaten his grandfather to death, the magistrate still has doubts about where barbarity lay. Others' pain elicits compassion but also doubt. He is not at all sure he wants to engage in what Bordo calls "sympathetic thinking," an interior closeness, a merging with what is to be known.[49] In an afterdinner debate with Joll's handsome lieutenant, the magistrate does say, "I wish that these barbarians would rise up and teach us a lesson, so that we would learn to respect them" (51). And yet he thinks to himself, "Do I really look forward to the triumph of the barbarian way: intellectual torpor, slovenliness, *tolerance of disease and death?*" (my emphasis, 52). A man very conscious of his sagging, aging body and his enjoyment of sensual pleasures, the magistrate wants distance from, if not control over, disease and death represented by the "barbarians." Though his ideology has very little of the certainty driving the Nazi state, he does here associate individual bodily vulnerability and a "disease" or corruption of civilization with the indigenous peoples. His fears blind him to the ample evidence condemning the colonial empire for bringing disease and torpor to those indigenous peoples docile enough to trust the empire's representative.[50]

When the magistrate takes into his home, into his bed, a girl crippled and almost completely blinded by the torturer, he moves nearer the body in pain. Wanting to read the signs of the girl's body, nightly he washes her crippled feet and then the rest of her body. But he is not the humbled and perfect Christ. He cannot read her, and she cannot put her pain into words he understands. At first she will say nothing and then she can speak only of the weapons that inflicted blindness but not of the pain itself. "You are always asking me that question, so I will now tell you. It was a fork. . . . They put it in the coals till it was hot . . ." (41). His pursuit of the girl's secrets (which he believes she willfully withholds) and his sexual desire are one—or so he fears—and as the one is truncated, so is the other. Though he is attracted to the girl, he cannot consummate this sexual desire. He can neither penetrate her forcefully and willfully nor merge with her sympathetically. In both guilt and frustration, he thinks, "Is this how her torturers felt hunting their secret, whatever they thought it was? For the first time I feel a dry pity for them: how *natural* a mistake to believe that you can burn or tear or hack your way into the secret body of the other!" (my emphasis, 43).

A man granted authority by his educated language, the magistrate credits the question more than the pain even though he knows the girl held no political secrets. The willful pursuit of an answer one desires he calls "natural." When his supposed good intentions are thwarted, he identifies with others in his civilization whose words create the world. And yet he cries, "*No! No! No!* . . . There is nothing to link me with torturers" (44). He continues to believe there is a clear difference between the civilian leader and the military leader. He resists an external enemy (sometimes the "barbarians," increasingly the torturers) without admitting the degree to which the other is himself. Arendt, Lifton, and Peters all contend even the most extraordinary, sadistic evil is not altogether other. An atmosphere created by certain overriding ideologies (such as the racial right to colonize) can produce sadists where there were none.

The magistrate struggles with the difficult distinction between sadism and desire never certain the two are truly separate. He does know his sexual pleasure felt in love-making with a young prostitute is quite different from his insistent attraction and resistance to the scarred, indigenous girl. Sartre offers a distinction between sadism and desire which demonstrates a significant yet tenuous difference. This passage speaks to the equally difficult question of the magistrate's culpability relative to Joll's in the novel, so I quote it at length.

> Sadism is a refusal to be incarnated and a flight from all facticity and at the same time an effort to get hold of the Other's facticity. But as the sadist neither can nor will realize the Other's incarnation by means of his own incarnation, as due to this very fact he has no resource except to treat the Other as an instrumental-object, he seeks to utilize the Other's body as a tool to make the Other realize an incarnated existence. Sadism is an effort to incarnate the Other through violence, and this incarnation "by force" must be already the appropriation and utilization of the Other. Sadism like desire seeks to strip the Other of the acts which hide him. It seeks to reveal the flesh beneath the action. But whereas the For-itself in desire loses itself in its own flesh in order to reveal to the Other that

he too is flesh, the sadist refuses his own flesh at the same time that he uses instruments to reveal by force the Other's flesh to him. . . . [Sadism] not only enjoys the possession of the Other's flesh . . . , it enjoys its own non-incarnation. . . . [The sadist] makes [the flesh] present in pain. In pain facticity invades consciousness.[51]

The magistrate's resistance to his own corporeal vulnerability thwarts his desire to know the indigenous girl's body and its scars. He tries to separate the scars as signs from the body, its pain, its being-for-itself. But he succeeds in neither sadism nor desire.

In a moment of insight, the magistrate admits to himself "the truth of what [he is] trying to do: to obliterate the girl" (47). Whether by a floundering cause and effect or simply by attrition, feelings of attraction and frustration and guilt result in the magistrate's decision to stop sleeping with the girl (with whom he has never had a consummated sexual relationship) and to return her to her independent people in the distant mountains. On the journey the magistrate and the indigenous girl do consummate their sexual relationship. His confusion temporarily resolves itself in desire. But the mutilated girl still chooses her own people.

When the magistrate returns from this very dangerous winter journey, he is imprisoned by the Third Bureau for "treasonously consorting" with the enemy (77). As a prisoner he soon becomes the body in pain. But before he suffers any physical abuse, he first feels elation because "[his] alliance with the guardians of the Empire is over" (78). He responds to the Warrant Officer's accusation by declaring, "We are at peace here . . . we have no enemies. . . . Unless I make a mistake. . . . Unless we are the enemy" (77). His new freedom from association—an association Adorno calls the unfreedom of a totalizing social system—temporarily clarifies his understanding of the word "barbarian" for he immediately thinks of the man who has usurped his desk as a "barbarian." Indeed, he understands how the new, Third Bureau barbarians have inverted, unmade, civilization. When forced to decipher the wood slips, he makes up this interpretation:

"It is the barbarian character *war*, but it has other senses too. It can stand for *vengeance*, and, if you turn it upside-down like this, it can be made to read *justice*. . . . Each single slip can be read in many ways. Together they can be read as a domestic journal, or they can be read as a plan of war. (112)

He understands the fragility of justice and of domestic life and the vulnerability of both to interpretation by "civilization" and inversion by torturers. Without irony or equivocation the magistrate shouts at the

Colonel, "*You* are the enemy, *you* have made the war . . .—starting not now but a year ago when you committed your first filthy barbarities here!" (114). But the magistrate does not here assert his earlier speculation, "*We* are the enemy" (my emphasis, 77).

To undermine the magistrate's inchoate clarity about civilization and barbarity, they torture him. Interrogation, again, is the rationalization for this torture—though the magistrate has always really known it is a fraud. "All I wanted from you was a clear answer to a simple question," Joll tells him (113). Torture undoes the voice, destroys the world—even the principles—of the magistrate.

> In my suffering there is nothing ennobling. . . . They were interested only in demonstrating to me what it meant to live in a body, as a body, a body which can entertain notions of justice only as long as it is whole and well, which very soon forgets them when its head is gripped and a pipe is pushed down its gullet and pints of salt water are poured into it till it coughs and retches and flails and voids itself. They did not come to force the story out of me. . . . They came to my cell to show me the meaning of humanity. (115)

On the Great Chain of Being, humanity resided between the animals and the angels because humans are both body and soul, as Augustine described us. Descartes raised the human self above its own body by its ability to think and articulate that thought without any dependence on the body, even the brain. The torturer perverts the Cartesian hubris and metaphysics. He eliminates the soul, the mind, the voice of others making himself the sole source of definition and defining humanity of others as the body alone, the "instrumental-object" Sartre describes.

Foucault argues that, in fact, "the surplus power exercised on the subjected body of the condemned man give[s] rise to . . . [a historical soul] unlike the soul represented by Christian theology." This soul, "born . . . out of methods of punishment, supervision and constraint," is that which the science and morality of humane punishment seek to control. Foucault further asserts that this technology of the 'soul'—the humanism the magistrate participates in—does not conceal or compensate for the technology of power over the body. Rather, it is one of the tools of that power.[52] In Foucault's terms, then, the torturer may eliminate the voice (and therefore the soul) as being-for-itself, but he creates another soul which is itself an instrumental-object like the body. The "meaning of humanity" the magistrate sees when he is tortured, this articulation of indescribable, solitary pain, is only a beginning of his understanding and, thus, his confusion. His complicity in the technology of the soul and thus the technology of power over the body—even his own body—is a meaning of humanity beyond any clarity in his narration. He lives in a context of survivors' guilt.[53] Nevertheless, he struggles to attach signifier to signified with his own pain (which is, for the reader, yet more signifiers).

The animals and angels—or rather, in the case of this novel, mechanical supermen—between whom the human resides are boundaries set on the first page of the novel. The animals (deer, pigs, bears, geese, ducks, and fish) are the prey of hunters: Colonel Joll, the magistrate, and various indigenous peoples. Joll tells of a hunt so successful "a mountain of carcases had to be left to rot," while the magistrate tells of "great flocks of geese and ducks" and "native ways of trapping them" (1). For both men animals are bodies, but for Joll the bodies are less than meat, food for life; they are an objective, quantitative measure of superior power. The magistrate's interest in hunting is process not product, though throughout much of the novel, he also accepts as necessary the sacrifice of animal life for human life. But after he takes in the tortured girl, he finds he cannot shoot a deer he has tracked. Apparently, the mortal body has become too present.

The supermen are Joll and his lieutenant Mandel. Joll wears sunglasses, a technological advance unknown to the magistrate and representative of the new Empire whose men can see or not see without being seen. The glasses also protect his skin from wrinkles, making it ageless. Neat, efficient, clear-headed, ageless, supported by scientific technology, and unfettered by conscience, Joll is superhuman (therefore subhuman). Mandel possesses an Aryan beauty so perfect he seems to be the culmination of flawless genetic engineering. These representatives of the Third Bureau are, like the Nazis Lifton describes, the male macho ideal: immaculately clean, erect, dignified. And like the Nazi professionals Lifton describes, Joll and Mandel are professionals with a misplaced confidence in their profession and professional selves.[54] The Nazi doctors told themselves, "because I am in a healing profession, whatever I do heals." Joll the professional soldier tells himself, "because I am in a protecting profession, whatever I do protects and defends." Between the heaps of carcasses—like the "pyramid of bodies" the magistrate imagines Mandel climbing to "reach the top" (84)—and the supermen are the magistrate, the fort residents, and the indigenous peoples.

Though the magistrate comes to believe that the torturers have inverted animal and angel, barbarity and civilization, he continues, in his narrative voice, to refer to the native peoples as the barbarians. His use of this word throughout the text implies the magistrate's insights cannot undo his habits of being. Neither as character nor as narrator does the magistrate point to the keen irony so evident in the etymology of the word "barbarian." The *Oxford English Dictionary* says of the Latin and Greek histories of the word "barbarous": "The sense-development in ancient times was (with the Greeks) 'foreign, non-Hellenic' . . . ; hence 'uncivilized, uncultured,' and later 'non-Christian.'" A barbarian is a foreigner. Imperialists must assert that wherever the empire takes itself, those not of the empire are barbarous. An empire convinces itself and usually history that the people native to a colonized land are the strangers there.

Imperialism is an assertion of objectivity as Bordo defines it. In the sixteenth and seventeenth centuries, Bordo declares, human beings lost a sense of a natural place, a home on Earth, and felt instead the arbitrary and impersonal allotment of one's place and time. Bordo argues that Descartes converted anxieties about this perspectivism into "the certitude of objectivity."[55] Imperialism converts anxiety about one's arbitrary location in time and space into an assertion that if nowhere is my home, everywhere is my home. I belong anywhere, everywhere—by virtue of my superior technology and civilization (the higher powers of the mind). If I am there, you are other. Peters notes that in the nineteenth century with its extensive colonization, torture, which had been outlawed in Western Europe, was reinstated, in the new areas of military police and espionage, as a necessity for the safety and security of the state.[56]

Of course, political definitions of "race" serve imperialism and torture. Though Coetzee's magistrate never acknowledges the etymology of "barbarians," he does for a moment consider the breadth and injustice of imperialism. "Where can that argument lead but to laying down our arms and opening the gates of the town to the people whose land we have raped?" he asks himself (108). But his outrage is mixed with doubt. For if the indigenous peoples belong in this territory, where in the world does he belong?—a crucial question for white South Africans and all the rest of us living on confiscated land.

In demonstrating the differences within civilization and barbarity, animal and angel, the novel asserts one kernel of certain truth. The novel's least moral character, Colonel Joll, provides the occasion for the appearance of this truth. Early in his acquaintance with the magistrate, Joll explains to him how torture leads to truth: "first lies, then pressure, then more lies, then more pressure, then the break, then more pressure, then the truth." The magistrate paraphrases to himself this lesson: "Pain is truth; all else is subject to doubt" (5). Joll is right as the magistrate interprets him even though the magistrate does not yet know the cost of this truth. He later pays the price and repeats the lesson. Torture produces the truth for it produces pain, and pain is certain presence. This is the metaphysics of presence Scarry addresses and Olsen does not.

The asking of questions in the pursuit of truth—truth in language rather than in pain—is a value held by all civilized peoples though, as Arendt points out, "No one has ever doubted that truth and politics are on rather bad terms with each other."[57] The extreme circumstances in which Joll the torturer is able to invert the value of pursuing truth, forcing it to devour itself, raise doubts about the value in less extreme circumstances. As the magistrate says of the wood slips, "they can be read as a domestic journal, or they can be read as a plan of war" (112). And as Scarry says of universal torture practices, domestic comforts are turned into weapons. Are domestic life and violent measures so distant from one another? To the degree the magistrate recognizes that his civil rule allows for Joll's more extreme military rule and that his seduction and questioning of the girl is like Joll's questions and willful penetrations of her intimate body, he begins to acknowledge his complicity as a man of language in a world of pain.

All readers of Coetzee's text are, through the very act of reading, also people of language. We share the magistrate's complicity. As a son of our civilized "first world," he derives his authority, his peace and comfort, even his pleasure from his ability to interpret and produce signs. When the silence and the scars of the tortured girl thwart his will—even his good will—he wants to penetrate, rape, possess her so that from her body will arise a certain interpretation of her complicated soul. But her spirit is part and parcel of her body. As a man of the "first world," he is accustomed to assigning meaning to sentient signs, particularly signs of the (barbarian) "third world." He can make presence or absence as he chooses. Just as his body possesses the vulnerability to transform him into a victim, his voice possesses the freedom to transform him into a torturer.

But language can make as well as unmake. It is not inherently a weapon. When Joll convinces himself the barbarians know the true answer to his question, when the magistrate believes the girl can interpret the scars on her body, when he sees her scars as signs for him (rather than as pain created by him), then certainty, manifested in one language, is evil.[58] The magistrate realizes too late that the girl could have taught him the language of her nomad people during the long nights they spent together. He learns too late that she could talk openly to his other female servants, that her nomad tongue could calm wild horses. The voice he wanted from her, the one that could explain the scars, could only be an object, a reflection of his own voice bringing some sense of order to his confused soul. Until they left the fort for the mountains, her voice remained as absent in the presence of the magistrate as it was in the presence of Joll's searing fork. But in the presence of the nomad leader only she can interpret the signs, translating for the magistrate.

If the magistrate's narration is "a monologue with nowhere to go, nothing to say, no one to say it to" as Olsen describes it, it is not so simply because of "the arbitrariness of language and its essential defectiveness for depicting the world."[59] It is because the existence of torture first presents the magistrate with the fact "pain is truth." It is because his search for a reassuring—however brutal—certain meaning to the girl's scars then presents him with his resemblance to the torturer. It is because his awareness of his complicity as authority and voice leave him without moral language. It is because torture of his body leaves him without any voice outside the boundaries of his body. In becoming Joll, he learns his complicity; in becoming the girl, he learns her vulnerability. Both experiences strip from him the habits of civilized language with its grace and authority. "In *grace*," Sartre writes, "the body appears as a psychic being in situation."[60]

The political implications in Coetzee's analysis of body and voice are clear. Coetzee indicts colonial barbarity, indeed, all interpretation of "barbarians" by barbarous authority and its ideology of otherness. He also implicates his own and his reader's authority derived from but one language—our own. The indictments are clear, but solutions are, by necessity, less clear. A novel does not owe its readers political solutions, perhaps not even hope, to be politically and artistically sophisticated. And yet, unequivocal despair—as Olsen describes *Waiting for the Barbarians*—in those of us not experiencing intense pain demonstrates a lack of imagination as artistically as it is politically unsatisfactory. Coetzee's text is not lacking imagination. As Adorno says of Nietzsche's Zarathustra, "the thinking artist understood the unthought art."[61]

Coetzee pushes his protagonist to the edge of conscious existence. Having been imprisoned, questioned, and tortured, the magistrate faces one more threat: his execution. One arbitrary day, Mandel and his men drag the prisoner from his cell, strip him, give him a woman's dress to wear and prepare to hang him. The hanging proves to be a public humiliation, a dire threat but, finally, a mock execution. This torture most explicitly imitates death, as Scarry argues all torture does. In death, the body is all; the voice, the world, civilization, perhaps even the soul are gone. Ironically, death returns humanity with its consciousness of death back to its animal state. Mandel intends to humiliate by making the magistrate a woman. But the magistrate no longer cares about the world that judges women and men differently. As he, in the dress, swings from the tree, conscious only that he wants to live, he has become the girl. And as he, on the cusp between humanity and animality, bellows in anguish, "someone observes, 'That is barbarian language you hear'" (121). Finally, he has learned the "barbarian" language.

This execution eventually proves his redemption; the "barbarian language," a salvation. Soon after his mock execution, the magistrate is released from prison as arbitrarily as he was hung. (Peters and Amnesty International note repeatedly that arbitrary treatment is a major contributor to threat in torture.) Having long since ceased his requests for a trial, he now wanders the streets begging for food like a poor, displaced native person. He even sleeps and eats among the dirty fisherpeople. But the Third Bureau has not destroyed him as thoroughly as they imagine. When he regains his physical freedom and some strength, he finds the moral freedom and strength to object when the torturers tempt civilians to join in the beating of "barbarian" prisoners. In the gap created by waiting, the Third Bureau has convinced the civilians that the "barbarians" are their enemies, but the magistrate has learned how insidiously the Empire pursues the civilian complicity it needs.

Wanting to be neither victim nor executioner—the moral position Camus defines and Lifton and Peters uphold—the magistrate realizes there is no room for him in the fort society when it permits torture. Peters ends his study of torture with these words: "[A] society which voluntarily or indifferently includes among its members both victims and torturers ultimately leaves no conceptual or practical room for anyone who insists upon being neither."[62] The civilians in the fort ridicule the magistrate and join in the beating, thus solidifying their allegiance to the torturers with what Lifton calls the "'blood cement' of direct involvement."[63] The torturers cannot allow other civilians to emerge from the killing ideology and atmosphere as the magistrate has done through his experiences and survival of pain. He has become a responsible person in a very imperfect world. In such a world matter and morality, body and soul cannot be separated. "What hope clings to," Adorno concludes, "is the transfigured body."[64]

Scarry's research leads her to conclude that "physical pain is so incontestably real that it seems to confer its quality of 'incontestable reality' on that power that has brought it into being. It is, of course, precisely because the reality of that power is so highly contestable, the regime so unstable, that torture is being used."[65] Joll's brutal behavior and the pain he inflicts are grotesque. But his power is ultimately unstable. ("Ultimately" can be a long time for those in pain, especially in places where one unstable, brutal regime replaces another. But in the fort Coetzee creates, the magistrate can take over when Joll's forces collapse—at least until the Empire sends another garrison from the Third Bureau.)

Singer refutes the truth of Scarry's contention in the nonfictional world with the fact that the Soviet Union, for example, is a stable regime which has used torture.[66] If one defines "stable" in political terms, then one cannot deny that Singer is right: regimes that have maintained power for decades have and do use torture. And yet Scarry's statement is not entirely inaccurate in psychological, philosophical, or even political terms, terms in which Coetzee writes his novel. For example, speaking as a legal historian, one of whose professed goals is a sophisticated understanding of twentieth-century torture, Peters writes,

> Paradoxically, in an age of vast state strength, ability to mobilize resources, and possession of virtually infinite means of coercion, much of state policy has been based upon the concept of extreme state vulnerability to enemies, external or internal. This unsettling combination of vast power and infinite vulnerability has made many twentieth-century states, if not neurotic, then at least extremely ambiguous in their approach to such things as human rights and their own willingness . . . to employ procedures that they would otherwise ostensibly never dream of.[67]

History, which has resulted in the paradox of vast power infinitely vulnerable, has also seen the reestablished use of torture. One could argue that, in this postcolonial century, vast political power has become its own political instability. And fear of instability instigates torture. Amnesty

International defines torture as "usually part of the state-controlled machinery to suppress dissent."[68]

In a psychological analysis of vast and vulnerable Nazi power, Lifton describes the Nazi professionals as individuals feeling both omnipotent and impotent at the same time. They had the omnipotence to make life and death decisions and yet felt the impotence of a cog in a vast machine of unseen others. Lifton says of this paradoxical state, "The very forces that provided its sense of power over others could cause it to feel itself overwhelmed, threatened, virtually extinguished."[69] A reality of seemingly omnipotent power is its important and vulnerable instability which often "necessitates" the tool of torture. Arendt concludes *On Violence* wondering if Paul Valéry was right when he said (as translated): "One can say that all we know, that is, all we have the power to do, has finally turned against what we are."

Arendt responds, "We know, or should know, that every decrease in power is an open invitation to violence—if only because those who hold power and feel it slipping from their hands, be they the government or be they the governed, have always found it difficult to resist the temptation to substitute violence for it."[70] Foucault similarly argues that in analyzing power "we should abandon the belief that power makes mad and that, by the same token, the renunciation of power is one of the conditions of knowledge. We should admit rather that power produces knowledge; . . . that power and knowledge directly imply one another."[71] Arendt distinguishes violence from power seeing the first as resulting from the loss of the second. She reiterates the contention that violence is the result of instability or perceived instability, but she also clarifies that power, defined as other than violence, must be held by government and governed for violence to be avoided. (In our postcolonial world where power and spirit are so far apart, even this power, this will to understand, is denied by that which is to be understood.) The "power" derived from torturing is violence predicated, paradoxically, on the excuse of eradicating pain and death by creating them. In the isolated fort community of the novel, Coetzee can display the full spectrum of political, historical, philosophical, and psychological ramifications of this paradox.

Significantly, the hill nomads defeat Joll's army through their knowledge of the terrain and weather conditions of their land. Unlike Joll, they are, body and soul, of this place and know its features. They do not simply will their location here. With the help of their knowledge and of nature, their victory is won by passive resistance. First Mandel and the soldiers desert the fort; then Joll retreats back to the fort with his defeated army. Returned to authority by default, the magistrate angrily and impatiently confronts Joll. Joll sobs, "We froze in the mountains! We starved in the desert! Why did no one tell us it would be like that? We were not beaten— they led us out into the desert and then they vanished! . . . They—the barbarians! They lured us on and on . . . they would not stand up to us!" (147). The magistrate replies, "Do you expect me to believe that?" The magistrate did tell Joll about the dangers of the season, but Joll chose to regard this fact as opinion.

Arendt remarks, "[Truth] is . . . hated by tyrants, who rightly fear the competition of a coercive force they cannot monopolize."[72] Joll has denied all truths of nature trying to replace them with the "truth" of his will. But as Arendt again warns, "Persuasion and violence can destroy truth, but they cannot replace it."[73] Finally, the magistrate can express his doubt, not of pain, but of Joll's words, his interpretation of the "barbarians" as cowards.

At least for a while, the magistrate can again define and articulate truth. But the scars of his body and his memory of the girl's scars have changed the truth about civilization that he knew before. The novel ends by bringing one of the magistrate's fitful obsessive dreams almost to life. The duality of dream and waking, mind and body, language and life are integrated when the dream of the mind must confront the sentience of life. Throughout the novel the magistrate dreams of the girl, with other children, making an elaborate snow fort in the middle of the existing fort. In one dream he is terrified because she is faceless; in another, he admires her beauty in her native costume; in another, he marvels at her ability to sculpt with hands "crippled" by mittens. But in all the dreams, the snow fort stands inside the other stone fort like one phase in a series of Chinese boxes: one civilization containing another containing another; or perhaps one civilization, carefully made, destroying or being destroyed by another civilization, carefully made. This conundrum of history confounds and haunts the magistrate. Even within the dreams the magistrate is confused. For example, in one of the later dreams he believes the girl is making a castle, but when she turns he sees that she has made an oven (109). He does not interpret his mistaking an image of domestic, bodily comfort for an image of wealth and power. But this dream, in particular, prefigures his dream come to life in the language of the novel.

One day, after Joll is gone, as the fort's remaining survivors wait out the winter, the magistrate sees children huddled together sculpting something out of snow. It is not, however, a fort or a castle, an elaborate barrier protecting a civilization. It is a snowman: a body with eyes, ears, nose and mouth. It is a clumsy body, a crude artistic text, defying humans' desire to make nature in our image and ourselves the center of the universe. It is, nevertheless, a kind of body, an individual, alive in the imagination, whose sentience precedes the civilization maintained within forts. Whether or not the body can continue to withstand, outlast, fort within fort within fort, in a world where vast power is infinite vulnerability remains to be seen. But in the meantime, Coetzee suggests, it is wise not to separate the vulnerability of the body from the will of the mind and voice.

Implicit in Coetzee's conclusion is a modest proposal. As the magistrate walks away from the children he thinks, "This is not the scene I dreamed of. Like much else nowadays I leave it feeling stupid" (156). He is on a "road that may lead nowhere" (156), but "feeling stupid" is neither despair nor humiliation. It is the absence of controlling language and disembodied certainty. It is humility, the humility he tried to achieve by the gesture of washing the girl's crippled feet. That was the beginning of this deconstructive process, this humility, that serves the body, the word, the soul, and the state.

"'Race' Is Not an Issue": J. M. Coetzee's
Life and Times of Michael K

The difference in races is not all it appears to be. In fact, we might say there is no clear difference at all, for "biologists are not agreed on the question of whether there are any human races."[74] But of course, this absence of proof is filled to overflowing with political definitions of racial difference. Japanese, Chinese, Germans, and Jews: many have claimed, or now claim, racial superiority in order to facilitate economic, military, and political domination of another group of people who are more easily controlled if they accept their inferiority and if their dominators wholeheartedly practice their superiority. Representation is all. Thus, for example, the English of the Romantic era, who professed abhorrence at the enslavement of the Noble Savage, found it expedient several years later to agree upon English superiority to African barbarism so that they might more efficiently colonize and control the African continent.[75] England may well have owed its success as a colonial power to its ability to believe in and sell ideas of racial difference. In contrast, Ian Buruma suggests, the United States may have lost its recent war in Southeast Asia because it was unable to declare its racial superiority convincingly and thereby daunt the Asians.[76]

The difference in races appears to be in the body: the texture of hair, color of skin, formation of bones, angle of the eye. But even these are "impossible to connect with a scientific definition of race." And yet, societies make of them a "badge of insult."[77] Lest this badge of appearance try to deceive society, it attempts to codify not always distinguishable differences. Thus, South Africans have carried passes, and citizens of Louisiana have officially declared their race based on the formula one thirty-second or more black equals black and less then one thirty-second black equals white.

Even those who mean to denounce racism engage in "usages of race which have their sources in the dubious pseudoscience of the eighteenth and nineteenth centuries," Henry Louis Gates, Jr., avers in "Writing 'Race' and the Difference It Makes." He continues,

> Race has become a trope of ultimate, irreducible difference between cultures, linguistic groups, or adherents of specific belief systems which—more often than not—also have fundamentally opposed economic interests. . . . Yet we carelessly use language in such a way as to *will* this sense of *natural* difference into our formulations.

Gates significantly adds, "Literacy . . . is the emblem that links racial alienation with economic alienation."[78]

In *Figures in Black* Gates again considers the importance of literacy to definitions of "race." In particular, he describes the role of literacy in the lives of Africans who had been transplanted into United States or European culture. He notes that since at least the seventeenth century literacy (i.e., the ability to write well in a European language) has meant political salvation for a few individual blacks. But those blacks lacking this literacy were judged inferior by no less influential thinkers and writers than Bacon, Hume, Kant, Jefferson, and Hegel. The irony of Hegel's judgment warrants particular attention: Gates quotes from Hegel's *The Philosophy of History* in which Hegel describes the African character as imprisoned in particularity. The African "consciousness has not yet attained to the realization of any substantial objective existence," and the African cannot distinguish between "himself as an individual and the universality of his essential being." Slavery is, therefore, a necessary "phase of *education*" for the African.[79] Meanwhile, Hegel's own literacy provides him a means to claim objectivity and universality for himself, his culture, and his language and to define as other, inferior, and deserving of oppression what his "objectivity" and "universality" do not include. Gates asserts that lack of writing, equated with absence of reason, mind, memory, history, and even humanity, became the sign of ultimate difference. If Gates's history and analysis are accurate, then one must conclude that the African confronted by European domination had nothing left to him (or her) but his body. And yet the appearance of this body was and is made the "badge of insult," the trope for all that is deemed inferior. An attempted reclamation of body and voice under these paradoxical conditions is the subject of Gates's study and J. M. Coetzee's novel *Life and Times of Michael K*.

Gates's analysis is of African-American writers, and Coetzee is a white South African. The differences between black and white, South African and United States art cannot be overlooked. Nor can I overlook this particular organization of variables into a black American critic and a white African novelist. I will return to these important differences. But for now, Gates's analysis of "race" as a creation of difference by dominating language that controls body and voice proves very useful. From it emerges a method for reading the politics of difference in *Michael K*. To demonstrate further that "race" is a trope of difference between those who have "fundamentally opposed economic interests" and that the emblem of literacy is a link between racial and economic alienation, it is revealing to compare *Michael K*, a South African fiction in which one assumes "race" is an issue, with Melville's "Bartleby," a familiar United States text in which one assumes "race" is not an issue.

Coetzee, Melville, and I all being—as far as I know—less than one thirty-second black, are therefore all white (or tea-rose as Nabokov described us). And yet, though white may be no color, white does not mean no "race," no badge. Judged by the principles of Hegel or Hume, the white badge has been less of an insult than those others wear. In talking to or about other whites, I might, in fact, assume "race is not an issue." Nevertheless, "race," that is, the economic segregation of people controlled by language which is given the political power to *mean*, is always an issue. The badge whites wear—the history of African slavery, the Native American diaspora, the bombing of Hiroshima, the Vietnamizing of the war—signifies whether we allow ourselves to see ourselves being seen or not.

Some white writers wear the badge perhaps too heavily and others too lightly. For example, in the course of her career Nadine Gordimer's consciousness of what it means to be white (particularly in South Africa) has developed enormously but developed to a point at which many of her white characters are without any measurable substance. Characters such as Joy in *Something Out There*[80] seem not to have a right to be anything but the badge of whiteness they wear. On the other end of the scale is, for example, William Styron whose narrative of Nat Turner[81] demonstrates no self-consciousness about the blithe, romantic voice it imposes upon the historical Turner. The effect is to silence Turner and foreground a voice which has every appearance of white, that is, nonslave, consciousness.

Between these extremes are Melville and Coetzee, both of whom write in a time when the irrationality of supposed racial difference threatens the annihilation of their native countries. Critics most often read Coetzee as a novelist who writes about language; some then accuse him of abstraction, or pessimism, or political detachment.[82] Critics have read Melville any number of ways, including as a commentator on "race," but "Bartleby" has not often been read as a comment on the "racial" struggle going on around him in the antebellum United States.[83] In Carolyn Karcher's book, *Shadow Over the Promised Land: Slavery, Race and Violence in Melville's America,* she eloquently argues that Melville was not only well aware of but also resisted prevalent pseudoscientific theories of innate "racial" difference:

> [Melville] showed whites developing the same traits under these [adverse] conditions as the Negro was thought to exhibit by nature; and he dramatized the various ways in which people of all races react to exploitation, from adjustment to passive resistance to outright rebellion.[84]

This agenda is no less true of "Bartleby," a markedly antebellum tale, than of "Benito Cereno." And yet, for the most part, it has been tacitly assumed that "race" is not an issue in "Bartleby" because there is no mention of color.

There is, as it turns out, no mention of color in *Michael K* either. Nevertheless, the reader is coerced (coerces herself) into seeing color by various characters' repeated use of such words as "monkey" and "idiot" to refer to Michael K. We may think we condemn the use of such words, but we "understand" nonetheless that they signify nonwhite. Coetzee, like Melville, uses indirection and the not-said to trick us (i.e., the white reader) into an awareness of our "racial" assumptions.

In both *Michael K* and "Bartleby," dominators define the dominated by building their rhetoric on the plinth of their own assumptions. Confronted with these assumptions and definitions, Michael and Bartleby quietly resist but with a language which is not permitted to signify. Though Michael and Bartleby do say something of what matters to them, because their auditors cannot place that language in their own contexts, Michael and Bartleby are perceived—even by the reader—as silent. Their voices are absent.

This similarity between the two characters and in the method of the two texts is illuminated by a major difference in the texts. While the reader of "Bartleby" gains information only from the lawyer who persists in explaining Bartleby's difference rather than acknowledging his own identity with Bartleby's inexplicable despair, the reader of *Michael K* learns about Michael first from the central consciousness and experience of Michael himself and only later, by contrast, from the first-person narration of a medical officer determined to insert his meaning into Michael's character.

While the method and amenable prose of "Bartleby" seduce the reader into sympathetic acceptance of the lawyer's language and his definitions despite Bartleby's words and our complete ignorance of Bartleby's experience, the method and controlled, flat style of *Michael K* lull the reader into believing the language and definitions of the medical officer despite Michael's words and our *knowledge* of his experience. In *Michael K*, as in Faulkner's "Pantaloon in Black,"[85] we first see the experience of the oppressed and then the interpretation of the oppressor. But unlike Faulkner's story, in which the reader engages in the tragedy of the victim Rider and then is shocked by a sudden shift in consciousness which parades before us the appalling racist assumptions of the sheriff's deputy and his wife, in *Michael K* we are not shocked by the medical officer. Instead, we are inclined to believe his language, whose struggle for meaning is familiar, and to discard our knowledge of Michael's experience (admittedly, available to us only through Coetzee's language), which is unfamiliar.

What we know about Michael is simply told. The novel's first sentence reads: "The first thing the midwife noticed about Michael K when she helped him out of his mother into the world was that he had a hare lip."[86] *Everyone* first notices Michael's harelip, his personal badge of insult. Some pity him, most ridicule him, but no one, including his mother, says of it simply, "This is this." The harelip is an emblem of otherness and "natural inferiority."

The harelip proves a powerful emblem for "race" and difference because a harelip affects the production of language. Like the creole or dialects spoken by Africans forced to communicate with Europeans in a European language, Michael's harelip speech elicits from his oppressors judgments that he is stupid, laughable, incomprehensible. The "humane" medical officer's response to Michael's harelip is that it could be fixed, should have been fixed long ago. If this were done, then Michael, like Africans educated in European languages, could lose all trace of his own voice and instead speak just like the medical officer. The harelip serves as an emblem of "race" more powerfully than usual signs such as skin color or hair texture would do because it is, as they are, an arbitrary result of genetics, and yet, it is not conventionally deemed racially linked.

Because of Michael's mother's embarrassment about her son's harelip, she isolates him from other children. "Michael K sat on a blanket watching his mother polish other people's floors, learning to be quiet" (4)—that is, learning to wear the badge, learning to be poor, learning to be passive. Known to be disfigured and perceived to be slow, Michael is quickly taken from regular school and placed in a special school where he and other "afflicted" children are "protected" by the benevolence of the state. Everyone, including the novel's reviewers, assumes Michael is a simpleton.[87]

Though the novel contains many characters whose opinions support this assumption, all evidence points to the contrary. Michael repairs a damaged radio; builds a cart out of junk which transports his mother across the country; cajoles his mother to ride in the cart; decides to forego the hopeless wait for permits and leaves the city anyway; finds a way out of Cape Town which evades the authorities surrounding the city; and later escapes twice more—once from a work camp and once from a camp hospital. In addition, when confronted by authorities, Michael always says just enough to survive but never so much that he undermines his dignity of which he is quite conscious. In one scene he advances on a youth who has threatened him and his mother with a knife because he "saw before him the prospect of being humiliated again [as they had been by the police who made them turn back] while his mother watched" (25). In a later scene when Michael is robbed by a soldier, he reassures himself: "It did not seem to him that he had been a coward" (38). And in yet another scene Michael, who loves food, questions his returning appetite for hospital food: "He was not sure that he wanted to become a servant to hunger again" (71). Michael is resourceful, decisive, and self-conscious. He fits neither a clinical nor even a Shakespearean notion of a simpleton.

Michael, like Bartleby, is in fact literate. He can both read and write. While he waits for the permits, he reads magazines from his mother's boss's deserted apartment. But the fact of Michael's literacy, like the other facts of his experience, does not signify with anyone in authority— including the reviewers. Michael and Bartleby are not literate in the language expected of them and so they are, for all intents and purposes of the authorities, illiterate. Knowledge of an oppressor's grammar is not enough to win them the right of self-determination.

Neither Michael nor Bartleby will deal with official documents in a way the authorities believe is necessary and expeditious. Bartleby, of course, refuses to proofread and then to copy legal documents thus showing disdain for or indifference to Wall Street's reverence for its paper work. He refuses to engage in proofreading, repetition of others' words, repetition *without* difference, and instead creates a repetition of his own. Bartleby's repetition of the curious phrase, "I would prefer not to," produces some new significance for these words that exceeds their conventional meaning. This new significance is most evident in the response of the lawyer to the repetition of the phrase. The power of the repeated phrase is such that the lawyer becomes incapable of a forceful resolution to his Bartleby dilemma—a *simple* resolution as his colleagues and my students see it. Gates argues that "we are able to achieve difference through repetition."[88] Though Gates concentrates his efforts on a black, critical difference, his emphasis on repetition as difference is relevant here. Arguing that repetition brings forth multiplicity, eclecticism, Gates quotes Said from *The World, the Text, and the Critic,* who reasons that in repetition there is "consciousness of two where there had been repose in one; and such knowledge of course, like procreation, cannot really be reversed."[89] Bartleby and his language disturb the lawyer's "repose in one." And yet, the nature of Bartleby's difference and his sameness continue to evade the lawyer.

If Michael K engages in repetition, it is in aporia and behavior of avoidance: escape, silence, evasion, fasting. Michael the gardener is a far more pastoral character than Bartleby the scrivener. Michael, however, does confront the official language of the state and its representatives. Michael refuses to sign a paper presented for his signature after his mother's death. Undaunted, the man "in a suit and tie" signs it for him; he assumes Michael is from an asylum, unemployed, illiterate, and, therefore, without control over his own name (31). The entire hospital scene is one in which the authorities are speaking one language and Michael another. Immediately after telling Michael his mother has died, the doctor asks, "Do you want to make a phone call?" (30). Michael, who has for days pushed his mother in the homemade cart to get her out of damp, unhealthy, war-torn Cape Town and who never had any relatives or friends there anyway, cannot interpret the question: "This was evidently a code for something, he did not know what" (31).

The next day a nurse presents Michael with two packages: one containing clothes, soap, and a razor and the other, his mother's ashes. When he does not move to take either, she asks, "Would you like us to take charge of it?" (32). Rather than respond with grateful compliance, Michael thinks of the burning corpses and of all the dying women he saw on the ward and asks, "How do I know?" (32). This time she is silent: "She refused to answer, or did not understand" (32). Like Melville's character, Turkey, who chafed at the gift of the lawyer's used coat, Michael thinks only of throwing away the charity. No one imagines Michael's experience and thus the feelings which would attend his mother's death. They do not credit his stunned quiet just as, in "Pantaloon in Black," the sheriff's deputy does not credit Rider's grieved rage.

Bigotry and charity—that "great safeguard to its possessor," as Bartleby's employer would have it[90]—create a language which codifies authority's assumptions and erases all experience they cannot (or will not) explain. After his mother's death, Michael is stopped on the road by a soldier who assumes Michael is a thief; therefore, he takes Michael's mother's money and then charitably flings a ten-rand note back at Michael's feet saying, "Tip . . . Buy yourself an ice-cream" (38). We see in this scene the etymology of "charity."

Neither Michael nor Bartleby accept charity; instead, they take what is necessary for independent survival of body and voice. Both occupy the apartments, offices, or abandoned homes of the dominators while subsisting, waiting for life—or for death, whichever comes. Neither can be trusted by the authorities because of his indifference to ownership. Bartleby's employer fears Bartleby will "in the end perhaps outlive [him], and claim possession of [his] office by right of his perpetual occupancy" (45). And the grandson of the boss whose abandoned house Michael uses assumes Michael is someone's paid servant who will help him desert the army. To Michael the grandson is a dangerous boy, a Tom Sawyer, to whom he must "play the idiot" until he can get away leaving behind the money the boy gave him. Michael had hoped the deserted farm "was one of those islands without an owner" (61), but the boy's first question, "Do you work here?" (60), leaves no doubt that the dichotomy of owners and workers cannot be easily escaped.

In the medical officer Michael finds a benevolent authority possessed of many of the same assumptions as Bartleby's lawyer-benefactor. Though the medical officer protects Michael from other authorities who would treat him more harshly and less patiently, the medical officer assumes Michael is too stupid, innocent, drunken or crazy to be the guerilla insurgent he is accused of being. He also takes for granted that Michael will prefer his, the medical officer's, definition of his character to that of the other authorities and therefore expects from Michael gratitude, even friendship, and mostly information to satisfy his curiosity. He never assumes, however, that compassion could be identity with Michael instead of charity separating him from Michael.

Neither Michael nor Bartleby will be grateful, friendly, or informative, though both are polite. And neither will give over control of their bodies to would-be benefactors. Bartleby prefers starvation to the special prison meals paid for by the lawyer. Michael, too, would rather starve than be dependent upon food he did not grow. Michael would also rather flee the hospital than submit to the cures for his emaciation and for his harelip proposed by the medical officer. Initially, Michael makes some attempt to explain his experience of his mother's death, but these explanations only strike the medical officer as other-worldly and convince him again that Michael is stupid, innocent, and possibly a drunk (130). The lawyer and the medical officer believe that the scrivener and the gardener cannot live without them. They do not imagine that Bartleby and Michael cannot live with them.

Though there is no vocabulary for Bartleby and Michael's experience in the lawyer or the medical officer's lexicon, when Michael is gone, has run away, the medical officer, like the lawyer in "Bartleby," nevertheless assigns meaning to the enigma of the starving man. At first, he imagines that he has saved Michael, a man who "can't take care of [himself]" (145), but after Michael's silence, fasting, and escape, he must abandon this explanation for another: "Your stay in the camp was merely an allegory . . . of how scandalously, how outrageously a meaning can take up residence in a system without becoming a term in it" (166). Like many of the lawyer's explanations of Bartleby, this construction is reasonable. But neither humanist interpreter can be baldly believed: each assigns meaning without knowledge of critical difference and sameness. Neither imagines how his repose in one is internally divided.

Melville prohibits our resting easy with the lawyer by having his narrator offer a relentless stream of explanations of varying degrees of credibility, ending with the dead letter allegory. This allegory, like the medical officer's, inserts meaning in silence—or rather *assumed* silence—in an attempt to control all enigmas with the language of those educated in the codes of authority. Coetzee prohibits our resting easy with the medical officer by having his narrator assume Michael's stupidity and ignore Michael's assertion that his name is Michael and not Michaels (131). Michaels, the name the soldiers have given Michael—perhaps misunderstanding his harelip pronunciation—is the name the doctor uses even after Michael corrects him.

Just as the medical officer "is not sure [Michael] is wholly of our world" (130), Melville's lawyer cannot offer "effectual succor" because "it was [Bartleby's] soul that suffered, and his soul [he] could not reach" (35). Neither the lawyer nor the medical officer wants to imagine that these men whose badges mark them as the dominated are of the same world as that occupied by professionals who have defined work, defined leisure, and defined status. They would rather see the starving men as souls or ideas (in a world protected by a transcendent signified) than as wasting bodies whose words are wasted on uncomprehending ears.

Most of all, the medical officer and the lawyer resist identifying with the gardener and the scrivener. Barbara Johnson explains such resistance in her paraphrase of Zora Neale Hurston's "What White Publishers Won't Print."

> The resistance to finding out that the other is the same springs out of the reluctance to admit that the same is other. If the average man could recognize that the Negro was "just like him," he would have to recognize that he was just like the Negro.[91]

Whether difference is designated as racial or acknowledged as political, this resistance to identification remains much the same. Though both the medical officer and the lawyer are isolated from a community of family or friends, neither wants to imagine that any vicissitude of life could leave him as verbally and culturally isolated or as physically decayed as Michael and Bartleby.

Many interpreters of "Bartleby" and reviewers of *Michael K* describe these characters as heroes possessing inward freedom.[92] Admiration for the self-determination of these passive resisters is appropriate, and yet the word "hero" is inappropriate, belonging as it does to a long, romantic tradition of conquerors. Other words, "noble," for example, also have a history which renders them inappropriate. To imagine Michael and Bartleby are free, albeit inwardly free, is a romantic notion like the lawyer's and medical officer's belief that the poor men's souls suffer. Characters are not necessarily free because they circumvent or even defy authority. Often such characters, or such people, are simply dead. Michael and Bartleby starve, not the medical officer and the lawyer. Even in attempting to praise these characters, commentators are reaffirming that the ongoing consciousness of the medical officer and the lawyer are more important than the bodies and voices of the gardener Michael and the scrivener Bartleby. Ours is a world whose words of praise do not suit these characters.

Claims to superiority are inherent in words of praise and gestures of charity. If an interpreter is to speak authentically about Michael and Bartleby's authenticity, she must face this internal difference created by a complicity in the construction of external difference or dichotomy. The line of difference separating "races" or classes runs through each individual. Analysis of this internal schism complicates the certainty of dichotomies and the ethics of one's political behavior. It moves racial difference inside the self but does not erase it. There remains a difference between what Wole Soyinka or Ishmael Reed could do with the character of Michael K and what J. M. Coetzee can do. Gates's theory, deriving from the figure of the Signifying Monkey, clarifies this difference.

The Signifying Monkey is an African-American figure, whose origin is in the Yoruba figure of Esu, divine messenger between gods and humans, the keeper of logos. From this figure African-Americans have derived the profane figure of the Signifying Monkey. Gates describes the Signifying Monkey as "the ironic reversal of a received racist image" and as "he who dwells at the margins of discourse . . . repeating and reversing simultaneously." "Signifying is a trope in which are subsumed several other rhetorical tropes,"[93] but signifying is definitely a rhetorical strategy or strategies and not a means of imparting information—at least not the information being sought.

Coetzee's Michael K—and Melville's Bartleby—do use such rhetorical strategies in a laconic, parenthetical sort of way and thus exhibit an individual authenticity. But Michael K is critically different from Gates's Signifying Monkey. The freedom to be gained by the black writer (or black individual in society) through the use of signifying, the assertion of a black-conceived voice, is not a freedom Michael K achieves. When characters use the word "monkey" in reference to Michael K, there is no ironic reversal worked by the character. Instead, the word effectively binds the reader to an ugly racist assumption. The reader ultimately recognizes her complicity in this racism by virtue of her participation in and understanding of language which defines "natural inferiority." Whether one labels the world of Coetzee and the reader the "white" world, the "first world," or the "bourgeois" world, the effect of the novel is not pity and fear of personal tragedy but complicity in and responsibility for public injustice. This is what Coetzee can authentically contribute to Michael K's freedom. But Michael K cannot, by his presence, ironically reverse the racist image of the monkey through signifying—or the black African equivalent of such assertive rhetoric. Though a white author can give a black character an African language, a fabricated language, or other tropes that signify an independent voice, the author's place in the world as a white finally prohibits his freeing his character through the creation of a black voice as Ralph Ellison or Zora Neale Hurston does.

The rhetorical strategies Coetzee has at his disposal must be different (even as they are the same because "racial" difference is only arbitrarily created difference). Coetzee's dialogue is ultimately with whites who wear their particular "badge of insult." To uncover just how the other *is* the same, and, therefore, the same is other, Coetzee lends his authorial voice to the consciousness of Michael. But unlike the medical officer and unlike commentators on the novel, Coetzee does not impose transcendent qualities on Michael. In the text the ongoing struggle of Michael's body and voice unfolds, a struggle whose obstacles the reader has helped erect. In such a rhetorical situation neither the author nor the reader can presume to set Michael free, to save him with any easy impulse of metaphysics or charity. Coetzee's Michael K is after all not Kafka's K, whose oppression, whose voice, indeed, whose body is his author's own. Nor is he Melville's Bartleby, whose repetition, silence, and enigmatic demise exert lasting control over his narrator and readers because, in part, his *is* the oppression of Melville. Coetzee's K is critically different from his author. "Race" is an issue because we have made it so. Within the *Life and Times of Michael K*, in the tain of the mirror, is a different text, a black text, in which Michael K has a voice whose literacy makes itself understood on its own terms, the terms of his harelip. But if this different text, this black text, *were* reflected from the mirror surface of Coetzee's novel and we, the white readers, "understood" its "objective" and "universal" significance there, Michael K would become just like us, his harelip fixed forever. Such is the paradox of politics and language.

We are poor passing facts,
warned by that to give
each figure in the photograph
his living name.

                        Robert Lowell, "Epilogue"

Chapter IV

Separation, Assimilation, and the State

Several years ago a delegation of white South African education officials were touring the United States to find out how we teach English as a second language. I was one of a group of instructors asked to meet with this delegation. We were prepared to be confrontational, if not hostile, but a member of the delegation quickly deflated our righteousness not by being less than imperious but by redirecting our comparison of the plight of black South Africans and that of African-Americans to a comparison of the plight of Native Americans and that of black South Africans. The official's reconception of the grounds of comparison was clearly well-rehearsed. It was, nonetheless, appropriate. The assumption of difference from which we had spoken should have been an assumption of sameness as well.

The paradoxes within the polarity of sameness and difference—the difference within difference itself—are perhaps the most important to study if one is in search of personal and public political understanding. Not considering the complexities of sameness and difference, one might confuse significant change with an old concept in a new set of clothes. And yet clear distinctions between sameness and difference can rarely be discerned. In her study of Zora Neale Hurston, Barbara Johnson makes a noble attempt to paraphrase the political complexities of difference Hurston describes.

> Difference is a misreading of sameness, but it must be represented in order to be erased. The resistance to finding out that the other is the same springs out of the reluctance to admit that the same is other. . . . Difference disliked is identity affirmed. But [there is a] difficulty of pleading for a representation of difference *as* sameness. . . . What Hurston rigorously shows is that questions of difference and identity are always a function of a specific interlocutionary situation—and the answers, matters of strategy rather than truth.[1]

The conventional assumption is that the self must define itself by its distinction from others. And so, for example, one feels a keen identity with the child in Elizabeth Bishop's "In the Waiting Room" when she asserts, "But I felt: you are an *I*, / you are an *Elizabeth*" after she has looked at the exotic pictures in the *National Geographic*. One would like to overlook the following, complicating line: "you are one of *them*."[2] Bishop's poem defines the persona *not* by her distinction from others but by a network of similarities running within apparent differences and by the internal differences within the child. The child is identified with the "foolish, timid" aunt and with the "first-" and "third-world" images in the *National Geo-*

graphic. The strangeness of her feeling finally brings the strange war—the First World War—into her young consciousness and her domestic experience as she sits in the dentist's waiting room in Worcester, Massachusetts, February 1918. Bishop's famous poem illustrates, from the white point of view, what Hurston and Johnson are working to explain.

Any juxtaposition of South African culture and United States culture struggles with the near indistinguishability of sameness and difference. I will presume to say that many people in the United States are consistently troubled by events in South Africa—more, say, than we have been by events in Cambodia—not because it is the only or even *the* most inhumane nation-state on Earth but because the struggles of its colonial history and its postcolonial politics are abhorrently different from and painfully similar to those in the United States. A study of any aspect of South African life or art leads anyone from the United States into a sticky web of complicity. Specifically, a comparative analysis of the fiction of a white South African woman writer and that of a white United States woman writer, such as I propose to offer here, brings into play these complexities of sameness and difference.

The fiction of Nadine Gordimer and the fiction of Grace Paley are linked to their respective cultures and political states despite and because of the disapproval of those systems demonstrated in their fiction. Edward Said helps to clarify this paradox when he speaks of two opposing pressures exerted on the critical consciousness (in which I am including these two writers of fictional prose). Said writes,

> the contemporary critical consciousness stands between the temptations represented by two formidable and related powers engaging critical attention. One is the culture to which critics are bound filiatively (by birth, nationality, profession); the other is a method or system acquired affiliatively (by social and political conviction, economic and historical circumstances, voluntary effort and willed deliberation).[3]

The critical consciousness no longer can rest in a Cartesian, colonial assumption that if the Earth is not the center of the universe and man has no ordained home, then he can call any territory he conquers home. The postcolonial critical consciousness, inheritor of the colonial assumption but participant in republicanism or democracy or socialism, finds itself bound to and estranged from this home on the American or African (or Australian) continent which European ancestors established. I find it important to remember that in both the United States and South Africa the European colonials have forced the earlier inhabitants of the continents to move from their home territories to "reservations" and "homelands" thus creating for them as well an estrangement from their new "homes."

Both Gordimer and Paley receive critical and even some general public support for their personal and artistic resistance to state injustices, that resistance affiliatively acquired. But I would like to look more closely at some of their filiative bonds in order to explore the internal differences, the struggle between filiative and affiliative bonds, in their fiction. In what ways is each woman's fiction a reflection of (the same as) her culture and in what ways is it a protest against (different from) that culture? And what similarities and differences, in the struggles seen in each woman's fiction, are revealed by the juxtaposition of the two women's work? Though the short fiction of these two writers differs considerably in style, setting, and tone, evident in both women's fiction is, to paraphrase Christa Wolf, characters' passion for what they do not want. Gordimer and Paley are both women with a keen sense of justice. Yet their stories demonstrate, with honesty, the strength of filiative bonds however morally suspect they may be.

One way to define these filiative bonds arising from nationality is to describe a national ethos rooted in a state's constitution and manifested in its history. The South African entry in the annual, *Constitutions of the Countries of the World,* explains that since its beginnings in the early twentieth century, South Africa—first the Union of South Africa, then the Republic of South Africa—has had three constitutions. Even a cursory examination of this constitutional history uncovers some provocative information about sameness and difference. The first constitution, the South African Act of 1909, was passed by the Parliament of the United Kingdom. Though it declared the equality of the Dutch and the English languages, only the English version was passed by Parliament. The Dutch translation was "unofficial." On the other hand, the second constitution, the Republic of South Africa Constitution Act 32 of 1961, passed by a bare majority of white electors (850,458 to 775,878), was official only in its Afrikaans version. The English version was not identical, and the difference between the two versions created confusion in the courts. Ironically, the focus of the discrepancy, according to the writers of *Constitutions of the Countries of the World,* was over the word for "conflict." The Afrikaans *verskil* means "clash," but confusion occurred when "conflict" was used to

mean mere discrepancy or difference.[4] The differences among whites and
a disagreement on the relative violence implied in the nature of difference
itself speak to various recalcitrant separations within South Africa.[5] The
more salient separation between Africans of color and white Africans,
apartheid, resides in a context defined by whites' differences from one
another and disagreement about the nature of difference.

The logic of apartheid develops with consistency over the seventy-five
years of South African constitutional history. For example, the voting
privilege awarded "nonwhites" in Cape Province (only) in 1909 was
eroded by a series of legal measures enacted between 1910–61. One of the
most interesting adjustments gives and takes ground on the separation of
men and women in order to assert further separation of black or colored
and white. In 1930 white women were given the vote but not "nonwhite"
women. Thus, in Cape Province the percentage of white voters relative to
"nonwhite" voters increased. Through a series of such measures culminat-
ing in the black national "homelands" idea, black South Africans were
systematically separated from the powers of the state that governed them.
Justified by the assertion that the "homelands" would be self-ruled, separate but equal states (the "white guardians" would engage in a "creative
self-withdrawal" from the "homelands") for black Africans, the white
powers of state were left then with the legal and logical conundrum of
assigning colored peoples—meaning imported Asian workers but not
black Africans—a place in the state. Denying these people voting rights
could not be justified by establishing "homelands" since they had none
any place in Africa. It is, therefore, logical that Article 52 of the 1983
constitution would reassign the voting privilege to colored peoples but
not to blacks.[6] While this move may appear a step toward liberalization to
people whose logical and legal assumptions are different from those in
evidence in the two earlier South African constitutions, in the context of
that constitutional history this liberalization, this bridge built between
whites and colored people, seems instead the logical conclusion necessary
to maintain the theory of separate "homelands" for black South Africans.
Acts seeming to minimize some differences—between white women and
white men, between whites and Asians—maximize others—between
whites and blacks, even between black women and black men.

This playing of one difference against another arises again in a 1986
speech by P. W. Botha. As though to build on the liberal changes in the
1983 constitution (and ignore its concentration of "emergency" power in

the hands of the president), he promises to end restrictions on blacks' movement and to enhance educational opportunities for blacks. The core of his speech is, however, a defense of South Africa and its laws as representing clear opposition to communism. Ironically, in asserting this difference from communist states, he moves into a comparison of South Africa's detention of political prisoners, namely Nelson Mandela, and the Soviet Union's detention of political prisoners, namely Andrei Sakharov and Natan Shcharansky. He ends by asking rhetorically if he releases Mandela, will Sakharov and Shcharansky be released too?[7]

The constitutions of South Africa consistently uphold an ethos of separation, but evidence of this pervasive ideology is amply available in cultural conditions as well as in legal documents. For example, in *Lifetimes Under Apartheid,* a book combining quotations from Nadine Gordimer's fiction with photographs of South Africans by David Goldblatt, are two photographs of black commuters: on the left-hand page are four men sleeping on a bus with their heads buried in their arms which lean on the backs of the seats in front of them; on the right is a row of seats each holding men who sleep with their heads dangling backwards or forwards on their necks. The caption on the left reads: "Busing to work: 4:00 a.m. on the 2:30 a.m. bus from Wolwerkraal, in KwaNdebele, to Marabastad, in Pretoria; one and a half hours still to go. 1983." The caption on the right reads:

> Busing from work: 8:45 p.m. on the 7:00 p.m. bus from Marabastad to Waterval; forty-five minutes still to go. The people of KwaNdebele, most of whom were compulsorily settled there in pursuance of apartheid policy, need to travel between two and eight hours per day simply to get to work in Pretoria and back to their homes in the resettlement camps of KwaNdebele. 1984.[8]

Employers would rather require of black laborers a 5½-hour daily commute, diminishing their time for work and rest, and, no doubt, their efficiency at work, than allow them to live in close, or closer, proximity to their employers. Difference and distance have been the primary value despite the economic cost.

Though in the 1950s in South Africa an interracial coalition acted against apartheid through peaceful resistance, by 1960 such integration and peaceful resistance floundered. The Sharpeville massacre of March 21, 1960, in which police killed sixty-seven antipass demonstrators—shot in the back, some witnesses said[9]—remains the watershed of this change, this reassertion of separation. The result was not only violent confrontation but a black consciousness conviction which very largely eliminated whites from the black anti-apartheid organizations and actions. (These organizations were declared illegal after Sharpeville but declared legal again in February 1990.) When in 1976, South African police killed over seven hundred of Soweto's children demonstrating against education in Afrikaans, black separateness was violently confirmed. By the late seventies whites, especially students, accepting the assumption of separation fundamental to black consciousness, responded with a theory of white consciousness. Not at all a white supremacist term, white consciousness, Stephen Clingman explains, "primarily denoted an attempt by whites to transcend the horizon of even an unwilling complicity in the patterns of supremacy by recognizing the real possibility of its existence, and thereby being able to construct an authentic alternative."[10] Those adherents to white consciousness accepted a necessary separation from blacks and further sought a separation from supremacist whites. Changes in "petty apartheid"—such as integration of beaches—notwithstanding, separation is, in 1990, still asserted. After a visit to South Africa in the spring of 1989, historian George Fredrickson wrote,

> "Petty apartheid" may be on the way out, but "grand apartheid"—the denial to Africans of the right to own land outside the 13 percent of the country "reserved" for them and the restriction of African political rights to the election of local authorities in "homelands" and segregated townships—remains in force.[11]

The reasons for this ethos of separation on all sides—black consciousness, white consciousness, and white supremacist—have been many, varied, and bound to the historical exigencies of more than three centuries. In *White Writing* J. M. Coetzee offers one provocative analysis of South African separation and its origins. He notes, for example, that in white writing about South Africa, from its beginnings in the seventeenth century, there existed an ambiguous alienation from the land and the colonial enterprise there. In his reading of early texts, Coetzee finds none of the talk of a new Eden or city on the hill which dominates early writing about the European settlement of North America. Well into the twentieth century, white Africans' search for an authentic yet Adamic language in which to describe Africa persists, a language sufficiently alienated to demonstrate appreciation of Africa's difference.

Coetzee notes as well a long-standing separation between the Boer settler and a European, especially English, ideology of appropriate imperialism. If the Boer was too slothful, ignorant, or cruel to the native, his behavior was perceived as a betrayal of imperial ideals. Imperialism demanded evidence of white labor, not black, yet also disdained white idleness as a dangerous imitation of Hottentot idleness.[12] One can imagine, in these conditions, not only the defiant assertion of idleness by blacks, which Coetzee describes, but also Boers' obscuring of black labor for the sake of imperial appearances to which they, nonetheless, did not wholeheartedly aspire. Eschewing the niceties of colonialism and progressive capitalism, the Boers asserted a feudal, patriarchal treatment of black labor to serve Boer ownership of the land. This ownership was understood to be "a blood-marriage too deep for words."[13]

Despite an uncertain colonial consciousness beneath this landowner-ship and despite subsequent farmer flight to the cities, this nostalgic feudalism remains, Coetzee argues, a salient ideology of South African culture. This feudalism also remains arguably different from the model of United States or European capitalism and celebrates instead independent white labor even as it depends upon the cheap black labor it tries to hide. South African economic successes notwithstanding, the separation, or obscuring, of black laborers in distant townships and "homelands" persists in defiance of pure capitalist profit motives. This persistence has already created dire poverty for many blacks, especially for the unemployed and women and children stuck in "homelands." It may result in an economic collapse destroying South Africa for whites and for blacks.[14]

The differences between the early Calvinist settlers of South Africa and the early Calvinist settlers of North America which Coetzee notes become more convoluted if one returns to the 1983 South African Constitution and compares its preamble to that of the United States Constitution. Because it is so revealing about that culture to which Nadine Gordimer is filiatively bound, I quote it in full.

> In humble submission to Almighty God, Who controls the destinies of peoples and nations,
> Who gathered our forebears together from many lands and gave them this their own,
> Who has guided them from generation to generation,
> Who has wondrously delivered them from the dangers that beset them,
> We declare that we
> Are conscious of our responsibility towards God and man;
> Are convinced of the necessity of standing united and of pursuing the following national goals:
> to uphold Christian values and civilised norms, with recognition and protection of freedom of faith and worship; to safeguard the integrity and freedom of

[South Africa]; to uphold the independence of the judiciary and the equality of all under the law; to secure the maintenance of law and order; to further the contentment and the material and spiritual welfare of all; to respect and to protect the human dignity, life, liberty and property of all in our midst; to respect, to further and to protect the self-determination of population groups and peoples; and to further private initiative and effective competition.[15]

The ambivalence, described by Coetzee, that early settlers of southern Africa felt about establishing a home on the old and tainted land of Africa becomes in this twentieth-century document a determined assertion of theocracy in language that would have been familiar to William Bradford and Cotton Mather. Responsibility to man is second to responsibility to a Calvinist god "who controls the destinies of peoples and nations." The "protection of freedom of faith" is second to "uphold[ing] Christian values" and attendant "civilised norms." The preamble defines a hierarchy based on theocratic principles ultimately associated with the furtherance of "self-determin[ed]" difference.

This 1983 South African Constitution casts an interesting light on the tension between Puritan idealism and Puritan materialism in early United States history. For example, if one is sympathetic to Jonathan Edwards's attempts to return the Puritans to the foundations of their faith and away from the acquisition of wealth—a materialism in which one is tempted to see the seeds of robber barons and junk bond dealers—then one may also need to recognize in the South African preamble one logical conclusion to the success of Puritan idealism: a "we" defined by God's control which "gave them this their own [land]." It is only this exclusive "we" which, the South African Constitution declares, stands united in pursuit of national goals. Perhaps, in part, the very optimism Coetzee notes in the writings of North American Calvinist settlers accounts for their ultimate rejection of God's control to which the Afrikaners ever more steadfastly adhere.

"We the people" of the United States Constitution stand first in the document undefined. Those who were socially excluded from the power implied in "we the people"—slaves, Native Americans, women, for example—are simply absent from the preamble. The preamble acknowledges no others, who would then serve to delimit the definition of "we," and no other higher power which could justify any action taken.

We the people of the United States, in order to form a more perfect union, establish justice, insure domestic tranquillity, provide for the common defense, promote the general welfare, and secure the blessings of liberty to ourselves and our posterity, do ordain and establish this Constitution for the United States of America.

The United States preamble differs from the South African not only in the undefined "we" it posits but also in its first order of business—"a more perfect union." Though this union may be comprised of disparate, differing parts (unnamed), it is apparently most important to the framers of the Constitution that it be made yet "more perfect." In pursuit of this goal the preamble proposes a "*common* defense" and "*general* welfare." The preamble posits if not downright sameness at least togetherness, unity.

While the South African ethos of separation promotes a misreading of sameness as difference, the United States ethos of assimilation promotes a misrepresentation of difference as sameness. The legal definition of "the people" has changed drastically in two hundred years of United States history, and yet, the United States collective imagination evident in advertising, political campaigning, and popular mass media productions casts a retrospective gaze on "the people" which does not acknowledge any difference in past and present definitions of the term. Nevertheless, the first article of the United States Constitution assumes some differences:

> Representatives and direct taxes shall be apportioned among the several States which may be included within this Union, according to their respective numbers, which shall be determined by adding to the whole number of free persons, including those bound to service for a term of years, and excluding Indians not taxed, *three fifths of all other persons*.

Only in the course of two centuries have slaves, women, and Native Americans been drawn into the ranks of "the people" through constitutional amendments. This hard-won democratic inclusion results not only in legal rights but also in a confusion about equality because of a representation of difference as sameness. In *A Way of Seeing* Margaret Mead and Rhoda Metraux assert that "for many Americans, democratic behavior necessitates an outright denial of any significant differences among human beings."[16] The Constitution's assertion of equal respect and equal rights—eventually extended to women and minorities—becomes confused with a more quantified assumption about equal opportunities or equal goals: to use Mead and Metraux's example, the learning-disabled child deserves the same education as the gifted child. Confusion about equality can also be seen in Americans' frequent misunderstanding of or disapproval of affirmative action laws which are an attempt to create equal rights through unequal numbers.

Despite cynicism, satire, and bitter history itself, the United States myths of the American dream and the melting pot remain viable economic and political currency. The United States capitalist state depends on the nuclear (though also patriarchal) family with its sexual division of labor and individual home ownership or on the vestigial desire for such a marriage and house in a society with many dual-career marriages and single parents. Citizens of the United States are united in their personal right to desire these political things. The positivist forces of both United States idealism and United States materialism have welded them to each other and to an ethos of assimilation.

Adrienne Rich challenges the value of assimilation. In a 1983 lecture she avers,

> To recover history, or herstory, means resisting two powerful pressures in present-day American culture—and, I suspect, in the culture being created globally by the multinational high-technology empires. These are very similar pressures, yet they are not the same. One is the imperative to assimilate; the other, the idea that one can be socially "twice-born."[17]

The assimilation imperative, Rich argues, abuses those who are not able to assimilate and those who are. Those who fail the imperative are cast irrevocably as other and are treated accordingly. Those who succeed give up their history, their names, their bodies (their alien appearance). To seek further refuge from the contradictions of history—especially personal history denied—assimilated Americans then desire second birth (epiphanic enlightenment) through the authority of a religion, a politics, or a science. "In the desire to be twice-born there is a good deal of self-hatred," Rich asserts.[18] If she is right, then self-hatred is the mate of United States positivism.

The pains and possibilities within each individual and within the state itself, the internal differences, operate amidst the South African ethos of separation and amidst the United States ethos of assimilation. These personal and public paradoxes are evident in the Botha speech asserting South African difference from communism by comparing South African treatment of political prisoners to Soviet treatment of political prisoners. One can see the personal and public paradoxes within the United States milieu in the career of Chief Justice Earl Warren. Though opponents of his civil rights decisions reviled him for "legislating racial equality from the bench," as Attorney General of California in the 1940s, Warren decided to intern Japanese-Americans in order "to avoid havoc after Pearl Harbor."[19] The tension of differences and similarities *between* the ethos of South

Africa and that of the United States may be seen in a line from Athol
Fugard's play *Master Harold and the Boys*. In the scene the adolescent
white male, Master Harold, is discussing "men of magnitude" with his
adult black friend, father-figure, employee, and whipping boy, Sam. Sam
suggests that Abraham Lincoln is his "man of magnitude," and Master
Harold replies,

> I might have guessed as much. Don't get sentimental, Sam. You've never been a
> slave, you know. And anyway we freed your ancestors here in South Africa long
> before the Americans.[20]

The internal differences within each state are brought to bear on the
meaning of any comparison between the two states.

The obvious power of separation and assimilation in South Africa and
the United States, respectively, does not point to any easy conclusions
about the two nation-states in relation to one another. But the ethos of
each and its play for totalizing influence, political control, provide contexts of filiative bonds which throw in relief the political protests and
paradoxes in Nadine Gordimer's and Grace Paley's short fiction. Even as
Gordimer and her characters struggle with the aegis of separation, Paley
and her characters with the aegis of assimilation, the dichotomy of separate and assimilated, different and same, is undone. These ethics complicate the relationships between black and white, male and female, production and reproduction, the personal and the political, land and language,
body and mind, home and world. The qualities of alienation, identification, change, and stasis in either woman's fiction under either ethos divide
internally leaving a complex grid on which we try to restructure definitions of our selves, our terms, and our theories of change.

Alienation and identification are terms in need of definitions and yet certain, stipulated definitions or normative definitions only limit but do not
illuminate understanding of the conscious and material self. In every instance, each text—each "specific interlocutionary situation," as Johnson
puts it—one must ask who is alienated, how, and from what? In twentieth-
century United States literature and literary criticism alienation has conventionally been the property of white male characters (and critics) inside
the ethos of assimilation but uncomfortable with it: resistant to marriage,
home ownership, or money-making work. Theirs is the struggle for
romance and freedom and individualism living within each successful
assimilated man or each man pursuing that same goal. It is not the
alienation of the worker from his capitalist work which Marx describes. It is

not the ambiguous alienation of women from child-bearing labor and motherhood which Gayatri Spivak and Adrienne Rich describe (and Marx does not).[21] It is not the alienation of the Boer farmer (and the white South African pastoral writer): an inability to articulate a consciousness which can speak to and for the African land they own. And it is not the alienation of subalterns that Gayatri Spivak analyzes: self-alienation which has been expressed as a failure of self-cognition, an inability to find or recognize their own voices in a theory or movement for change.

The poor and disenfranchised are, conventionally, objects of some other subject's history or idea about political change. And yet, quoting Antonio Gramsci, Spivak argues, if the "'lower classes . . . achieve self-awareness via a series of negations,'" if they see themselves not simply as victims of crisis but as "themselves bringing hegemonic historiography to crisis," if they can imagine the defining subject as effect and not cause, then they may conclude "that failures or partial successes . . . do not necessarily relate, following a progressivist scale, to the 'level of consciousness' of a class."[22] To use Rich's metaphor, if subalterns perceive the power in their wounds, they may recognize their ability to create crisis, to undermine the plans and ideas of politicians and political theorists who use and define them. Whether or not the children of Soweto succeeded in getting Afrikaans removed from their schools, their effort was the assertion of a group consciousness which poses a threat to their persecutors. At the 1976 demonstration not only did they suffer the effect of others' decisions; they were the cause of crisis for themselves and for others. For them that crisis was and is one of pain and grief and terror. But also for them, their persecutors, and those who learn of their history, their action creates uncertainty about dichotomies of success and failure, progress and regression, identity and alienation, power and hopelessness. Alienation and identification, (de)positing someone inside and someone out, some defining and some defined, may be deconstructed. Such rereading creates possibilities in uncertainty and reconsiders theories of change.

Everything, Nothing, and This Here Now: The Short Fiction of Nadine Gordimer

From her earliest work in the 1950s, Nadine Gordimer has explored the personal and political properties of white marginality and domination in South Africa by representing the full network of fractures in South African society. Fellow South African Stephen Clingman warns that "to give the basic division between black and white is to note only the most obvious aspect of social fracture in South Africa."[23] Dividing people into categories by region, color, class, religion, gender, ethnic origin, and language, the South African state would seem to have rendered all groups marginal, as marginal as the ruling white minority. To claim a South African identity which is not alienated is difficult for any group. Because of white wealth and military might, whites have wielded the most obvious power over the process of defining, and yet, they are as much caught as catching in their quarantined enclosure.

When the Indian fisherman first appears in Gordimer's early story "The Catch," the reader sees his body, without his voice, as it is seen by the young white vacationers lying on the beach. The point of view is theirs. And yet the sunbathers are described as "washed up" on the beach,[24] like the fish the Indian catches, like the remnants of a wrecked ship, like a failing leader who won't quit. When the Indian does speak, they notice not his voice but his "strong uneven teeth . . . like the good useful teeth of an animal" (36).

In "the frame of their holiday freedom" they envy the Indian his fishing life and its isolation from the world. They are surprised to learn when they do finally speak to him that, like them, he is on holiday—he from a sugar refinery; they from city white-collar jobs—and fishing for leisure. Though they are all on vacation from work, they seem to remain separated by the difference between leisure and idleness. In his essay "Idleness in South Africa," Coetzee notes a distinction, derived from Rousseau, between idleness and leisure. Leisure is the time for self-improvement, or, in Rousseau's words, "time devoted 'industriously' to the elaboration of 'conveniences.'" Leisure promises the development of culture; idleness promises stasis.[25] Coetzee argues that in the settling of South Africa Europeans perceived the Hottentots as an emblem of idleness which the Boers were in danger of imitating. The imperial, Christian ethic demanded white labor and white leisure as proof that the colonials deserved the confiscated land. But Gordimer's young vacationers sit on the beach and "idly watch" the fisherman until the heat drives them to the hotel's veranda. The Indian, on the other hand, spends "his annual two weeks . . . fishing . . . because that was what he liked to do with his Sundays" (37). His industrious leisure is productive. It not only puts the alienated factory worker back in touch with his body and its labor but also produces benefits: fish which he can eat, sell, or give away. When the young white man envies the Indian, his wife skeptically imagines her husband in his suit in the city "carrying a bottle of gin" (37). His weekly and yearly idleness are decidedly separate from the Indian's industrious leisure.

The language of the story criticizes white idleness for its unmoving decadence and exploitation, but white idleness differs from itself as in other circumstances Hottentot idleness had. While it may be decadent, suspension in white idleness also makes possible some intercourse between white and Indian. The young couple feel an intimacy with the Indian and a light-heartedness in this interracial holiday—freedom from "confinement in a close dark room" (37). In this their idleness is an opportunity for (i.e., perception of the possibility for) change. But the narrator does not trust these characters, reminding the reader "they almost forgot he *was* an Indian" (37)—almost. Idleness is not to be trusted. The young couple reassert their wary distance from the Indian when he tries to sell them a fish. Too late, the young woman realizes she had "mistaken a privilege for an imposition" (38): the Indian does not usually offer his fish for sale at their hotel. Still, he is " 'their' Indian" and he smiles at them in "the proud, almost rueful way one looks at two attractive children" (39). Suspended in free time, the "races" can mingle, and yet, their mingling adheres to economic and social conventions narrowly defining kindness. He is to be owned like a clever and carefree animal; they are to be admired like dependent and delightful children.

The dangers of this paternal intimacy with its inchoate potential for useful crisis are felt when the Indian's leisure becomes more than industrious and the whites' time is no longer free. Urged on by his own boast and the young couple's promise that he will be photographed, the Indian catches a huge salmon, in excess of what he alone can carry or even sell. This excess production makes the Indian dependent not only on the white hotel guests' praise. He also needs the white man's help to carry the fish, and later, he needs to be carried with the fish in the white man's car. The excessive catch, the prize fish, is a burden for the Indian and for the whites.

Meanwhile, the couple's idleness is changed to white leisure when friends of theirs arrive from the city.

> The young man and his wife suddenly felt certain that they had had a very dead time indeed up till now, and the unquiet gnaw of the need to "make the best"—of time, life, holidays, anything—was gleefully hatched to feed on them again. (45)

They play golf, talk of city life, and drive to the city to enjoy its nightclubs. With their white friends in white leisure they reassert separate white culture. However decadent their idleness by Enlightenment standards, it allowed for a suspension in free time—time marked only by the Indian's comings and goings—away from the most dominating claims of their culture. Their leisure has no place for the Indian and his leisure, and yet his burden is their burden. He is their burden and they are his.

Throughout the story the narrator speaks of the white couple with metaphors of fish, part of a cycle of eating and being eaten, being washed up or caught. So when the whites in their car reluctantly offer a ride to the exhausted Indian and his huge fish, the nature of his catch has been defined. The white woman says, "So your big catch is more trouble than it's worth" (47), and the Indian later echoes the same phrase. The fish and the whites are an expensive, rotting weight he cannot carry. And yet his alien presence in the car—his salt-stiff clothing amid their colognes—is for them a burden also. Their relationship, however meager, with the colored laborer has made his difference a much more salient burden than it otherwise would have been. If he had not been "their" Indian, they would not have felt compelled to pick him up and drive him in their car.

His onerous presence in the car makes obvious, to the reader, their childish, evil inadequacy but also their uncertainty and even hysteria. They do not know what to do with the Indian. In their car he is as "oddly helpless" as the voiceless body of the salmon. Their white culture has defined him by class, color, religion, and work and rendered him dependent on their culture from which he is excluded. They have caught him as they have caught all of South Africa. In experience, colored peoples and white are each caught—one weighing on the other—by a totalizing system of separation and exploitation. "What on earth can he do with the great smelly fish now?" the young woman asks her friends (49). With all the ambiguity of Chaucer's Troilus, they laugh hysterically and she laughs with them. Like the Indian the whites in their Mercedes are confused and "oddly helpless" (48). Interracially shared confusion, helplessness, and uncertainty divide the totalizing system of separation from itself. In the experience of uncertainty is the possibility for change.

Though Gordimer has rejected the usefulness of feminist ideas for change in a culture based on racial otherness, consistently in her fiction she has presented experiences in which the private life of man and woman is publicly implicated or violated or in which this intimate connection is internally divided by unexpected, often unacknowledged, connections between different "races" or classes. The feminist assumption that private life is public and public private is evident in Gordimer's fiction even as she reveals the limitation of racial intermingling socially when it is denied politically.

South African critics like Clingman (those whose works are available in the United States) particularly admire Gordimer's rejection of liberal attitudes toward apartheid and her adherence to a more radical position.[26] And yet Clingman's perception of liberalism as based on subjectivity which he equates with "personalism" and his perception of radicalism as based on the political realities of impersonal history[27] separate private and public life with a certainty not evident in Gordimer's fiction. In her characters' private lives, especially in marriages, there are internal differences which undermine theories of change grounded only in the separateness of black consciousness or the impersonality of history. Subjectivity is not confined to bourgeois personalism. On the contrary, subjectivity's variety and contradiction are what Gordimer gives us to read. The difference within a subject, be that character subaltern or bourgeoisie, complicates dichotomous definitions of politics in South Africa.

"The Catch," "Six Feet of the Country," "The Gentle Art," "Something for the Time Being," and "A City of the Dead, A City of the Living" are among many stories[28] in which Gordimer questions the assumptions of marriage, that purported enclave dividing private from public, employers from employees, black from white, that source of new but still separate generations. Like "The Catch," "The Gentle Art" looks at a white, middle-class couple on vacation from the city in relation to a man of the outdoors. But in "The Gentle Art" that man, admired for his independence and physical skill, is a white crocodile hunter not an Indian fisherman. The absence of a racial barrier can simplify the white couple's admiration of the hunter as they sit idly while the hunter and his assistants demonstrate the night-killing of a crocodile with the aid of a bright light that freezes the crocodile in fear. Also, unlike the Indian's fishing, hunting is the hunter's work not his leisure. His work is, however, solely for the purposes of white leisure. He demonstrates crocodile-killing for the edification of city whites and for the skin of the soft underbelly, the source of ladies' high heels and handbags.

The white society in the boat, afloat in an exotic, alien place, is unified in its sameness and in its separation from what is alien by strict adherence to a code of manners. Vivien is abject because "she might have kept the crocodile-hunters waiting" (202). Jimmy Baird, the hunter, is solicitous of one ailing (white) employee: "No, no, Mike old man, you better hang on to that [coat], you're not yourself yet" (203). In the boat Vivien and Baird keep up a steady stream of mannered conversation. She lavishes praise upon his virility; he caters to her need for entertainment. Together they justify the hunt, crass destruction for their purposes.

Though Vivien repeatedly and rhetorically addresses Ricks, her husband, and Baird speaks to or of his two employees, these other three men who occupy the boat are less a part of Vivien and Baird's mannered white society than their silence first suggested. While Vivien exclaims, "That's how I like a man to look, as if he's really got a job to do. It drives me mad to see poor Ricks shut up in a blue suit in town. Isn't that a wonderful outfit, Ricks?" (204) or (when Baird's shot turns the crocodile's skull to "a soft pink mess of brain" [212]) "What a man! Wasn't that wonderful Ricks?" (213), Ricks is chagrined to learn that they shoot the crocodiles at a distance of only two yards. " 'Two yards!' said Ricks" (206). And when the crocodile Baird shoots turns out to be "less than half-grown," Mike, disgruntled by expeditions to entertain ladies from Johannesburg, says, "Just a teenager, eh, Jimmy?" (213). With a crocodile tooth in her purse, Vivien asks excitedly, "Ricks? How do you feel about Johannesburg now?" And though he responds "Oh fine, Vivien, fine," she goes on, "This'll make my poor husband just impossible. He loathes cities, anyway. This is a life for a *man*" (214).

Vivien and Baird's conversation, which provides each sex a role necessary for the perpetuation of alienation from otherness and of wanton destruction, reveals Vivien's difference from her husband and Baird's separation from his employees. But the three men are also internally divided. They see the perfidy in the system Vivien and Baird create and yet they aid this system even if it humiliates them. Because the sense of inclusion is seductive or a vision of any option on the shore is absent, they acquiesce.

On the shore is Baird's wife, separate because she is a mother. She cannot go on the boat leaving the children alone in the camp. Of course, her labor producing children is necessary for the continuation of the system Baird and Vivien articulate. She is, nevertheless, largely alienated from the benefits of that system. Her responses to Vivien's enthusiasm about Baird and, later, the killing are laconic. The only comment she initiates paradoxically identifies her with both the paralyzed crocodiles and the isolated white culture, each made vulnerable by the very behavior supposed to save them: "I didn't see you coming. . . . You gave me quite a scare. You can't see beyond the light of the fire, when you're sitting there in it" (215). She makes as if to push her husband's encircling arm and tender look away but stays within them. When Vivien asks her what she has done while they were away, she replies, "I waited," a response which sends Vivien "back to the company of the men" (215–16).

Mrs. Baird is alienated and marginalized because of and despite her necessary role as mother. But in her conversation with Vivien is evidence of the women's sameness as well as their difference. The conventional gender roles Vivien participates in will ask motherhood of her as well. She may prefer her role in the company of men but in that company—as it exists in this story—she cannot escape the expectations of the system she helps to perpetuate, expectations that keep her separate from those men. Vivien's rhetorical zeal and sexual maneuverings and Mrs. Baird's silence and passive motherhood serve the system of white solidarity in the jungle even as they are alienated from it and from one another. They do not see or accept their identity with the hunted crocodiles.

Blacks exist in the story on the margin between the boat and the shore. Whites see blacks without seeing as they push the boat into the river and later pull it ashore: "They saw the two black men, for a moment, gasping, leaning forward with hands hanging where the boat had been wrenched from their grasp" (205). "A moment, between boat and bank, when each one of them saw the dark water beneath him, wriggling with light from the oil lamp an African held—and then they were on land, lively and stretching" (215). The "sullen" blacks push the whites from the margin or light their way so that these whites can imagine they are heartily together squarely in the boat or on shore. If the three men in the boat (Ricks, Mike, and the other employee), the woman on the shore, and the woman in the boat acknowledged their alienation from white unity, their internal difference, then for them a margin would exist where they now see only a void. White man meets white man and white woman meets white woman in the center of the jungle, but they do not confront one another. These characters would rather flee identification at the margins for the alienation at the center of "The Gentle Art." They lack the white consciousness which sees its internal difference and recognizes its complicity. They cling instead to white culture. If the story suggests any theory of change, it begins with accepting alienation and the possibilities in uncertainty, possibilities that exist in the dangerous water at the margin.

A white reader of "The Gentle Art" can easily condemn the cruelty of the crocodile hunt, the man who sells such barbarity and the woman who enjoys it. She can even separate herself from the woman who would marry such a man, the man who would marry such a woman. The white reader can be safely separate from these white characters as she remains safely wedded to white culture. She can criticize the characters rather than the conventions of marriage or motherhood or manners that she shares with them and that make them and her what they are. But even if she goes this far in her flight from complicity, the image of the Africans off-balance and empty-handed in the water asserts itself. Their difference undoes the rights of white culture. If I wax philosophical about their status from my position on the shore or in the boat, I become like Jimmy Baird seeking acceptance of and compassion for his own cruelty. Baird tells Ricks, "Sometimes when I've got five or six big crocs in one night, I look at them spread out on the river bank and I think, that's a thousand years of life, lying there. It seems kind of awful, a thousand years of life" (214–15).

In "Six Feet of the Country" another white couple from the city have left that milieu not for the beach or the bush but for a farm. The African farm, the owning and cultivating of the African land, is the Afrikaner's historical claim to South Africa, Coetzee argues. The Boer farmer asserts he has made something out of nothing. And yet this justification for white rule, founded on farms and living on as myth in city and suburbs, is paradoxical. The Boer farmer, the feudal lord of the frontier, has always wanted independence from all centralized rule.

A white man, a travel agent in Johannesburg, narrates the story of his experience as a farm owner. He defines himself and his wife by negation: "My wife and I are not real farmers—not even Lerice, really" (69). They have entered this alien land "to change something in [themselves]" and their marriage. His goal: "You long to hear nothing but a deep satisfying silence when you sound a marriage" (69). For him the farm is smelly, sickening, but beautiful, a place to show to city visitors with pride because they tell him he's "got it both ways," the best of city and country life. He knows this triumph is short-lived, that a third way occurs "you had not provided for at all" (70). Change threatens to intrude in the way one had not planned. Still, he lives this idea of "having it all," commuting between city and country, between capitalism and feudalism, grounded in apartheid.

The farm divides the narrator and his wife. Lerice, a former actress, has permanently left the city to breed fowls and cattle. When she gazes at her animals she "look[s] dreamily for a moment, the way she would pretend to look sometimes in those plays" (70). The husband and wife were, however, divided before they came to the farm: "She calls my 'jealousy' of her capacity for enthusiasm as big a proof of my inadequacy for her as a mate as ever it was" (70). She breeds animals but will not herself be bred. When the narrator is annoyed with Lerice, he too is defiant. He sleeps in a separate bed because, as he explains, "I didn't want to find myself softening towards her simply because of the sweet smell of the talcum powder on her flesh after her bath" (71). He resists the physicality of the farm and of his wife—these two fields for cultivation which the Afrikaner farmer and pastoral writer always spoke of as one fertile field needing the plow.[29] But in this text the *wife* is the feudal farmer—the object having become its own cultivator. And yet she doctors the blacks, "the poor devils, . . . like babies" (71); her role as feudal farmer carries with it not just physical involvement but also patriarchal and paternal conventions and assumptions. Meanwhile, her husband is the voice that articulates the position of their farm in history—a "pretransitional stage," a "relationship with the blacks [which] is almost feudal" (70).

Despite this conventional split of silent, physical femaleness and speaking male mentality, what the husband wants of marriage is silence; Lerice wants talk. The narrator tells us, "I really haven't the time or inclination any more to go into everything in our life that I know Lerice, from those alarmed and pressing eyes of hers, would like us to go into" (73). So her silent looks of "urgent uncertainty," in fact, desire talk, while his narration desires "satisfying silence" (73 and 69).

Juxtaposed to this white family is a family of black farm laborers and their community of fellow farm workers. Crisis arises on the farm when a brother of the laborer Petrus, having walked from Rhodesia to work in South Africa, dies on the farm apparently of pneumonia caught on the road. The narrator and Lerice did not know of this illegal alien's presence but must respond to his death. Consistent with her paternalism, Lerice is hurt she was not informed about the sick man. She believes in her own paternal behavior as an idea. Her husband's response is grounded in city life and civil authority: "I'll have to notify the health authorities. . . . It might have been something contagious" (73). Though he expects the authorities to be, at worst, tedious, she sees them as superfluous, perhaps even dangerous. The couple's history and style of disagreement is, however, so imbedded in their appearance and behavior, it is impossible to separate any public ideological division from their private division or internal difference.

When the narrator speaks to the police, they are rather more than tedious. Ironically, their city assumptions are of his feudal role which he has failed to live up to. Why didn't he control his natives, know their affairs? His defense is a capitalist one: "So long as my natives did their work, I didn't think it my right or concern to poke my nose into their private lives" (73–74). Private life and public labor are assumed separate by the narrator, and yet, in fact, he does not want to poke his nose into his own private life either. He brings a desire for silence and ease to both realms. He is as annoyed by the policeman's "look of insanely inane certainty" about "the master-race theory" (74) as he is by his wife's look of "urgent uncertainty" (73). Both threaten his life in the best of both worlds.

The police have done an autopsy on the body and disposed of it. But only at his wife's insistence does the narrator tell Petrus the full story about his brother's body. Petrus will not accept the result; he insists on another crisis—the narrator must get the body back. "[Petrus] just kept on looking at me, out of his knowledge that white men have everything, can do anything; if they don't, it is because they won't" (75). Like Lerice and the police, Petrus understands the feudal power structure in which the white male is authority, and yet Petrus finds some power for himself by demanding a crisis. The white man may be the narrator, but he plays the role of effect and not cause in the plot. The black man turns his brother's body into an insistent subject. The white woman joins in the black man's request on the similar assumption that the struggles with official authority are the domain of white men.

The narrator hopes the government will refuse to return the body thus absolving him of responsibility from this feudal burden. When the authorities say they can exhume the body, but only for twenty pounds, the narrator is relieved feeling certain Petrus cannot afford this. In the world of money and affordability, the narrator feels safe. But Petrus challenges even this safety by collecting the money from the community of farm laborers. This precipitates from the narrator a capitalist analysis of life and death:

> I took [the money] in irritation . . .—irritation at the waste, the uselessness of this sacrifice by people so poor. Just like the poor everywhere, I thought, who stint themselves the decencies of life in order to ensure themselves the decencies

of death. So incomprehensible to people like Lerice and me, who regard life as something to be spent extravagantly and, if we think about death at all, regard it as the final bankruptcy. (76)

The body securely bought and paid for, the narrator feels free to forget about the burial in the old burial ground on the farm—"a relic of the days when this was a real farming district" (76). He insists on his separation from the "real" historical farm and its influence on ideologies of power in the present, as his wife insists on physical identity with that rural past and denial of its violent manifestations in the present. While the white man practices his approach shots on the veld, the funeral passes by.

Petrus's father has come the many miles from Rhodesia to bury his son. Unlike the white family the black family has been divided by physical distance created by the need for work. And it is physicality again which makes the father realize the body in the coffin he helps to carry is not his son's. It is too heavy. But it is the old man's incomprehensible mutterings, his voice, like the mumbling of a prophet, that arrest the progress of the mourners. They stop and turn from the mutterings of the old black man to the silence of the white golfer. Speaking in his own tongue, the black man says something even the white man recognizes as "shocking and extraordinary." His assertions are even leant an ironic "special validity" by his long mustache "grown in emulation of early Empire-builders" (78). With the collective, paradoxical authority of prophets, white empire builders, his own language, and finally, English, the old man holds white and blacks spellbound. "He was mad, but they had to listen to him" (79). He wins; they pry the lid from the coffin and prove him right. The body is not his son's. But the moment his voice wins, he is again a body that loses: "very old, very weak and unable to speak, . . . he abdicated . . . he was no good any more" (79).

His helplessness is matched by the state's when the narrator tries to recover the right body: "in the confusion of their anonymous dead they were helpless to put it right" (79). The state, infinitely powerful, is infinitely vulnerable to its own anonymous machinery.[30] The state can be certain of its master-race ideology but never get its details right. In this it is indifferent to suffering but also vulnerable to the myriad possibilities for crisis. Indignant at the civil system's inability to get it right—perhaps intimidated by the implications of this—the narrator pursues the matter with more and more energy: "'It's a matter of principle,'" he declares (80).

In his failure he sees Petrus and Lerice become more silent and more alike. They have become the silent couple the narrator had hoped he and his wife would be.

> She and Petrus both kept their eyes turned on me as I spoke, and, oddly, for those moments they looked exactly alike, though it sounds impossible: my wife, with her high, white forehead and her attenuated Englishwoman's body, and the poultry boy, with his horny bare feet below khaki trousers. (79–80)

Every night the narrator's voice sounds weaker as he tries to reassure them of white male authority's ability to make it right within the system he created and tacitly supports even as he speaks of it with disdain. The white man's power is internally divided. The black man creates a crisis for the white man which the white woman can amplify, and yet what these two, the black man and the white woman, can make of their power is subject to internal difference. The power of the old black man, derived from prophets or imitation of the white aggressor, fails as soon as it succeeds. And the white woman's retreat to a female feudalism is regressive in its notions of humane behavior and isolation from urban racial tensions. The young black man, Petrus, did force the white man to confront the cruel stupidity of the white man's system, but Petrus's power of crisis in confrontation seems to depend on his failure. If Petrus had succeeded in burying his brother on the white man's farm, this would not have granted the brother greater identity[31] and would not have precipitated any necessary crisis for change. Like all subalterns Petrus needs the ability to turn collective failure into collective crisis.

The unity of the black man and white woman in joint recognition of white man's absurdity and weakness is not, in the story, sustained. When Lerice joins in her husband's struggle and neither she nor her husband can recover the blacks' twenty pounds, the white couple do not themselves offer the money in reparation for the mistakes their government has made. This would at least be consistent with the capitalist ethic that money be refunded when the middleman fails to deliver the service. Instead, they give the old black father a worn, old suit of Lerice's father's in the charitable tradition of paternal feudalism. Where the narrator saw sameness in his black servant and his white wife, he found it "odd" and "impossible," so instead he, with his wife—because of and despite *their* differences—asserts difference between master and servant, the life-loving and the poor. In also asserting the hopelessness of waste, he, like Jimmy

Baird, seeks compassion for his cruelty: "The whole thing was a complete waste" (80).

In "Something for the Time Being" the possibilities within racial, gender, and class differences are considered in a more direct juxtaposition of black laborer couple and white bourgeois couple. Within this matrix the story develops the multiple significance of the words "something," "everything," and "nothing."

Having been imprisoned repeatedly for political activity, Daniel Mngoma has been released again to discover that this time he has lost his job as a skilled packer of china. His wife Ella had married him "because he didn't merely want something for himself, . . . but everything, and for *the people*" (218). He changed her awareness of herself, but now she knows with ironic understanding, "she would never get something from him" (218). While he goes in and out of prison, she lives in a rented room without their only child, a daughter, who lives with a grandmother in the country. As Daniel talks confidently of getting a new job, Ella sits silent but demanding, running her fingers over her scalp looking for the flaw in herself that will explain why "these things that she knew had deserted her, [why] she had lost her wits" (218). Why has she separated from herself?

Daniel's solution is to look up Flora Donaldson, a white woman who helps political prisoners. Though "he got on all right with those people, ... [to Ella, Flora] looked just like any white woman who would automatically send a black face round to the back door" (218–19). But instead of finding black faces indistinguishable, Flora Donaldson, purportedly, does not distinguish white from black, and this confuses Ella. She is isolated not only from whites but from her daughter, her husband, and the people. Her husband changed her awareness but not her black female circumstances. While he suffers for the people apart from his family, Ella sits alone amidst the absence of her family sewing a dress for her daughter. It is a quotidian something for the time being.

Despite Daniel's confidence and his indifference to a job and despite Ella's confusion and her desire that Daniel have a job, her skepticism about whites and about Daniel is borne out by the circumstances of the story. Flora Donaldson gets Daniel a job with white industrialist William Chadders whose own marriage unfolds with the plot. The juxtaposition of the two marriages reveals a matrix of difference, and sameness, of good intentions and self-service, an undoing of marriage and of separation.

William Chadders married Madge because he is enchanted by her heartfelt but diffuse protests against the color bar. He believes in "absolute personal freedom as strictly as any bohemian" (220) and so he, unlike Daniel, swears he would never try to change his wife. She, on the other hand, "would not hesitate to go ahead and change anybody" (220), and it seems she has changed her husband, at least enough for Flora Donaldson to seek jobs for blacks from him, another capitalist confronted with apartheid.

The morality of Madge and William differs in conventionally gender-specific ways. While she is erratic in her response to apartheid, doing "what she felt" without considering "the varying degree of usefulness of the things she did" (220), his position is "backed by the impersonal authority of a familiarity with the views of great thinkers, saints and philosophers" (220). When, after their marriage, he does act on his repugnance to the color bar it is as a capitalist "through the setting up of an all-African trust company and investment corporation" (221). Also, consistent with conventional gender arrangements, he accepts her erratic behavior because it "enchants" him while she admires his views on racial immorality because they are sounder and his economic projects because they are more effective than anything she does. Yet she believes her contribution comes in seeing, touching, talking to, caring about the people. Madge and Flora Donaldson seem to have access to the people from whom Ella is isolated. Even this right of birth has been denied Ella and given to Madge who has the wealth to engage in unpaid, sometimes ineffectual work. Madge has everything and Ella has nothing.

When William tells Madge he has no skilled packing job for Daniel Mngoma, in fact, no skilled labor for blacks at all, she does not object to the inherent assumption but says instead, "He'll understand. It'll give him something for the time being" (223). But her husband, a man of systematic principles, is more accurate in his assessment of Daniel, another man of such principles. I have "nothing for him," William says, knowing Daniel will not stick with an unskilled job (222). Madge thinks Daniel will understand if William sees him personally and explains. She has no inkling of Daniel's desire for everything and not something, a desire Ella understands but materially and emotionally cannot tolerate.

Though Madge has been in touch with the people, it is William whose reading of Daniel is more accurate. But in the process of this reading William also demonstrates a division between his interests and Daniel's and between his wife's sympathies and his own. On Daniel's first and only day of working at William's factory, he wears an outlawed African National Congress button. William tells him he cannot wear it. When Madge hears this, as she and William undress to go to bed, she argues that William was wrong. "Vulnerable and naked, he said authoritatively, 'You can't wear a button like that among the men in the workshop'" (223). His body's sexual vulnerability to his wife is overridden by the public authority of his voice. But his wife's sympathetic defense of Daniel replaces her husband's principle with some idea of her own. "He's not there *representing* anything" (223), she says, and "It is exactly the same [as] . . . a Rotary button, or an Elvis Presley button" (223).

Her argument renders Daniel's behavior meaningless or frivolous, even as it makes a claim for free expression. William says it would not be fair to his more conservative partner if he allowed Daniel to wear the button, but he knows the real risk is not something for the time being but everything: the end of apartheid and the white-controlled state. Madge says to her husband, "You'll let him have anything except the one thing worth giving . . . his self-respect" (226). But her conventional, humanist argument never faces Daniel's desire for everything, not anything, for a *total* change in the political and economic and labor conditions of South Africa. Madge never asks herself or her husband if they will "let Daniel have" everything. She never asks if self-respect is something she and William can give or if it is *self*-respect that Daniel lacks. She never questions that it is up to them to let Daniel have anything or everything or nothing.

The argument divides Madge and William. She eventually makes him *feel* his nakedness before her. And when she looks at his face she sees a stranger. "I'm not angry," she says coldly. "I'm beginning to get to know you" (226). But as she feels herself separating from her husband, she does not also feel a difference within herself. She does not see how her sympathies for the people depend upon her husband's political and economic decisions and her own political and personal complicity in this arrangement. She does not know herself. She also does not know Daniel, whose struggle for everything is like her husband's. And yet because of the men's all-or-nothing conflict, her conventionally female, contextual morality, something for the time being, may in fact be a necessary ameliorating alternative. The story's absent answer is the answer to the question, Does Madge know Ella? If Madge could know the people in the isolation of their everyday practical experiences, then she might know Ella better than Daniel knows his wife.

Daniel does not include his wife or his daughter as complex individuals within his sense of the people defined by principle. When he returns from a political meeting he says triumphantly to Ella, "I've got them to accept, *in principle,* that in future we won't take bail. . . . We lent the government our money interest-free when we paid bail" (226–27). Like William, Daniel argues in principle, capitalist principle. But he also adds, "*In principle.* Yes, it's easy to accept in principle. We'll see" (227). Change must be measured in practice, Daniel implies. William applies principle to change, but he separates sharply from Daniel in practice. And yet like William's, Daniel's practice is hampered by principle. In the public political arena, he practices his principles. He has been in jail repeatedly and without taking bail. But he separates effective, public practice from private life—or rather, he doesn't. He lives his private life as though it were public, always on principle, never on individual relationship. His wife's tears exasperate him. Daniel does not see his wife's pain and fear and confusion, or rather, he cannot change her experience to fit his theory of change, his vision of the future. She will not be the people. He lashes out at her individual vulnerability, a recalcitrant challenge to his political vision.

Impatient, he reveals to her, "You think straight in prison because you've got nothing to lose. Nobody thinks straight, outside" (228). After all, he is not a man who has transcended experience through political principle—nor could anyone be. His political commitment and bravery notwithstanding, his "clarity" is the result of isolation in prison. In prison where there is nothing, he can imagine everything. Ella, on the other hand, has been isolated in the context of the world where she has her absent daughter and her absent husband to lose. She must live practically with the effects of political principles. "Don't cry. You're just like any other woman" (228), Daniel says to comfort her. She might be equally comforting or condescending declaring him just like any other essential, principled man. But in fact, all four characters must live any theory they devise in their experiences as paradoxical members of the people. The differences and sameness among them depend upon specific interlocutionary situations.

"The Catch," "The Gentle Art," and "Something for the Time Being" are all stories of the 1950s. In Gordimer's novels of the same period (*The Lying Days, A World of Strangers*), Clingman traces the novelist's beginnings in conventional, humanistic fiction and complains that in exploring subjective consciousness this fiction tolerates, even celebrates, paradox. In these novels Gordimer deals with apartheid as a social phenomenon and posits multiracism as its most effective opponent. Clingman sees these assumptions as consistent with South African history of the 1950s, but he also describes Gordimer's and South Africa's movement away from such bourgeois liberalism to a more political understanding of "impersonal history."[32] There is truth to this perception of the development in Gordimer's work. I have made similar observations about her short stories.[33] But there is also a deconstruction of conventional separation and sameness in these early stories which belies any strict progressivist perception of her art or her political acumen. There is no single definitive origin of the trace. The stories' plural subjects challenge not only certainty about change but also who will be the subjects and who the objects of change. The stories read paradox in the text of South Africa. It is there to be reckoned with.

In much later stories, stories of the 1980s, Gordimer creates a greater number of black characters, occasionally in stories without whites. And yet, this bow to separate black consciousness—if that is what it is—can be achieved, of course, only by the white woman writer presenting the characters' behavior and speech. The white writer cannot eliminate her own voice. In these later stories Gordimer seems tempted by the syllogism: in South Africa all blacks are victims; all victims are virtuous; therefore, all blacks are virtuous. But she resists it. Whites, however, are given less reign for their subjectivity and become more typified in the later stories. With exceptions, the mode of the later stories is most often satire and not the subtler woven web of complicity.

In "A City of the Dead, A City of the Living," a story of the 1980s, all of the characters are black, but the complexities of internal difference are still apparent. A young woman, a mother, finds herself harboring a political fugitive in her small township house, where her life is defined entirely by women's labor in childbearing and domestic chores. The world of the whites where her husband works or the larger world her husband reads of in the newspapers, a world where this fugitive has been, are not what she knows. She cooks and cleans for the fugitive, as she does for her husband, but is confused when he helps with what she assumes is woman's work. She is also confused by his showing her his revolver when he does not show her husband. And she is confused when he holds the baby as though it were his own. Nevertheless, after her early objections, she is helpful and, according to her husband's instructions, unquestioning.

And yet one Sunday, after days spent shut in the small dark house with the fugitive, her husband, and her baby, she walks out, on the excuse the baby needs milk, walks to the white police station, like the one the man blew up, and turns him in. No one asks her why, and though she asks herself, she cannot answer. Is it because his laughter made her forget herself and feel like a girl? Is it because it became too tense, too impossible to learn nothing of him so they could not tell the police? Is it because he did not remain separate enough for her to act in impersonal political unity? Not knowing the world outside her home, she cannot imagine how the politics of that world are applied personally in her home. The woman does not articulate any of these questions or any conclusions about how the fugitive threatens her with change.

The fugitive inadvertently provides one answer to her question: Why? In arguing with her husband, Samson, for black solidarity in action, he says, "Isn't the truth what you *know?* Don't you listen to the ones who speak the truth?" (17). In this and all arguments the men ignore the woman. The fugitive inadequately grasps what the *woman* knows: she thinks to herself, "*We'll never have a car . . . and we'll never have to run away to those far places, like him. Lucky to have this house; many, many people are jealous of that*" (23). Her truth is what she knows and what she fears, not what the fugitive would have her know. She acts on her truth. But no one seems to know or fear her truth. It is not a part of their strategy.

After she turns the man in, creating an unexpected crisis for him, she wonders why "*nobody in [her] house asks*" (26). Only another woman, Ma Radebe, the shebeen queen, bothers to spit at the betrayer. In this confrontation at least the women see one another as subjects. They have their own roles in any movement for change.

Abdul JanMohamed explains Gordimer's acquisition of affiliative bonds this way:

> While writing and educating herself, Nadine Gordimer experienced a radical psychological rupture which she calls a "second birth"—she discovered the "great South African lie." The realization that white society was trying to conceal the simple fact that blacks were people led her to understand that her identity as a South African had to be formed through a resolution of the black/white dichotomy, that the two races had to be unified under a central, definitive experience of black-and-white as people with undifferentiated claims to life, whatever else—skin, language, culture—might distinguish them from one another.[34]

That Gordimer's "second birth" would be expressed as a direct opposition to the ethos of separation, as in fact assimilation, is what one would reasonably expect, and yet, one can also see in this South African "second birth" traits of that United States phenomenon Rich describes: resistance to first birth and even self-hatred. What the narratives of these short stories can do that a committed statement of affiliative bonds cannot is show—and again I quote Johnson—"that questions of difference and identity are always a function of a specific interlocutionary situation—and the answers, matters of strategy rather than truth." Whoever articulates a theory and undertakes action for a change promoting greater justice faces the complicating uncertain conditions of each situation and the paradox of politics. Given this challenge to change and the recalcitrance of "grand apartheid," it is not surprising that Gordimer's affiliatively acquired commitment has come to manifest itself in her late fiction as satire (*Something Out There*) or as wishful thinking (*A Sport of Nature*). Separation asserts itself in the personal and political consciousness of her fiction. In her best fiction one sees that political divisions remain as much because of internal as because of external difference. But in the recognition of internal difference, useful commitment can take root.

A Few Facts: The Short Fiction of Grace Paley

Like Nadine Gordimer, Grace Paley has been writing fiction for forty years, and like Gordimer's characters Paley's characters have demonstrated in that time a salient evolutionary change from lives of private preoccupations to lives of public action.[35] But in both women's fiction, theories of public action are always challenged by the details of personal experience. Outside as well as inside her fiction Paley, unlike Gordimer, expresses faith in a feminist vision of private and public correspondence. Paley's language is mostly comic and always conversational. Everyone has a voice which, with all the other voices, the narrator weaves into conversation. The sullen silence and immovable physicality with which the marginalized (colored or white, female or male) assert themselves in Gordimer's fiction is, in Paley's fiction, turned to complaint. Unlike the African beach or bush or farm or even the hideout within the crowded township, the United States city of Paley's fiction is a noisy place in which everyone gets a say though she may not be heard.

All of this suggests the United States ethos of assimilation asserts itself in Paley's fiction, and it does. Adam Mars-Jones, a British reviewer of Paley's most recent collection of short stories, *Later the Same Day,* even accuses her of an aggressive but selective assimilation which creates an insular world.

> The world which Grace Paley in most of these stories puts all her energy into saving is not a shared and vulnerable planet, but her private world of unified emotions and assumed politics, which she must perpetually repair without ever actually admitting that it has been exposed to damage.[36]

Whether or not Mars-Jones has accurately described Paley's fiction, his accusations address a United States which assimilates emotions and politics in the nuclear family, in the neighborhoods, and even in the world abroad. Paley's stories are, as the United States is, preoccupied with the sexual and economic seduction of the American dream. While admirers of Paley's socialism or feminism see *these* affiliative bonds manifested in her fiction and Mars-Jones sees instead the ethos of assimilation, I think Paley's fiction is marked by a tension between affiliative and filiative bonds, between attraction to and abhorrence of the American dream.

In *The Little Disturbances of Man,* Paley's first collection, she introduces Faith, a character with two sons and at least as many husbands. Often her own narrator, Faith is easily identified with Grace (Paley). Faith *is* frequently the mouthpiece for Paley's humor; she is, however, as frequently a victim of it. In early stories Faith suffers from her simultaneous devotion to and intolerance of men. In later stories she seeks love and understanding in a larger world but with a similar confusion of sentiment and sarcasm. Faith may well be a typical United States white working-class (Jewish) mother in her particular internal division, but she is not Grace.

"The Used-Boy Raisers" is one of two stories about Faith presented together in the first collection under the title "Two Short Sad Stories from a Long and Happy Life." Faith narrates incorporating the words of her ex-husband, dubbed Livid, and her present husband, Pallid, into her wry voice. As the three talk over breakfast, Faith embroiders a Bless-Our-Home sampler "for the protection of my sons, who were also Livid's."[37] Faith's sewing, unlike Ella's, is ideological rather than practical. She embroiders this picture of a ranch house and a Norway maple with the same skeptical optimism evident in the "Long and Happy Life" of the title.

Even as they express differences, Faith sees her husbands as the same. Though Livid has gone off to work in "the British plains in Africa" (127) and is himself British and Pallid goes off to work in the city outside her door, from Faith's position at home the two are the same because they share a decorous, kindly imperturbable distance from her sons. Livid writes Pallid from Africa:

> I do think they're fine boys, you understand. I love them too, but Faith is their mother and now Faith is your wife. I'm so much away. If you want to think of them as yours, old man, go ahead.
> Why, thank you, Pallid had replied. . . . Then he implored the boys, when not in use, to play in their own room. He made all efforts to be kind. (127–28)

Livid passes to Pallid ownership of these products of Faith's labor. But when the children enter wild and affectionate, playing "horse thief" and "crack shot," these American ruffians overwhelm both fathers. Faith sees herself and the boys as separate from these men who are alike.

In the conventional sexual division of labor in the nuclear family, men *are* after all separate: Faith eventually sends them both off to work. But Faith's conflation of the two fathers defines the men's role as silly. In this polygamous situation Faith trivializes their sexual and emotional contribution to women and children. The role in the American dream that the men play is rendered no more serious than the boys' games they criticize. Yet if Faith were not attracted to the American vision of the conventional nuclear family in the first place, its inadequacies would not so much disappoint her.

Faith simultaneously makes and unmakes the American dream. This is her internal difference, her struggle with assimilation. Faith raises the children, does the domestic chores, sends the men to work, and even embroiders a suburban house in lieu of the one neither Livid nor Pallid has bought. She fulfills her tasks and maintains the domestic schedule as though they are part of the sampler she makes "for the protection of her sons": "You'd better go to work, I suggested, knotting the pearl-gray late-afternoon thread" (127 and 133). And yet she must pierce this embroidery like a balloon in order to make it: "as one talked of time past and upon us, I pierced the ranch house that nestles in the shade" (128).

When the three adults talk of marriage, she says ironically, "I don't know, it just ties a man down" (129), all the while knowing, in her experience, that it does not. Faith does not acknowledge that marriage can tie a *woman* down, but the text's presentation of her passive anger reveals her confinement nonetheless. More destitute than Penelope, she weaves and unweaves the dream at the same time without clear consciousness that she does so. And yet when she puts her experience together with the promises of the dream, such made unmaking appears her only choice. To have other choices, she would have to have a different theory of labor and marriage; she would have to have theoretical thinking itself. Before a theory can be subjected to the multiplicity of experience, one must first have some system of thought reaching beyond the repetition of quotidian life and the filiative bonds one inherits.

When the men argue about the significance of the church and parochial school, Faith gives no credence to their ideas or their difference because she gives no credence to ideas. She judges them by only one criterion: how much are ideas mere echoes of childhood experience? She is right to see that "recalling childhood and home [religion and parochial schools], poor Livid writhed in his seat" (130), that Livid's experience has engendered his ideas, but she is wrong, therefore, to discredit the ideas. Pallid argues that "we free-thinkers . . . are never far from our nervous old mother, the Church. . . . I myself, although I lost God a long time ago, have never lost faith"(130–31). Yet his Faith is furious when she is drawn into this argument. As though to avenge the treatment of Hawthorne's Faith by Young Goodman Brown, this Faith, in narrating the story, dismisses all arguments about God and faith. And yet her reason for this summary dismissal is again confirmed when Pallid asserts, "I inadvertently pray. . . . It is not to God, it is to that unifying memory out of childhood" (131). Each man's ideas are only assertions about his childhood. Without the generalizing of ideas, however, one's experience has little private and no public power. Change is left to be defined by those who will express ideas and strategies defined by their experience.

When Pallid draws Faith into their argument, she does express one opinion about the world outside her home. Like the men, she also finds her ideas in her experiences even if she does not acknowledge the connection. Faith asserts that she believes in the Diaspora, the wandering of the Chosen People. "Once they're huddled in one little corner of a desert, they're like anyone else. . . . Jews have one hope only—to remain . . . a splinter in the toe of civilizations, a victim to aggravate the conscience" (132). She then says separately of herself, "I rarely express my opinion on any serious matter but only live out my destiny, which is to be, until my expiration date, laughingly the servant of man" (132). An American product on a grocery store shelf, she will live her "long and happy life" serving man—not humans. The proximity of Faith's declarations about Jews and herself implies that women too are "victims to aggravate the conscience."

But Faith does not grant women the dignity (or hegemony) of being chosen people. Nor does she admit any feeling of loss at having given up her Jewish heritage to marry Christian Livid, then Pallid. To assimilate with other American women in the roles of wife and mother, she has, ironically, left the Chosen People—both the community of Jews and the community of women. Faith's struggle with the identity and difference of women and Jews exposes the schism in her character.

Faith's idea proposes that Jews have moral power, just as her experience demonstrates to her that she has moral power. Furthermore, she associates moral power with long-suffering, her own and the Jews. The power can only be exercised if these people are diffused. And yet she wants the Jews to wander as she, a woman, does not wander; they must be the homeless conscience of the world while she stays at home. As Faith embroiders an even more stable, assimilated, suburban home for her sons, she implies, nonetheless, that a home will dull the moral acuity of the Jews. In her identity as a Jew and as a woman, however, Faith is isolated from any political or social body. So her idea that Jews must be diffused to be the bearers of conscience acts as justification for her inertia as a woman. In fact, her conscience at home is conventional. She never challenges her husbands' behavior or her own assumption of separation from them. She does not address the fact, for example, that it is not she but her husbands who wander in the world like the mythic Jews. She stays at home working to assimilate with that which she views with wry skepticism.

Though Gordimer's characters experience forced separation in their society and Faith finds encouragement to assimilate in hers, the effects of the two ethics are not altogether different.[38] United States assimilation urges participation in the nuclear family, and the conventional ethos of such family life requires women's labor as mothers be isolated from men's labor. Assimilation further urges private home ownership—and, if it is not affordable, the semblance of such privacy. Thus, one nuclear family is separated from another; women in these homes are isolated most of all. Mother-isolation alienates mothers from their labor even as mothers make every effort to protect their products. Like Samson's wife in "A City of the Dead, A City of the Living," Faith behaves according to a truth separate from that the men in her home articulate, and yet her behavior also maintains their behavior and the national ethos.

Faith calls Pallid "the used-boy raiser," but she who "takes good care of her men" (133 and 128) is and has been the raiser of boys and men (used-boys) and contributes to the continuation of the very qualities she mocks at a wry, if not cynical, distance. At the story's end she says the men "set off in pride on paths which are not my concern" (134). In her acute alienation from men, she treats them as though they are moral illiterates undeserving of anger. This indifference keeps Faith assimilated into the United States enterprise and separate from the power to change.

In *Enormous Changes at the Last Minute,* Faith reappears in a tree. Like Italo Calvino's baron of *Baron in the Trees,* Faith of "Faith in a Tree" finds her leafy vantage point difficult to give up, but compared to the baron's years of traveling in trees, her stay is momentary. Child-bound to the park, Faith longs for "important conversation, a sniff of the man-wide world," but then she defines this worldliness as a language of sex: "one brainy companion who could translate my friendly language into his tongue of undying carnal love" (77). Longing to escape the children she must watch over, she sits in a tree.

Beneath her are children who control their mothers' movement and mothers whose only apparent freedom is in their talk: "Wherever the children ran, their mothers stopped to talk" (77). Above her are "His Holy Headquarters," he "who unravels the stars to this day with little hydrogen explosions," like those reproduced by man in the "man-wide world" (77). God and Faith look down upon the various women and their children, representatives of different social classes. The opinion of God, like that of man, is so distant and separate as to be of no relevance in the park. But opinionated Faith speaks with disdain of the wealthy and with affection for her laboring friends. "I can only see Kitty, a co-worker in the mother-trade—a topnotch craftsman" (78).

Her socialist mother has told Faith: "You're an American child. Free. Independent" (80). But Faith is skeptical of independence declaring, "I have always required a man to be dependent on, even when it appeared that I had one already. I own two small boys whose dependence on me takes up my lumpen time and my bourgeois feelings" (80). Though Faith's humor asks that her life be accepted in the spirit in which she says she accepts it, her contradictions challenge a reader's inclination toward simple empathy with a woman-victim.

For Faith, having a man does not remove the strain of requiring one. She overdoes desire—for sex or the completed family—as she overdoes mothering, babying her boys "well beyond the recommendations of my friends" (80). Her excessive desire to acquire and maintain the nuclear family results ironically in a challenge to that American dream. And yet she maintains the desire. She maintains it even though she now has not two men but none. Her husband Ricardo has left her for "a new under-developed nation."

He writes to her:

> I am not well. I hope I never see another rain forest. I am sick. Are you working? Have you seen Ed Snead? He owes me $180. Don't badger him about it if he looks broke. Otherwise send me some to Guerra Verde c/o Dotty Wasserman. Am living here with her. She's on a Children's Mission. Wonderful girl. Reminds me of you ten years ago. She acts on her principles. I *need* the money. (82)

While Faith is up a tree, rooted in motherhood, Ricardo acts on principle not just in the public world but in the international, underdeveloped world. He also admires a woman who acts on principle—and who provides him a home. He has separated himself from insular, money-making, home-buying, family-responsible maleness. He remains, nonetheless, a used-boy Faith is asked to raise, providing sympathy for his sickness and money for his independence.

Meanwhile with experience, but not with "principle," Faith is on a Children's Mission of her own. Her desires are assimilated into the United States ethic, but her experiences are thwarting her "American independence." And yet if she were more thoroughly successful in her bid for assimilation, she would be less exhausted but not more free. Her freedom depends on separating from as well as adhering to motherhood. Tree-sitting is an attempt at some physical and fanciful separation. But to imagine being publicly responsible—as Ricardo describes Dotty Wasserman—threatens her sense of being personally responsible. Her husband is, after all, apparently publicly responsible at the expense of separation from responsible fatherhood.

So Faith lives reacting to children—their appearance, their crises, their potential. She defines the public world of the city, including its integrated schools, as the important object present for the subjective appreciation of her sons. Separating herself from any evaluation of relative worth, she does not consider that she is the subject narrating her children and the world. She sees her sons as cause, not as effect. Even as she introduces the world to them, she yearns for her sons to guide her. "If you would only look up, Anthony, and boss me what to do, I would immediately slide down this scabby bark" (87). She is separated, alienated, from her sons by her devotion to them and by her romantic abnegation of adult responsibilities in lieu of the safe innocence of child guidance. Skeptical of the god of hydrogen explosions, she instead looks down for help.

She believes she receives guidance when Vietnam protestors, young parents wheeling babies, enter the park. They carry posters: one with the picture of a well-fed man and child and the question "Would you burn a child?"; the second with the words "When necessary"; the third with the picture of a napalmed Vietnamese child. Infuriated that the local cop expels the protestors from the park and that the other adults do nothing, Faith's son rewrites the question and the answer on the sidewalk. Faith then expresses her response to her son's outrage as an epiphany. "That is exactly when events turned me around. . . . I thought more and more and every day about the world" (99–100).

It seems all the children working together—those whose parents are protesting, the healthy child in the picture, the burned Vietnamese child, and her own child: essential child—have made Faith conscious of a world outside the playground. And yet her perception of all children as one, her definition of them all as cause and herself as effect is not strong evidence that she sees herself as subject or as anything other than essential mother. She has seen the different economic classes of children beneath her in the park. She knows the difference in their lives, yet she immediately assimilates the Vietnamese child into her mother's embrace. The kindness of this impulse does not, unfortunately, bear with it an understanding of Vietnam or the United States involvement there. Only adults can thoroughly study this and take responsibility for it. Young children cannot lead armies into or out of war however much those wars brutalize them. The protestor incident and her son's reaction separate Faith from the playground but tie her to motherhood as firmly as ever.

Paley's text respects mothers' labor while remaining mindful of the uncertainties and internal difference inherent in the work. As mother and narrator, Faith's authority is dubious. In a tree Faith is herself: rooted in motherhood and fancifully removed from it. Motherhood limits her experience and this limitation often turns her wry humor in on herself, but at the same time her pride in her product is such that she believes her children lead her. Faith asserts the moral guidance of children; Paley's text asserts that it is adult interpretations of children's behavior which defines innocence as moral, politically responsible, worthy of following. Like all interpretations, this interpretation holds meaning in the scars of its internal difference.

Some—perhaps many—readers of "Faith in a Tree" take Faith's assertion of child guidance as Paley's. "Wise mother to be led by a child," writes
Blanche Gelfant.[39] Such readings assume the natural, innocent morality
of children. Such readings also deny or ignore the prevalent use of children, in images and words, for purposes of persuasion. Faith uses her son
as the protestors use their children they wheel in carriages and the pictures
of children they carry on posters. The children lend the assumption of
natural morality and innocence to the adults' political positions. Whether
those positions are just or justifiable may be argued on many grounds,
including the tragic loss of valuable young lives. One could certainly
argue, for example, that the South African police and military were wrong
to fire on the children demonstrating in Soweto. One could argue that the
adults of the South African movement could have and should have pre-
vented the children from demonstrating or that the children were a
necessary sacrifice in a war against a violent, recalcitrant opponent. All of
these arguments might be defended as moral, but none of them is natural
or innocent. The internal difference of motherhood—the promise of
power in assimilation, the absence of freedom in isolation—makes mothers vulnerable to arguments which conflate nature and human will.

In "The Long-Distance Runner" Faith is again led by a child,[40] a black
child. Though in "Faith in a Tree," Faith tells her son she has stayed in the
city because of all he will gain from integrated schools, in "The Long-
Distance Runner" it is clear that most of those others in the integrated city
live ghettoized in neighborhoods some distance from hers. The neighborhood Faith visits is the one where she grew up—the same one near the
same beach, but now it is different.

Having "spent a lot of life lying down or standing and staring" (181),
Faith decides at forty-two to run. Although, she says, "I was stout and in
many ways inadequate to this desire" (179), she decides to take up running. Having finished her training in the country, she instructs her grown
sons, "Go lead your private life. . . . Only leave me out of it" (180). She
leaves them watching the news on television, "which proved with moving
pictures that there *had* been a voyage to the moon and Africa and South
America hid in a furious whorl of clouds" (180) and runs to Brighton
Beach where years ago her mother "had been assigned by her comrades to
halt the tides of cruel American enterprise with simple socialist sense"
(181). Besides cruelty, American enterprise produced the innovation of the
moon voyage and the television on which her sons watch it.[41] Faith runs

between the assimilating reality of the television in her sons' generation and the criticism of conglomerate brutality in her mother's; she runs before "urban renewal" destroys the city and old age destroys her.

In the visit to her past, she is surrounded by familiarity and otherness: the same apartment buildings and streets; blacks and their speech. She works to make the other the same saying, "I like your speech. . . . Metaphor and all." "Right on. We get that from talking," they respond. "Yes my people also had a way of speech. And don't forget the Irish" (181), she says. The difference is all valued the same. But when a small black boy does not know who the Irish are, another tells him "cops" (182), a significant other. Faith, however, refuses if not all difference, all insult in their language. "You blubrous devil!" says one young man, but she sees behind his horn-rimmed glasses "that intelligent look that City College boys used to have when I was eighteen and first looked at them" (182). And when this bespectacled, young man leads the others "in contempt and anger" (182), she jumps in with "some facts" asking them how many wild flowers they can name. Though wild flowers are a deflection and a long distance from the ghetto, her age as an adult is, nevertheless, also a long distance from their youth. This difference lends her some modest authority. As Faith says in "Friends" (*Later the Same Day*) to her son's ideological reprimands, "Hindsight, usually looked down upon, is probably as valuable as foresight, since it does include a few facts" (89).

Cynthia, a Girl Scout and Faith's child-guide, takes Faith into the sanctuary of her old apartment building. But as they near Faith's old apartment, she becomes afraid, refusing to go on. Her excuse is a lie: "my mother's dead" (186). Later, when she cries at her old apartment door "It's me! . . . Mama! Mama! let me in!" (187), it seems the one who died is the all-protecting mother who had been behind the door, the one Faith imagines she had and certainly the one she was before she sent her sons into the world to lead private lives, the same one the Girl Scout swears she cannot do without. When Faith tries to soothe Cynthia's anxiety (and her own) saying, "you could come live with me [if you lost your mother]" (187) for the first time the child is afraid of Faith, afraid of this white woman who would usurp her mother's role and pull her into the white world ignoring her difference. Faith cannot be the essential mother of every child. When she later learns the mother of the woman in her old apartment has died there she persists: "I remained quiet because of the death of mothers" (194). There is for Faith still a quality of motherhood deserving reverence though experience demonstrates that one mother cannot replace another. In fact, it is because one mother cannot replace another that Cynthia's fear is justified and the old woman's death is poignant.

For about three weeks Faith lives in her childhood home with Mrs. Luddy, her son, and three baby girls and tries to form a bond of essential motherhood with Mrs. Luddy. Again she offers "a few facts," this time about herself, because she wants to "talk lovingly like sisters" (191–92) with Mrs. Luddy. She talks and Mrs. Luddy talks but also repeatedly asserts, "Girl, you don't know nothing." This phrase both pushes Faith away and, by its familiar rhetoric, draws Faith in. In Mrs. Luddy's idiom, the phrase asserts that Faith knows nothing (about life in general or about Mrs. Luddy's life in particular). But in the artistic idiom of the text, the phrase can also mean that Faith knows not nothing (that is, something), and that Faith doesn't know nothing (doesn't know what it is to have nothing). Still, Mrs. Luddy talks. This is what Faith wants from everyone. In talk Faith does not hear cacophony; she hears unity. Yet when Mrs. Luddy finally tells Faith to leave, it is because Mrs. Luddy hears "a lot of noise" (195) in the apartment. She is skeptical of any possibilities in multiplicity. She wants separation: "Time we was by ourself a little" (195). After Faith leaves Mrs. Luddy's to run home, she goes by the playgrounds to warn young mothers, "you girls will be like me, wrong in everything" (196). When her offer to (mis)represent the other as the same is denied, Faith makes a totalizing assumption about truth which blinds her to the significance of Mrs. Luddy's strategies. She prefers certain defeat to uncertain possibilities.

Faith was, it seems, not wrong about running. When she is out again after three weeks in Mrs. Luddy's apartment, she discovers everyone is jogging. "I was only one person doing her thing, which happened like most American eccentric acts to be the most 'in' thing" (196). Greeted by fellow-runners, she is assimilated into that United States culture in which she is accepted and lost, that culture from which Mrs. Luddy is excluded. Being again among her own kind, Faith is relieved and saddened.

At home Faith talks sentimentally to her son about her return to the old neighborhood at Brighton Beach. "Cut the baby talk" (198), he replies. He wants no part of her sentimentality about being a baby or of her belief in babies' essential virtue—all the assumptions inherent in her tone. Both of Faith's sons and her lover Jack say they do not know what she is talking about when she tries to explain her trip home. The joggers took her in but from those in her private life she is separate. Still, for Faith, talk is almost as good as communication. They, after all, let her repeat herself, and she admits it isn't simple. Though she cannot communicate it, she asserts about her experience that "she learns as though she was still a child what in the world is coming next" (198).

Has Faith gone to Brighton Beach looking for what Rich calls second-birth, or has she gone to recover her first-birth before assimilation made her another American incapable of keeping her eccentricities for herself? Her sense of wonder, like her leap to the fact of wild flowers, is an avoidance of the ugly gutted sofas lying in the empty lots of her old neighborhood. Yet despite her sentimental explanation to her son, her trip was not simply nostalgia, a coopting of the past. In fact, she runs back-ward to see what is coming next, not to control what lay behind her. But how much can she recover of her first-birth in a place so different from it? Is her denying of the insult in the blacks' language a derailing of their difference and their anger and the crisis it would precipitate? Does her experience with them give her power but not them? If Faith is right, if there is true egalitarianism in the democracy of talk, however eclectic, then her journey back to the root of (her) motherhood has been of some success. But what of the silence that is absent in the story? Every morning Faith's mother—still living after all—reads the newspaper and every morning she says to her husband, "Everyday the same. Dying . . . dying, dying from killing" (187). This is the silent horror perhaps all joggers are running to avoid.

Dying asserts itself in Paley's most famous story, "A Conversation with My Father." In a note at the beginning of the collection, Paley explains that this father is her father. Though she never says the daughter is herself, the persona Faith is absent. The daughter is a writer and it is about her stories that she and her father talk. While they argue, he is dying: "His heart, that bloody motor . . . will not do certain jobs any more" (161).

He asks her to write a simple Chekhovian story. The daughter writes of alienation between mother and son, the result of excessive mother-love. When the son becomes a junkie, the mother becomes a junkie—to fore-stall his guilt and keep him at home. But when the son gives up drugs for health food, the mother cannot. So her son moves out refusing to see her. This is essential child guidance and essential motherly devotion com-pletely undone. It is the simple story offered the father, a wise and kindly figure unlike Livid, Pallid, or Ricardo whose behavior as fathers Faith treats as beneath contempt. Even as "A Conversation with My Father" presents the daughter's adherence to "the open destiny of life" (162) and the father's insistence that she face tragedy, it dismantles the ethic of mother-love and dismissal of fatherly possibilities the daughter's persona Faith has expressed. The story asserts the difference between Faith and Grace even if they share struggles of internal difference.

The father's physical frailty in the story also insists on the silent presence of dying no matter how vociferous his daughter's commitment to open destiny. Like Milan Kundera's story of a conversation with his dying father in *The Book of Laughter and Forgetting,* this story's conversation evokes the irrevocable physical presence of individual loss. And yet it demonstrates the power of words as it undermines them. In that paradox is the open destiny in which the daughter believes.

In "Somewhere Else," from Paley's most recent collection *Later the Same Day,* she writes of another medium of representation, photography. "Somewhere Else" is an overt exploration of the relationship of images and language and the political uses of both; similar questions have already arisen in regard to the Vietnam protest posters in "Faith in a Tree" and the video of the moon shot in "The Long-Distance Runner." In "Somewhere Else" Paley juxtaposes United States citizens touring and photographing mainland China to one of those tourists, a white man, filming the Bronx. In both places the people object to being photographed, and the United States marxist-sympathizing tourists ask themselves why.

The story undoes the unity of ideology with both the complexities of cultures and the quirks of individuals. Politics requires a continuous rereading. While the Americans see China as a totality because they are in love with the Chinese revolution and people, the Chinese see Westerners as one unit because they have distrusted Western photographers ever since Michelangelo Antonioni made the film *Chung Kuo* celebrating China's "archaic charm" (47) and denigrating its new technology. The socialist Americans are eager to identify with the Chinese people but in doing so reveal their filiative bonds to the United States rather than any affiliatively acquired marxist resistance to their homeland. They take thousands of photographs to display later in American church basements. Though the Chinese government is eager to control what those images will be, in fact the Americans as much as the Chinese want to erase any image that diverges from their expectations. Even in confrontation, they are alike in this. Yet in their practice of ideology the Americans display much less control than the Chinese, as the narrator's humor makes evident: "We do it [that is, take pictures] with politics in mind, if not in total command" (47), she says. And when they are detained she observes, "We hoped we were not about to suffer socialist injustice, because we loved socialism" (48). Assimilating the Chinese into a United States yet socialist vision requires outright denial of the facts.

Though in rote repetition of their rules, the Chinese officials seem inscrutable, the tourists' individual quirks are obvious (to a United States reader). Even a group of twenty-two left-wing Americans quickly divide into fragments, thus in their individualism proving to be much the same. Socialist solidarity notwithstanding, United States individualism abides. East separates from West, that is, New York from California. Some of the New Yorkers think the Californians' tennis shorts and golden tans are an offense to the Chinese. Youth separates from age. When one man is accused by the Chinese of taking a photograph without the subjects' permission, the older people cry, "No! No!" But "three young people, who liked to see us older folks caught in political contradiction or treasonous bewilderment, simply laughed" (50). The timid separate from the adventurous. "Some of our people with poor character structures . . . [had] been a little ashamed of their timidity . . . but now that [the accused] was being spoken to [by the Chinese official], they were proud of their group discipline" (52). When the Chinese official, Mr. Wong, leaves the tourists "some of us gathered around Fred [the accused]. Others gathered as far from Fred as possible" (53).

In this nonviolent encounter the dichotomy of East and West (the international East and West) is shattered by a comic conglomeration of misperceived difference and sameness. When Mr. Wong tells them which is the offending photograph, the narrator offers to the reader the tourists' more-marxist-than-marxist interpretation of the images. And when they learn who is accused of taking the illegal photograph, it is the man who hates cameras, not the one who took 4,387 photographs before his camera shut its eye in exhaustion.

Later, the Tientsin Women's Federation invites them to share their United States folk heritage. They sing "I've Been Working on the Railroad" (although none of them seems to be of the laboring class: one tourist is an attorney, another a filmmaker, and so on). In this choral presentation they provide a unified and largely false idea of the United

States and of themselves. And yet everything about their individual differences within their dogged political rhetoric is characteristically of the United States.

Back in New York, on the night of their "China reunion," they hear from Joe, the adventurous one, about his filming in the Bronx. Joe has gone to the Bronx to help young people film the building of playgrounds, "just to keep a record" (56), but he has also filmed burning gutted buildings. That day, without their permission, he inadvertently films a group of young Hispanic men sitting on a stoop. They take the camera and film from him, but when he pleads for the return of the film the children shot, they return that film and the camera to him. Then, inexplicably, he presses the young men to keep the camera. They reject it vehemently, "you crazy, man?" but he "shove[s] the camera into their hands" (59).

If one takes pictures "to remember the Chinese people better," "just to keep a record," then it is reasonable that the young men do not want the camera. It is not likely that they or the Youth Corps children who, Joe observes, never turn to look at burning buildings will forget their neighborhood. Can the camera's selective seeing—art's selective seeing—show them something about their home they do not already know? In "The Long-Distance Runner" Faith says that she behaved as though "remembering was in charge of the *existence* of the past. This is not so" (186). If Faith is right, if the existence of the Bronx was and is whether it is recorded or not, and it is the existence which has contributed substantially to what the young men are, then the camera is superfluous.

When Joe tells his fellow-tourists of his Bronx encounter, Ruth exclaims, "What in the world!" to which Joe responds, "Forget the world" (59). On the night that they have gathered to remember China—as though it were their alma mater—Joe moves them closer to home and first birth; they must think again about photographs and memory. Martin, the avid photographer, says that Joe gave away his camera because he wanted to show that a person who owns a camera does not own the world. But Joe resists this marxist photographer's guilt. To appease Joe, Martin says, "Let's be calm" (60) and look at the slides of China. The group resists rereading the two confrontations and potential crises, one with distant and one with near outsiders. Instead, for all their differences, they join together in the activity of "remembering the Chinese people" through the slides. It seems a narrow, assimilating activity.

In *On Photography* Susan Sontag observes that "people robbed of their past seem to make the most fervent picture takers, at home and abroad. . . . In certain countries, such as the United States and Japan, the break with the past has been particularly traumatic."[42] Paley's tourists take pictures of the Chinese consuming and assimilating them as they have been assimilated by the United States ideology of independence and consumption despite their socialist resistance to these forces. Their intent is to verify their understanding of socialism with their photographs thereby making themselves like the Chinese and the Chinese like them. But the effect, most evident in Martin, the avid photographer, has been to replace experience with images. The imagery consumes not just the lives of the Chinese but their own lives as well.[43]

By pressing his camera upon the Hispanic boys, Joe may have avoided consuming them and thus himself. But his act is also the result of an inadequate United States ideology. In the name of socialism and the code of tourism, Joe can participate in photographing the Chinese, but neither socialism nor tourism can explain what Joe sees in the Bronx. Sontag argues that ideology, not photography, determines what constitutes an event and names it.[44] The assimilation promised by United States ideologies of equality and capitalist competition excludes destitute places like the Bronx. Exiled from assimilation, the Bronx is, by Sontag's reasoning and Rich's, a non-event with a non-name. Perhaps Joe, the assimilated American—despite his left-wing politics—gives away the camera because he has no philosophy through which to name images of the Bronx that he reproduces. The separations within the myth of assimilation are more difficult to confront than challenges to United States notions of East-West difference. Experiences in distant lands are also easier to replace with images than are experiences in neighboring boroughs. The first birth is the painful one.

And yet the films of the Bronx and photographs of China have, as selective imagery, the same rhetorical potential, political power, as the television clips of the voyage to the moon that Faith's sons watch in "The Long-Distance Runner." They have the political potential manifested in Antonioni's *Chung Kuo* because of and despite the fact that the Chinese government dislikes it.[45] The photographs will misrepresent their subjects—whether those subjects give their permission or not—as memory is bound to misrepresent existence, even carefully recorded memory. Perspective is a quality of the real.[46] Whether or not the photographs' political power can be something more than corroboration of a prenamed ideology depends, in part, on the photographers' consciousness of their own perspective and their struggle with filiative and affiliative bonds.

Despite their avoidance of immediate crisis and their naive socialist expectations of the Chinese, the United States tourists are right to take photographs "with politics in mind, if not in total command" (47). The deconstruction of totalizing meaning is the special political possibility of art though all practitioners of artistic media do not always realize this potential. Martin, the compulsive photographer, cannot remember anything about the subjects or locations of his photographs. Joe, the adventurer, must remind him of the particular existence that allowed for the art. The particular existence undoes the totalizing influence of the assimilation ethos to which the Americans and their picture-taking are subject. Their socialist convictions do not separate them unequivocally from their first birth in their own culture. "A few facts" can enable them to understand that they do see through the lens of their culture even though they resist it.

∗   ∗   ∗

The relationship of art and political change is an uncertain one. To consider the political possibilities and pitfalls in the practices of art, specifically in the language of fiction, it may be helpful to approach the question through comparison with the uses of photography. From the young white South Africans who promise to photograph the Indian when he catches a big enough fish in Gordimer's "The Catch" to the American zealot who takes 4,387 photographs of the Chinese in Paley's "Somewhere Else," photography plays an important paradoxical role in these characters' assertion of themselves by trying to record and remember others.

John Berger argues that, in the present world of easily reproduced images, "the art of the past no longer exists as it once did. Its authority is lost. In its place there is a language of images. What matters now is who uses that language for what purpose."[47] Berger fears that photographs of agony, like the one used by Paley's Vietnam protestors, may only "arrest" the viewer making her feel a personal moral inadequacy and thereby accusing everybody and nobody for the atrocity. This is the kind of outrage expressed by Faith's son. But this language of images obfuscates the politics impinging upon the subject of the photograph and the presentation of the image. It obfuscates the viewer's complicity.

Berger prescribes an antidote for this problem: adding words to images. His solution follows the thinking of Walter Benjamin, who was "troubled by the way photography inexorably beautifies" and recommended captions to "confer upon [photographs] a revolutionary use value."[48] Berger suggests the photographer think of herself as a recorder for those involved in the events and not as a reporter to the rest of the world. Then the photograph must be represented in a context of words and other photographs so that the whole works radially, like memory.[49] The Goldblatt and Gordimer collaborative effort, *Lifetimes Under Apartheid,* follows Berger's prescription. But can Goldblatt's photographs escape the pitfalls of aestheticism and moral inadequacy? Do they have not only "revolutionary use value" but also deconstructive use value? Can they undermine a totality of meaning with the presentation of paradox?

Lifetimes first of all makes evident the complications in Berger's distinction between recorder and reporter. A desire to misread sameness as difference or misrepresent difference as sameness intrudes when a recorder attempts to take down a life not his own as Goldblatt photographs the Africans, especially those living according to their own non-Western customs? Even if one assumes Goldblatt can be a recorder and not an interpreter of a people other than his own, his photographs are published for audiences other than the black and white subjects of the photographs. The photographs' selection and arrangement, the captions, and the excerpts from Gordimer's fiction together are the verification of an ideology if not the presentation of an argument directed at an audience not featured in the photographs.

The difficulty with *Lifetimes* is not that it has designs on the viewer. The photographs are not nature recorded somehow without bias; they are a perspective in service of an idea. The difficulty is that the viewer will forget or suppress this perspective, the specific interlocutionary situation. Then the photographs truly do steal the images of their subjects—as some have always feared—and offer them to the viewer for the price of accepting a truth, a prescribed ideology of separation: white subjects are frozen in pursuit of kitsch; blacks, in pursuit of survival.

The greater, though less apparent, difficulty is that like the photographs of advertising in which the future is continually deferred,[50] these engaging photographs seek, yet defer, the change which will undo the injustice the images convey. It is not that the black subjects of these photographs will defer change (though they may risk creating the image the photographer expects as does the Indian fisherman in Gordimer's "The Catch"). It is the "first-world" viewer who will feel neither complicity in the injustice nor responsibility for change: the photographs ennoble blacks' suffering and trivialize whites' lives such that the white viewers, who cannot place themselves among the blacks, do not place themselves among the whites. The moral clarity of the separation ethic evident in these photographs may be too comfortably certain for concerned United States or European white viewers to give up for some murkier world of black liberation. The white viewer must confront Gordimer's fiction unexcerpted for an uncovering of the vertiginous planes beneath the ground of certain separation.

Edward Said's discussion of vision and narrative in *Orientalism* is, I think, relevant here to my argument for the political usefulness of artistic language relative to photography (if we imagine that the idea of orientalism may be applied to more than the Orient). Said writes:

> Against this static system of "synchronic essentialism" I have called vision because it presumes that the whole Orient can be seen panoptically, there is a constant pressure. The source of pressure is narrative, in that if any Oriental detail can be shown to move, or to develop, diachrony is introduced into the system. What seemed stable—and the Orient is synonymous with stability and unchanging eternality—now appears unstable. Instability suggests that history, with its disruptive detail, its currents of change, its tendency towards growth, decline, or dramatic movement, is possible in the Orient and for the Orient. History and the narrative by which history is represented argue that vision is insufficient, that "the Orient" as an unconditional ontological category does an injustice to the potential of reality for change.[51]

Literary language, with its special tolerance for uncertainty, ambiguity, and paradox, can peer into the fluctuations of politics and find in that movement both pain and potential for change. The reader has a responsibility for both. Bishop's Elizabeth in the waiting room does not feel her own strangeness because she has looked at the photographs in *National Geographic* but because she has done so within the diachrony of her aunt's scream, the ongoing war, and the falling sleet. In her inchoate sense of complicity is ours.

In "Epilogue," a poem from Robert Lowell's final collection *Day by Day*, he writes of the paradoxical difference between photography and painting as a metaphor for his struggle with the medium of words. Words record and complicate the facts so that they are both frozen images and interpreted images, and yet are neither of these. They are the individual voice struggling to see, through the paradoxes of language, those words, what happened and what could happen in an uncertain world.

I hear the noise of my own voice:
The painter's vision is not a lens,
it trembles to caress the light.
But sometimes everything I write
with the threadbare art of my eye
seems a snapshot,
lurid, rapid, garish, grouped,
heightened from life,
yet paralyzed by fact.
All's misalliance.
Yet why not say what happened?
Pray for the grace of accuracy
Vermeer gave to the sun's illumination . . .
We are poor passing facts.[52]

The juxtaposition of the description in Gordimer's fiction and the conversation in Paley's illuminates the scars of separation and assimilation shining light where internal difference lies. These women's language challenges the reader to move beyond the certainty of outrage to an understanding of complicity conducive to change.

It is despair that nothing cannot be
Flares in the mind and leaves a smoky mark
Of dread.

> Thom Gunn, "The Annihilation of Nothing"

Chapter V

Theory, Madness, and the State: Ibuse Masuji's *Black Rain* and John Hawkes's *Travesty*

The reasons to speak of Ibuse Masuji's novel *Black Rain* (*Kuroi Ame*) and John Hawkes's novel *Travesty* in the same essay need explanation. *Black Rain* is a novel of historical catastrophe, a nuclear holocaust novel from the only nation that can produce one.[1] *Travesty* is an apocalyptic novel in the United States tradition. Douglas Robinson argues that images of the end abound in United States fiction where they both undermine and express basic "American ideologies of the self, of nature, of God and the supernatural, and of the community"[2] and, he could have added, of the state. He further argues that Poe is central to the tradition of apocalyptic unveiling. Though Hawkes does not figure in Robinson's argument, he well could. Besides being an avowed admirer of Poe, Hawkes creates an art of last things beyond the veil of the familiar. *Black Rain* and *Travesty* are both fictions of the end though one is distinctly Japanese; the other, American.

From a discussion of the two novels together one can derive only the thinnest speculations about the current polarity of Japan, the economic miracle, and the United States, the debtor nation.[3] Though distinct characteristics separating Japan and the United States, as well as *Black Rain* and *Travesty,* elicit respect for the integrity of each, the two novels considered together can provide a rich unraveling of numerous conventional dichotomies of art and politics. The novels' sameness and difference uncover the internal differences within popular polarities. These dichotomies fall into four categories, or clusters: madness and reason; life and death; self and state; art and morality.

Before delving into the complexities of these interlocking clusters, it is useful to consider briefly each novel. *Black Rain* is a collection of diaries recording events in Hiroshima on and immediately after August 6, 1945. The transcription of these diaries is precipitated in about 1950 by the protagonist's desire to free his niece, Yasuko, from rumors of radiation sickness. Shigematsu, the protagonist, addresses his efforts to a marriage-broker and the family of the man interested in Yasuko's hand. Just as the subject matter of *Black Rain* is a weaving together of traditional marriage customs and the nuclear age, the form of the text links the traditional Japanese diary with the narrative experiments of the modern novel. John Treat emphasizes Ibuse's use of diaries and other historical documents throughout his writing. He also notes the tradition and prevalence of diary-writing in Japan.[4] J. Thomas Rimer describes the traditional diary (*nikki*) as a vehicle less for fact than for poetry. Those diaries, written in

Japanese rather than Chinese, were of private rather than public matters and were usually composed by women using a "false I." The famous "Tosa Diary" was, however, written by the male poet, Ki no Tsurayuki, using a female persona. By the Kamakuran period the diaries had become mostly travel accounts recorded by pilgrims,[5] a form of writing akin to the castaway accounts (*hyōryūki*) of the eighteenth and nineteenth centuries which Ibuse used in several of his works.[6] These conventions of the diary tradition seem to permeate *Black Rain* even though it is known for its use of contemporary diaries of "real-life" facts. In bomb-ravaged Hiroshima where—as many have noted—the normal and abnormal were inverted, fact may only be credible as reality if the reader is approached through various personae, or I-masks, reporting reality through traditional imagery.

Both Robert Lifton and John Dorsey focus particularly on the novel's transcription of life. Lifton, a psychiatrist researching Hiroshima victims, has reservations about Ibuse's medical inaccuracies and claims the text's documentary style is not radical enough to avoid comparison to scientific fact.[7] Dorsey discusses Ibuse's novel with John Hersey's *Hiroshima*, a nonfictional account of Hiroshima victims.[8] Both men's concern is with the devastating content of the novel. The diary conventions are, however, also a powerful presence. For example, even as the novel amasses facts, it distorts them because myth replaces the Hiroshima citizens' ignorance of the weapon that has destroyed them. Or to offer another example, when Shigematsu, a conventionally patriarchal male, rewrites his niece's diary in his hand, he takes on her persona in that he becomes intimate with her dilemma as an unmarried female victim of the bomb in a situation which makes female beauty an important asset. While none of the *Black Rain* diaries seems to create a "false I," each is separated from Ibuse and the reader by both the fallibility and the precision of its immediate, firsthand accounts of the devastation. And when the extent and nature of the destruction defies the diarists' powers of description, however poetic themselves, the diarists allude to the poetry, myths, and folklore of historical Japan. Finally, the diaries, most especially Shigematsu's, are the bizarre accounts of pilgrims with no remaining shrine to travel to. The pilgrims move in and out of hellfire seeking normal life, which is absent.

When Lifton and Dorsey evaluate *Black Rain* by the standard of fact—as those from the United States may be compelled to do—they might add the history of literature and myth to the facts of science and war. Yet when

Rimer, who links the novel to the historical roots of modern Japanese fiction, goes beyond Dorsey's focus on survival to an assertion about comfort and hope,[9] Rimer might remember the unique political context of the novel and his own place, as an American, in that context. By placing *Black Rain* in the context of Ibuse's works about catastrophes, castaways, and the importance of written record, Treat provides a convincing analysis of the novel as writing about the necessity of writing. But in his pains to place *Black Rain* within the process of Ibuse's career and remove it from any easy political position which might claim it, he assumes a conventionally narrow definition of politics and political reading. A reading of internal difference and political paradox in *Black Rain* can instead enhance appreciation of its art which undoes dichotomies such as that dividing politics and art.

John Hawkes's *Travesty* also elicits dichotomous conclusions about art and life. In her analysis of *Travesty* Brenda Wineapple argues for the need to separate life and fiction.[10] Jean-Louis Brunel concludes his "Reading *Travesty*" with the assertion that form, form without meaning, is more important than content.[11] While Donald Greiner initially stresses the morality of Hawkes's fiction, he concludes that "art is more important than morality in *Travesty*," "that imagined life is more sustaining than remembered life," because "among other considerations *Travesty* is a travesty of the traditional realistic novel that relies on logic and cause and effect."[12] To all appearances *Black Rain* and *Travesty* are themselves polar opposites despite their mutual concern with last things. Patrick O'Donnell writes that the end of *Travesty* is a black hole;[13] William Van Wert, that the novel is an end game.[14] Thomas LeClair asserts instead that it is the parody of an end game.[15] *Travesty* is clearly of last things, but no one measures its success by fact or claims to find comfort and hope at its end. It is instead evaluated by its distance from fact and from the banality of comfort, if not hope.

Travesty is the monologue of Papa, a "privileged man" driving a car at top speed toward a planned accident. The accident is to be a murder as well as a suicide because with him in the car are his daughter Chantal and her lover, the poet Henri. Henri is also the lover of Honorine, Papa's wife asleep in their château. Papa, who likes pornography and maimed people (he himself has only one lung), swears he feels no guilt or jealousy but is staging this accident as the perfect artistic paradox of design and debris. Papa's language rings with clarity of purpose yet is full of illogic and

rhetorical excess, as Christine Laniel has documented.[16] Many readers of
the novel have concluded that Papa's voice is the novel's only character,[17]
despite Hawkes's statement that he does not "want to be left with nothing
but the narrator. . . . I think the accident the narrator imagines is the
accident that occurs."[18] Shigematsu narrates his family's journey walking,
sometimes crawling, through a vast landscape of corpses; Papa narrates
his plan as his family, enclosed in a beige luxury car, hurtles through a
rural landscape toward the crash. And yet these two novels speak to one
another. When Papa concludes his monologue with the words "There
shall be no survivors. None,"[19] I see not the twisted metal of the artistic
accident Papa has described but instead, in Shigematsu's words, "corpses,
and yet more corpses. Driven by the heat and trapped by the smoke, they
had flung themselves face down in their suffering, only to be unable to rise
again and to suffocate where they lay."[20]

Travesty and *Black Rain* are about the logic of madness. In *Madness and
Civilization* Michel Foucault argues that in the Age of Reason the mad
were no longer banished from the cities but were instead confined along
with the poor for the sake of the monarchy, the bourgeoisie, and even the
church. As it fused poverty, madness, and animality, confinement separated madness from reason, privilege, and even disease. "It was this
animality of *madness* which confinement glorified, at the same time that it
sought to avoid the scandal inherent in the *immorality of the unreasonable*."[21] Confinement still separates reason from madness but now does so
not only through public enclosure of the insane but through private
enclosure of the privileged in private homes and private transportation,
the car.

Whether *Travesty*'s narrator Papa is mad or only the vehicle for a
travesty of the psychological novel, his narration is a product of unreason.
Papa's monologue places the reader under the skin of madness. Papa is
confined as both the madman and—as he refers to himself—the "privileged man." In his luxury car privilege is not separated from madness.
Though Papa accuses his passenger Henri of reason, he also reveals that
Henri once "gave [himself] over to the sullen immobility of the mental
patient," a fact, Papa asserts, that "applies to you but not to me." "You
think that my brain is sewn with the sutures of your psychosis," says Papa
and then denies it (120–21). Though Papa makes a futile attempt to
distance himself from what he asserts is *Henri*'s madness, he more powerfully assimilates all the characters of his narration into his voice—in true

mad or true American fashion. Furthermore, the "you" he addresses collapses the distinction between Henri, the character and passenger, and the reader. Charles Baxter argues that the reader is trapped in the suicide seat with and by Papa as long as her passivity will allow.[22] Reader = Henri = Papa. Not only are madness and privilege confined together in the car, but also madness and whatever conventions of reason on which the reader imagines she can rely. Papa and the reader are trapped together with the craziness they fear inside the privileged vehicle designed to save us from such contamination.

The automobile set America free to go where it wanted when it wanted and to take one's home along. The comfort of the familiar, private environment inside the car makes all car trips like the one in *Travesty* as Laniel describes it: the car seems to sit still as the scenery moves.[23] Freedom and enclosure, movement and suspension, become one. While, as Foucault records, the eighteenth-century arbiters of reason (and guardians of authoritarian rule) believed political freedom and idleness induced madness in the populace,[24] Papa's freedom and idleness as a privileged modern man, his confinement in privilege, have turned his free movement into stasis. The faster he drives and talks, the more suspended he seems, like the still point of a top whose colors whirl around it. Papa describes the confinement of his mind inside his memory and their confinement in the car not only as "a fist in glass" (15) but also as "a clock the shape of a bullet" (16). The violence of the fist and the bullet are restrained by the clock which moves in time but not in space. Though Papa implies that the freedom and speed of his car separate him from the "sullen immobility" of the mad incarcerated in public institutions, his movement is suspension in time, suspension in madness. All that matters in madness is inside the stillness of the car filled only by Papa's controlling voice. And Papa *is* the car: "these yellow headlights are the lights of my eyes" (15).

Everywhere Papa pitches his voice, he sees himself. Foucault writes that "the symbol of madness will henceforth be that mirror which, without reflecting anything real, will secretly offer the man who observes himself in it the dream of his own presumption." When Papa looks into the Fountain of Clarity, his reflection, the privileged man, looks back (103). With the logic of privilege and an obsession for clarity, Papa, in Foucault's words, "generates his madness like a mirage."[25]

Only the driver of the car can entertain the possibility of the delusion of freedom; the passengers—Henri, Chantal, the reader—feel the confinement, the inability to separate themselves from violence or insanity. In one of his most provocative remarks about the creation of *Travesty,* Hawkes explains that though he was thinking of Camus's *The Fall* and Camus's death in a car accident when he wrote *Travesty,* he learned only after the novel's completion that Camus was a passenger, not the driver of the car.[26] Camus was, as we are, trapped without the possibility or delusion of free choice. And yet, Baxter argues about Papa's narrative, "its freedom lies in our ignorance." In as much as the reader, like Henri, only provides the most "banal explanations for black-box behavior,"[27] she cannot expect to separate herself safely from violence and unreason.

As auditors of Papa's monologue, Henri and the reader are in the position of silent analyst observing the analysand, but this power of the medical person, whose absence is total presence, is denied by our place-ment within the bullet of our own destruction. The auditor scrambles for the explanation that will be the immediate cure even though Papa will not allow reason's conventional authority to be heard. Papa fills the air with all the usual familial details for a successful analysis, and within them is the usual Freudian paradox that the family is both the source of madness and the bastion of reason. Foucault notes that in the nineteenth century asylums even modeled their structure and treatment on the family. In the familial model madness is childhood attacking the father. "The prestige of patriarchy is revived around madness in the bourgeois family."[28] The father, Papa, is reason itself bombarded by the madness of his daughter "the porno brat," his son the oedipal conqueror of Honorine, his wife the infidel. It is Papa, however, who has promoted the sexual behavior of his family. It is he whose bird of passion has been beaten to death by his mistress's garter belt because he spanked her; he who loves pornography and disease. Papa promotes his own madness, calls it reason, and thereby regains the possibility or the delusion of control. Meanwhile the auditor and analyst cannot separate the reason of the Father—"I am the kindest man you will ever meet" (15)—from the madness of the child—"as a child I divided my furtive time quite equally between those periodicals depict-ing the most brutal and uncanny destructions of human flesh . . . and those other periodicals depicting the attractions of young living women partially or totally in the nude" (21). Nor can the reader distinguish her own adult reason from her desire to lie with Chantal on the floor behind the driver's seat and cry. *Travesty* is a black comedy of "reason dazzled."[29]

The familial madness of *Travesty* is not really private madness. It is cultural and national: the madness of patriarchy and privilege. In explaining the accident which will balance design and debris, Papa considers "the triteness of a nation incapable of understanding highway, motor vehicle, pedestrian" (19) but admits that he has always been attracted to accidents. He imagines his appreciation of their incongruities to be superior to the triteness of a nation yet accepts that he is a part of that nation that lives and dies in and by its cars: "You and I are two perfect examples of our national type" (99). The privilege of free movement and privacy becomes self-absorbed madness and the dream of apocalyptic death. W. S. DiPiero has noted that all of Hawkes's fiction of the 1970s dramatizes "self-absorption (which is becoming more and more a high fashion of American culture),"[30] but a student required to read *Travesty* for my class has brought Papa's American character more vividly to life. She told me that she loved the novel because it made her feel the way she does when exiting the interstate on a raised clover-leaf structure. She imagines she can forego the demands of the turn and instead allow her Trans Am to fly straight out into space. She could so easily imagine Papa's control which is out of control. Papa's language is the rhetorical excess, white noise, illogical clarity of salesmanship, be it the sale of detergent powder, political candidates, or systematic theories. It bedazzles itself and its audience with its madness—as, perhaps, Papa Hemingway's clarity bedazzled him into suicide.[31]

Foucault argues that at the end of the fifteenth century in Europe mockery of madness replaces fear of death: "From the discovery of that necessity which inevitably reduces man to nothing, we have shifted to the scornful contemplation of that nothing which is existence itself. . . . The head that will become a skull is already empty. Madness is the *déjà-là* of death."[32] Papa's rhetorical excess is just such a mad emptiness propelling him toward the more restful emptiness of death. Foucault further writes that confinement of the mad in the Age of Reason had a paradoxical justification. While it asserted the clear difference between reason and unreason, it was also intended as a correction of madness through the suppression of madness and fulfillment of nothingness in death. The many deaths of inmates were the annihilation of nothing.[33] The annihilation of nothing is, in this sense, a clarity of clarity, a certainty of certainty. Neither life nor death can surprise us. But what if Papa is wrong when he declares "There shall be no survivors" from the confinement in the car? What then can provide protection from madness?

In *Black Rain* the excess debris resulting from the precise design of the Manhattan Project is an excess irreducible to nothing because survivors remain. In that the explosion destroyed all operation of normal life and turned domestic scenes into images of horror, it rendered Hiroshima a mad world. But this madness is confined neither by reason nor by privilege. Instead ubiquitous madness confines the survivors. Shigematsu remembers "a man whose legs were moving busily as though he were running, but who was so wedged in the wave of humanity that he achieved little more than a rapid mark-time" (58). Shock and pain reduce each being-in-the-world to a self confined in its own body, just as in the process of torture Elaine Scarry describes, pain and threat reduce the individual's world to the parameters of his body in pain.[34] In Hiroshima it is the madness of abnormality and the reason of war strategy which confine the individual inside his own animality. The freedom and idleness, that is, homelessness and joblessness of the survivors, further confine them in their bodies. Like the military man's favorite horse shivering with severe burns or the ordinary carp with nerves paralyzed by shock, each, regardless of rank, is confined within his body.

Shigematsu is an exception it seems. Though his face is cut in the explosion, ironically he feels no pain. He is, therefore, both free to see and forced to see the insanity around him. And yet when he finally sees himself in a mirror, he does not recognize his own face. He does not want to accept that the madness has touched him. "My heart pounded at the idea, and the face in the mirror grew more and more unfamiliar" (143). He is afraid that the face is unfamiliar and afraid that it is familiar. He has behaved as though sanity were carefully confined within his body but the mask of madness is on his face—or half a mask. Shigematsu's face is half blackish-purple shriveled flesh and half pale smoothness. Unlike Papa, Shigematsu does not want to look at the world and see this face, his own reflection. He does not want to assimilate what he sees, but he has no choice: the ambiguity of madness and reason are on his face. When he pulls on the curled skin and feels pain, he knows then that the face is his. Madness is something, not nothing. And he is a part of it.

Unlike Papa, Shigematsu does not have the privilege of directing his own movements within the privacy of a car. Also, no landmarks of Hiroshima remain so all survivors risk moving in a direction other than that they intend. And while Shigematsu feels compelled to walk by a baby girl clutching at the breasts of her dead mother because he does not know what he can possibly do for her (107), he is nonetheless locked in intimacy with his neighbors. His next-door neighbor's kitchen, for example, has been blown into his bathroom (84). Private space has opened up allowing one to penetrate another. Whatever madness the family generates and cures is subsumed by this world in which father must desert son, or the son the father, but either might have a stray chance to save a stranger. Charcoal messages to family members are left unanswered and a wife searching for her husband can find him only by luck. At the edges of the destruction the wounded crowd onto the trains which move inefficiently among the debris. The people complain that the national railway—the symbol, like the emperor, of Meiji modernization and nationalization[35]— is deteriorating.

Shigematsu, his wife, Shigeko, and his niece Yasuko do seem to reach a haven separate from the madness. At the glassworks a familiar boss-employee hierarchy maintains order but only until unreason encroaches in the form of bodies needing burial and a national ethos running amok. Shigematsu has been defending the government against the complaints of his fellow survivors, but when he hears that the vegetable woman was proud of her son's attendance at a human torpedo school—"a top secret military establishment" that everyone has heard of—even he has to conclude that "war . . . paralyzes people's power of judgment" (142–43). He is faced repeatedly with the knowledge that the war and the Japanese war effort are a madness even larger than the destruction of Hiroshima out of which he has just crawled. He is learning what Ibuse told the reader early on through the speech of a headman as he sends the voluntary labor unit off with bamboo spears: "take care not to drop those symbols of your invincible determination to fight on to the bitter end" (13).

Even time does not act as a shield from unreason. Five years after the war's end Shigematsu, his wife, and niece live in Kobatake village, a traditional Japanese haven separate from the confusions of the modern city. But the war has followed them in the form of radiation sickness. As, in the transcribing of his 1945 diaries, Shigematsu becomes increasingly aware of the lunacy of the war, his niece's radiation sickness in 1950 becomes increasingly apparent. His reason for transcribing the diaries is null and void—as is all reason. The logic of Yasuko's distance from the blast has not saved her. The same illogic which in 1945 often resulted in rescuers dying from contamination by the rescued invades Shigematsu's family. It does not, after all, survive intact.

When Shigematsu reaches the dual realizations that the war is crazy and Yasuko is dying, he records in his diary the formal celebration in 1945 marking Yasuko's honorable discharge from the glassworks. Shigematsu, who has worked hard to hang onto meaning, slips into a maimed world of non-sense. He and his drunken boss recall a children's nursery rhyme and Shigematsu observes that he never understood what it meant. Then when he falls asleep he dreams "a one-legged man in a kimono too long for him came hopping after me with a long spoon over his shoulder" (285–86), and when he wakes he finds that he is wearing his wife's bathrobe. Neither dream nor waking life will offer up clear cause and effect.

Shigematsu cannot succeed in using his reason to confine unreason. He cannot clearly distinguish reason from unreason and thereby render madness nothing. In 1945 the rumor among the remaining citizens of Hiroshima was that nothing would grow in Hiroshima for seventy-five years, but Shigematsu thinks this is wrong: "Hadn't I seen weeds running riot all over the ruins?" (282). Shigematsu fears something worse than nothing. Dr. Iwatake, suffering from radiation sickness, longs for an explicable disease (268) just as Papa likes imperfection he can see—coughing, one-leggedness. Instead radiation sickness with its odd symptoms infects not only Dr. Iwatake and Shigematsu, both of whom were in the city at the time of the bombing, but also Yasuko, who was on the outskirts of the city. When Yasuko suffers from the disease's symptoms, Shigematsu must accept that illogic is something, not nothing. Even death is not nothing. Hundreds of thousands of bodies in Hiroshima remained after their deaths and had to be buried.

From his interviews with victims of the Hiroshima bombing, Lifton derives something of the Japanese sense of nothingness. It is no less paradoxical than but is apparently different from Western thought. On the one hand, Lifton notes that the Japanese refer to the remaining Hiroshima victims as victims (*higaisha*) or as explosion-affected persons (*hibakusha*) but not as survivors (*seizonsha*) because guilt at having survived when so many did not taints the word *seizonsha*. On the other hand, a Hiroshima writer explained to Lifton that while Westerners feel that annihilation, specifically nuclear annihilation, will wipe out humanity and therefore result in nothing, Oriental thinking suggests that "no matter what the degree of annihilation, something [not necessarily human] will be left." And yet one *hibakusha,* a history professor, believes the Dome commemorating the Hiroshima victims is a disingenuous memorial and should be

replaced by nothing symbolizing the power of the bomb to turn everything into nothing. This is consistent with this man's and other *hibakusha*'s conviction that silence, like the stillness after the bomb ex-
ploded, is the only authentic response. "It is also said that on the occasion
of his being awarded the Order of Cultural Merit (on Culture Day,
November 3, 1966) [Ibuse] told friends that *Kuroi Ame* was a failure
because it did not capture the *hibakusha*'s special form of silence."[36] While
Papa seeks control through a clear language of illogical excess, the *hibakusha* seeks meaning through silence, and yet, Papa's goal is the silence
of death while the *hibakusha*'s life bespeaks survival.

In *Travesty* and in *Black Rain,* life and death are not distinct. Papa works
to undermine the existential absurdity death makes of life by erasing the
line between life and death. Through the illogical clarity of his talk, he
proposes to render the debris of life uninterpretable and, thereby, the
emptiness of death knowable. He says that his artistic accident will be
"our private apocalypse," a revelation of the future, but the future he sees
is "no survivors, none." His art will be the apotheosis of nothing in life
and in death.

Papa does, however, occasionally admit to some possible hitches in his
plan. He regrets the fire from the exploding gasoline. Like a mad scientist
qua artist, Papa says that if we could

> remove from it the convention of fierce heat and unnaturally bright light, so
> that this very explosion occurs as planned but in darkness, total darkness, there
> you have the most desirable rendering of our private apocalypse. (58)

But we cannot remove the fire, which changes apocalypse into holocaust,
especially when that "private apocalypse" is not personal (my) but public
(our). Papa also regrets the intervention of society's rescue efforts: police
lights, ambulances, tow trucks, photographs (60). He seeks an act and an
art untouchable and uninterpretable, yet he wonders what they will say
of his act. Art, after all, requires the continuing consciousness of life.
Though life is the source of uncertainties: fire, interference, rain—the
hazard Papa did not predict but does not credit, it is also the source of
response. In pursuit of a private apocalypse filled with emptiness *and*
response, Papa risks our holocaust.

The Hiroshima victims' experience was what Lifton calls death-in-life
because of the kind and degree of the heat and blast, the fire, and the contamination. All appear supernatural. Ground zero and madness, which is

"the zero degree of [man's] own nature,"[37] occupy the same non-space. Those people vaporized by heat at the epicenter are for Shigematsu a mystical burden but those dead and dying damaged by blast, fire, and contamination remain a moral and material burden. It is they who immerse the living in death. In addition, the conflagration following the blast produces a fire outside the natural laws of life. In observing the burning of bridges, Shigematsu notes that the fire defies water. "The strange thing was that though the next high tide ought, in theory, to have put the fire out, the next morning found it smoldering again, so that little by little all the timber was eventually consumed" (157). Those who escape this bizarre fire must in turn recreate it in the form of crematoria on the river bank to burn the dead. The rescue efforts Papa fears, those impositions of life on death, are not possible in Hiroshima because the social and medical services themselves are destroyed and then because radiation contaminates the rescuers. It is in Shigematsu's world, not Papa's, where the veil of the familiar is lifted to reveal the unfamiliar, but the apocalypse uncovers a future of yet more uncertainty. It is a world in which Shigematsu cannot distinguish the living from the dead. Days after the bombing he sees a body with a blackened face which appears to be breathing. He approaches "to find swarms of maggots tumbling from the mouth and nose and crowding in the eye sockets; it was nothing but their wriggling, that first impression of life and movement" (161).

Unlike the corpse, Shigematsu does survive the blast and even the fire. He is alive. But the logic and decency by which he thought he lived before the bombing prove no match for radiation and bureaucracy after the bombing. Together they bring reason to a standstill. Whether one obeys the state, like Shigematsu, or condescends to it, like Papa, one cannot escape the intricate relationship of self and state.

Nuclearism—the weapons themselves and all that goes with them—are the common subject of *Black Rain* and *Travesty*. While *Black Rain* provides facts which cannot be imagined, *Travesty* presents an imagined strategy which cannot be physically deployed. The vehicle of Papa's strategy, like the vehicles of nuclear strategy, is so destructive that it will annihilate the very goal he means to achieve. And so he cannot act; he can only threaten. In his analysis of the arms race, Jacques Derrida emphasizes that nuclear war cannot be anything but talk.[38] The arms *race* is in the speed of the scientific-military-government talk. "I . . . violently increased our speed and hence interrupted our lively conversation and signaled the true state of things," says Papa (39). But it is not only the car's speed which is the state of things; that speed is his solitary fast talk.

Papa insists that what he has in mind is kindness, not threat; apocalypse, not murder (47), just as nuclear strategists explain that increasing numbers and kinds of nuclear warheads is deterrence and protection. The text of this fast talk needs to be understood. Yet when we hear clear arguments about the relative humanity of counterforce (mutually targeted missile silos) and countervalue (mutually targeted cities), we know we must first understand that we are hearing reason dazzled.[39]

Perhaps by necessity, maybe by incompetence, this talk is nonetheless the rhetorical excess of reason dazzled. Lifton writes that a common ethos of the nuclear age is nuclear fundamentalism, a reductive response to the threat of fundamental structures. Lifton mentions religious and physical structures but could include logical structures as well. Nuclear fundamentalism conflates the bomb's man-made technological power with the infinite power of a deity, therefore concluding that the bomb has an unquestionable ability either to protect this world or to connect the destruction of its end with the creation of a new beginning. Papa is a nuclear fundamentalist "seek[ing] in a technology of annihilation a source of vitality, of sustained human connectedness or symbolic immortality."[40] In his passion to invent the very world he is quitting, he forgets that he has made his invention equivalent to his quitting the world and taking others with him. The only apocalypse resulting from Papa's self-destruction is one that says we have seen the future and it is now.

Papa believes he is a "privileged man" above the "triteness of a nation." "One and all they are driven by the twin engines of ignorance and willful barbarianism" (98–99). He also admits to sharing in these national qualities but only in conjunction with the other national qualities of charm, good humor, and handsomeness. With a focus on American personality, he dismantles his own political charges as he has dismantled accusations of murder, guilt, jealousy, and insanity. In so doing he ignores the state and thus becomes it.

Shigematsu is proud of his contribution to the order and discipline which make Japan strong. When he leads his family out of the wreckage, he takes them to the glassworks which has been engaged in war work and where he is employed. His wife and niece follow his orders as he follows the orders of his boss: to act as priest in the burial of the dead and to return even a second time to Hiroshima in search of coal. While from the perspective of 1950 he seems to hear the absurdity in the admonition to the bamboo spear-carriers, even amidst the rubble of 1945 he defends the government. He defends the Defense Section of the Municipal Office from the complaints of a stranger on a train. When the same stranger goes on to ridicule the military, Shigematsu only implies that these stories were in bad taste (121–22). To another malcontent he remarks, "You ought to keep defeatist talk like that to yourself," though he knows he feels something of the same way himself (130).

At the novel's midpoint an army unit with false papers steals food from the civilians at the glassworks. From this point on Shigematsu has more and more difficult encounters with the army and the state bureaucracy. Like Kurasawa's protagonist, Shimura, in the 1952 film *Ikiru,* Shigematsu goes from office to office unable to find anyone who will answer his questions about coal, clothing, and food. While Shigematsu is transcribing that part of his diary about his "los[s] of patience with such stupidity" (170) and loss of all heart for the horrible war, his niece is showing symptoms of leukemia caused by the radiation. The juxtaposition of the two, as Shimura's cancer and the bureaucracy are juxtaposed in *Ikiru,* suggests that the bureaucracy itself is proliferating contamination of the Japanese spirit. It is in many cultures customary to associate contamination with otherness; Sander Gilman has documented this tendency in *Difference and Pathology.*[41] But in *Black Rain* and *Ikiru,* the self has been infected by its allegiance to the state which, in turn, rejects those who recognize their own illness.

The Meiji ideology campaign designed to modernize and nationalize the thinking of the Japanese and turn them into citizens[42] had worked with Shigematsu. Though he lacks the nationalist zeal of another Ibuse character, Lieutenant Lookeast, Shigematsu nonetheless identified himself with the Japanese state. But then that state's bureaucracy undermined itself. He learns to hear the absence of morality and plethora of absurdity in official language; not only United States propaganda leaflets but also Japanese bureaucratese and even the emperor's surrender speech take on an eerie but empty Big Brother quality.

Shigematsu eschews the emptiness of the denatured modern Japanese state and relocates his identity in nature. When the emperor's speech is broadcast on the radio, Shigematsu does not listen with his fellow-employees: "I made no effort to follow the sense" (296). He is instead watching baby eels swim upstream. When Yasuko is dying in the hospital,

Shigematsu divides his time between her bedside and a pond where he and some other friends weakened by the long-term effects of radiation are raising carp. Their carp are reminiscent of the magnificent carp in Ibuse's story "Carp," a symbol of the fortitude of nature and of friendship.[43]

The sad difficulty with Shigematsu's relocation in nature may be seen if we step outside the time limitations of the text. If one refuses confrontation with the bureaucracy and eschews the distasteful wrangling of partisan politics (as Carol Gluck argues most Japanese do and Karel van Wolferen argues Japanese have had no choice but to do),[44] but one also lives in a small nation whose wilderness has all been brought under bureaucratic control, then a relocation in nature is only temporary and probably delusional avoidance of one's bond to the state. After his immersion in death, Shigematsu has to verify his survival in nature, but nature, human and otherwise, is nonetheless subject to state control.[45]

Travesty and *Black Rain* each have a theory of art which tries to locate the moral place for an individual in a politically paradoxical world. In both cases the authenticity of the morality depends upon an undoing of the theory proposed. *Travesty* is, in virtually all its critics' estimation, a novel about art. O'Donnell calls *Travesty* a "burlesque of the confessional novel and the existentialist récit" and argues that "along with the self, [Papa] desires that the world be subsumed into the final manifestation of a 'clarity' where the troubled relation between things and the signs that stand for them simply disappears." In other words, Papa desires pure metafiction separate from any representational baggage of realism. In his conclusion O'Donnell moves from speaking of Papa to speaking of *Travesty* when he writes, "It forces us to behold, through 'clear glass,' what is at the bottom of the narrative impulse and the act of reading—the desire to signify the end of signification."[46] Laniel concludes her analysis of *Travesty* with the statement that "the creativity of desire can only be asserted through the absence and destruction of its object."[47] Greiner concludes that, though Hawkes is a moralist, *Travesty* demonstrates that "art is more important than morality": "suicide is secondary when one considers the task Hawkes sets for himself—to conceive of the inconceivable."[48] Ironically, only William Gass, a novelist whose work is arguably more metafictional than Hawkes's, and Hawkes himself place Hawkes's fiction in the world of the signified (that is, things, politics, moral responsibility). Gass writes,

> In our civilization, the center has not held for a long time; neither the center nor the place where the center was, can now be found. . . . Inside the silence of unmoving things, there are the sounds of repeated explosions. Perhaps it is

catastrophe breathing. Who has rendered this condition more ruthlessly than Hawkes has, . . . for his work has always refused ruin in the act which has depicted it. . . . [His is] a healing art."[49]

In a 1979 interview with Thomas LeClair, Hawkes said that the creative act is "a thing of beauty . . . knowledge and moral meaning"; it is "a risk, an assault on the world as we think we know it, and as such can be viewed as dangerous, destructive, criminal."[50] Though it is impossible, it is important to separate Papa from *Travesty* as a creation of Hawkes.

Travesty demonstrates the travesty of everything Papa says whether it is true or not, and everything Papa says is an articulation of illogical systematic theory. Part of his theory is a paradox playing on the word "nothing": "nothing is more important than the existence of what does not exist" (57). This, he says, spares us from wasting "the last of our time together by passing between us the fuming bottle of cognac" (57). His theory replaces memory, comaraderie, and loss. Also, his "theory tells us that ours is the power to invent the very world we are quitting" (57). This, he implies, will provide us an end that we can understand. In the next breath he adds, "My theory does not apply to exploding gasoline" (57). We could achieve the art of perfectly balanced design and debris, the private apocalypse, if we could control "the convention of fierce heat" (58). Papa—and often *Travesty*'s readers—confuse the phenomena of reality with the conventions of realism. While human behavior may not be attributable to clear psychological causes and conditions, fire *is* attributable to exploding gasoline. We can try to theorize a disassociation of the word "fire" from the natural element, but we must be prepared to be humbled by the fact that gasoline burns.

More unusual and ingenious than *Travesty*'s attack on realism is, I think, Hawkes's creation of Pascal as Papa's response to the artist's anxiety of influence. Writing of this question of anxiety of influence in Mallarmé, Barbara Johnson notes

a supplementary twist to the traditional oedipal situation. For if the father survives precisely through his way of affirming himself dead, then the son will always arrive too late to kill him. What the son suffers from, then, is not the simple desire to kill the father, but the impotence to kill him whose potency resides in his ability to recount his own death.

It is perhaps for this reason that the so-called "fathers of modern thought"—Mallarmé, Freud, Marx, Nietzsche—maintain such a tremendous authority for contemporary theory. In writing of the subversion of the author, the father, God, privilege, knowledge, property, and consciousness, these thinkers have subverted in advance any grounds on which one might undertake to kill off an authority that theorizes the death of all authority.[51]

The point of Papa's entire monologue, and his proposed artistic crash, is the assertion of his authority through its abnegation in his own death. But Papa does not merely subvert the son's desire to kill him; he kills his son Pascal before his own death is announced. On the one hand, he offers no objection to Pascal's full enactment of his oedipal instincts; on the other hand, Pascal—a name hearkening back to a philosopher of conventional authority—mysteriously dies, of unexplained causes, in this oedipal phase. To the degree that Papa is the artist and madman whose voice has created or assimilated all the other characters, the creation and destruction of Pascal is a perfect example of patriarchal and artistic wishful thinking, for it is a total subversion of any tradition or any newness whose authority might supersede Papa's own.

Travesty is as much a parody of totalizing contemporary theories as of bourgeois reason or banal realism. It does not demonstrate that art is more important than morality but instead that an art of paradox is moral because it undoes totalizing theories of the self, the state, and art. In his introduction to Hawkes's *The Owl*, Robert Scholes asserts that Hawkes is a moralist because he immerses the reader in a disturbing consciousness. "The point of this immersion in the abhorrent is to force readers to acknowledge a kind of complicity, to admit that something in us resonates to all sorts of monstrous measures, even if we recognize and condemn the evil consciousness for what it is."[52] I am convinced that *Travesty* works this way, and yet I have some doubts about the kind of complicity it achieves. Aristotle writes of emotional as well as intellectual effects of literary forms. I am not sure that the complicity *Travesty* elicits is more than intellectual. Scholes states that Hawkes's methods *force* readers; Baxter describes *Travesty* as an *attack* on the reader;[53] Hawkes himself uses the word "*assault*" to describe his art. Force can, in a willing reader, produce an intellectual acknowledgment of her own monstrousness, but it cannot elicit a heartfelt sense of responsibility for a violent world. For that the reader needs both the distance of travesty and the proximity of pain.

Early on in his transcribing of the diaries, Shigematsu says to his wife Shigeko,

> "It's no easy matter to put something down in writing."
> "I expect it's because when you write you're too eager to work in your own theories." ["some sort of 'isms.'" (216)]
> "It's nothing to do with theories. From a literary point of view, the way I describe things is the crudest kind of realism." (60) ["crude realism" (216)]

After this exchange Shigematsu does add increasing—though still mod-est—amounts of opinion to his record of August 1945. His theory of ethics becomes a simple one: war is lunacy. He admits that he had "slipped into the habit of hoping, for our sake, that Hitler would win." But after the bomb was dropped he notes, "I began to feel that what I had been believing was a lot of nonsense" (282–83). He realizes that what people used to say in olden times was right: "in an area badly ravaged by war it took a century to repair the moral damage done to the inhabitants" (149) ["regions where wars have been especially terrible need one hundred years for their people to recover from the damage done their characters" (230)]. The crudest realism is the logical proof of such a theory. Though Shigematsu may not see in his crude realism an aesthetic theory, Ibuse does. The novel's materialism, its amassing and juxtaposing of chaotic, physical details, is a theory of undoing, the undoing of systematic theory which undermines moral impact by clarifying madness which is not clear.

Black Rain is, nonetheless, a collection of Japanese rituals and tradi-tions, as Treat frequently notes. All of the novel's diarists—Yasuko, Shige-matsu, Shigeko, Dr. Iwatake, and Mrs. Iwatake—are all ritualistically Japanese and typically Ibusean in their perception and presentation of the present through allusions to the past. They make references to fairy tales, folk cures, agricultural festivals, Civil War heroes, historical routes, and a host of poems. The cumulative result is the reassurance that Hiroshima will have a future because it had a past. Shigeko reinforces this belief in the future by suggesting to Shigematsu that he must write his diary in writing-brush ink and not in pen so that it will be preserved for posterity (40). Shigematsu, his family, and his neighbors order the crude realism of their writing and their lives by a number of conventional theories.

In Ibuse's hands these characters and their diaries are arranged to demonstrate the spiritual value and poignant limitations of their theories. When Ibuse juxtaposes Shigematsu's record of the dinner honoring Ya-suko's discharge from the glassworks, including its memory of the non-sense children's verse and Shigematsu's nonsense dream, to Yasuko's imminent death, the novel shows the reader the limits of sense in allusions and in the body. The woman who is younger than her uncle and was further from the epicenter is dying and he is not. This fact renders the innocence of childhood nonsense a nasty dream and subverts the respect-ful tradition of allusions. The anxiety of influence here is not that the past knows best how to explain the present but that it does not.

And yet Ibuse shows that the aesthetic of allusions cuts at least two ways. When Shigematsu discovered that the blackened face he thought was alive is actually covered with maggots, he remembers lines from a poem. "'Oh worm, friend worm!' it began . . . [and then]: 'Rend the heavens, burn the earth and let men die! A brave and moving sight!'" Calling the poet an idiotic fool, Shigematsu declares he should have been in Hiroshima on August 6 "when the heavens had been rent asunder, the earth had burned, and men had died" (161). The poem's easy feeling and acquiescence to death are an affront to the destruction and anguish Shigematsu has witnessed. On the other hand, in the diary of Dr. Iwatake, who was gravely injured, is the recollection of his encounter with "women [who] were unrestrained in their expressions of sympathy." Reminded of a poem by Li Po, he realized for the first time "that it was not just a piece of skillful description, but a work of intense emotion" (252). There is a correspondence between the physical reality of the women's weeping and the words of the poet which enhanced the beauty of each.

Amidst the hardships of war, it may be that the best that can be done with words—especially one's enemies' words—is to send them up in smoke, as Shigeko records they used an entire English dictionary for smoking papers during the war (69). It may also be that the pain of holocaust will always lie too deep for words. Yet from amassed descriptions of physical horrors, Ibuse creates beauty which arises from the transition of time. That beauty is acute in *Black Rain* because the bombing speeded up the course of time tenfold—perhaps a thousandfold. This sense of beauty is connected to what Rimer calls "the highest aesthetic virtue" in Japanese literature: *mono no aware*—the "ahness of things." A necessary ingredient of this emotion is transience. In the fourteenth century Yoshida Kenkō explained, "Were we to live on forever . . . then indeed would men not feel the pity of things. Truly the beauty of life is its uncertainty."[54] This aesthetic is also an ethic for it is understood that *aware* is not achieved without the self-consciousness which comes only from transience. Because of Ibuse's ability to render the physical manifestation of accelerated time while forestalling the control or comfort of any totalizing theory, *Black Rain* elicits in the reader an intellectual and emotional self-consciousness which is complicity.

The text is beyond the ease of accusation; its effect, beyond the certainty of guilt or rational defense. The novel presents the United States not as feared enemy or even as hated other. The United States is an absence from which falls disembodied propaganda leaflets and the bomb, the bomb that transforms everything into nothing. Even as the Western reader identifies with the struggle against the presence of contamination and bureaucracy, she remains a part of the absence from which the bomb fell. For the Japanese reader, I can imagine, the novel elicits a sense of complicity with the nationalist war effort and with the desire to explain away madness through allusions to the past. But for the United States reader there is also the uncomfortable identification with absence.

The theory of *Black Rain* cannot be reduced to the American adage "no ideas but in things." Ibuse's arrangement of things defies, embraces, complicates the ideas that approach it. The novelist Ōe Kenzaburō laments the current theory craze of Japanese intellectuals, observing that one European or United States cultural theory after another—Foucault, Barthes, Lacan, Derrida—is translated and "discharged," but "almost no effort was made to interpret them meticulously in view of specific situations in which Japan found itself."[55] Ibuse did what Ōe now desires. But in creating an antitheory theory of crude realism or materialism out of Japanese traditions, Japanese experience, and Japanese documents, Ibuse has formed a novel of what my Western mind thinks of as negative dialectics. Adorno's book *Negative Dialectics* and Ibuse's novel are linked because each arises out of a response to holocaust. Each recognizes that after 1945 we all became survivors of holocaust who need an art that can respond to vast destruction and extraordinary immorality. In "After Auschwitz" within *Negative Dialectics* Adorno writes,

> Spellbound, the living have a choice between involuntary ataraxy—an esthetic life due to weakness—and the bestiality of the involved. Both are wrong ways of living. But some of both would be required for the right *désinvolture* and sympathy. Once overcome, the culpable self-preservation urge has been confirmed, confirmed precisely, perhaps, by the threat that has come to be ceaselessly present.[56]

While readers frequently find hope in *Black Rain,* I think it is a carefully deconstructed hope. It resides in its choice of symbols. The white pidgeon, for example, will not do. Emerging from a frustrating encounter with military bureaucrats, Shigematsu is struck by a desolate lotus pond. In it is a dead body but beside it is a white pidgeon. When Shigematsu examines it he sees that it is blind in one eye and missing some feathers. He considers eating it but instead tosses it in the air on the chance that it will fly. It does, but then, as he watches, "it lost height and plunged into the waters of the pond" (171).[57] The bird's white innocence cannot survive. The common baby carp Shigematsu and his friends are raising to avoid idleness are all that abides.

But the most interesting, the deconstructed, symbol is the multicolored rainbow Shigematsu wishes for in the end. As conventional as the white bird, the rainbow, if it appears, will cure Yasuko. Or so Shigematsu tells himself, knowing it is not true. Compared to the image at the end of Ibuse's medieval novella, *Isle-on-the-Billows (Wabisuké)*, the rainbow is especially intriguing. That novella ends with an earthquake which sends a prison island beneath the sea. The protagonist, watching the island sink from a distant vantage point, observes red poppies against the white waterspout before the island disappears under the water. This evocation of the Japanese flag indicates that the island sinking is Japan itself weighted down in that novella by its aristocratic insensitivity to its own people.[58] The rainbow of *Black Rain* may instead mark the end of Japanese isolation and the beginning of an ambiguous international age. With this internationalism will come extensive progress, like the modern progress the Meiji ideologues promoted, but ironically that progress is of a piece with the technology that produced the bomb.

The colors of the rainbow actually appear in the novel only in the massive cloud which rose up from the explosion, the same cloud which produced the black rain, the fallout responsible for Yasuko's contamination: "The head of the mushroom would billow out first to the east, then to the west, then out to the east again; each time, some part or other of its body would emit a fierce light, in ever-changing shades of red, purple, lapis lazuli, or green" (53) ["Just as one thought that the top was billowing towards the east, the wind would shift and move it towards the west, then back again to the east. Each time different parts of its mushroom body would change colors—red, purple, azure, and green" (220)]. On the novel's last page, Shigematsu says to himself, "Let a rainbow appear—not a white one, but one of many hues—and Yasuko will be cured" (300).

The white rainbow is, as Treat notes, a bad omen earlier in the last chapter and elsewhere in other Ibuse works. Ibuse has even written a piece called "All About Rainbows," in which he contrasts the Genesis depiction of rainbows as offering hope to the Early Han *Shih Chi* perception of rainbows, specifically white rainbows, as portending military insurrections.[59] In wishing for a multicolored rainbow, Shigematsu makes some attempt to disarm the old omen of the white rainbow and perhaps even adjust to a new age. Unlike Papa, Shigematsu hopes for life. But he does so with an image of hope he cannot really believe in. In *Black Rain* Ibuse has let the reader know the price, and some very modest possibilities, of hope.

Having argued the importance of material existence in the detotalization of theory, Adorno concludes in his "Meditations on Metaphysics" that "metaphysics must know how to wish."

> The need [for hope] is what we think from, even where we disdain wishful thinking. The motor of the need is the effort that involves thought as action. The object of critique is not the need in thinking, but the relationship between the two.
>
> Yet the need in thinking is what makes us think. It asks to be negated by thinking; it must disappear in thought if it is to be really satisfied; and in this negation it survives.[60]

Rather than "despair that nothing cannot be,"[61] we, challenged by the facts of our times, must think a theory which in negating hope insures its survival.

Uncertainty: A Conclusion

What about action? That is the question that arises when politics is spoken of as a use of language within a web of paradox. Deconstruction, feminism, negative dialects are just more naive intellectualizing in a world of realpolitik, more white man's and woman's craziness in a world of injustice. At the risk of trying the questioner's patience I have to respond, "But what is action, what constitutes action in the present world?"

If I accept Seweryn Bialer's argument that bureaucracy is the obstacle to radical change from whatever source; if I accept that the arms of the Earth's two huge bureaucracies stretch worldwide; if I accept Lawrence Freedman's assertion that nuclear strategy is an oxymoron, and Jacques Derrida's that nuclear war is a battle of words or nothing at all; then I conclude that political action begins with an analysis, a deconstructive analysis, of systems, theories, and texts. If I also accept Theodor Adorno's argument that all of us living are Auschwitz survivors, and Václav Havel's that all citizens are a part of the bureaucracy, then I conclude that in analyzing contemporary systems and texts, I am analyzing myself. I am a part of their madness, clarity, immorality, and wisdom. I am complicit in the recalcitrance of bureaucracy.

While a nuclear war will cease to be a war the moment it becomes one, the everyday wars and violence of the waning twentieth century are not talk or nothing. The daily assault on human flesh and all physical facts of life are not simply battles of words. Though the action they require may be an intrusion of words, they do require action. If I assert that we live as uncertain creatures in uncertain times, I do not remove the necessity of the ability to act. No authority does not mean no responsibility. Whatever face of leadership a moment demands, the fact remains, I would argue, that power—the power to heal that the world requires—arises from wounds born of identity with victims and complicity with victimizers. While shame hangs its head and guilt seeks forgiveness, complicity acts to undo what it has done.

The value of the fiction I have discussed here lies in its ability to understand and elicit complicity in an age of uncertainty. Those of us who love art are tempted to claim for it the powers of salvation. It will comfort us, cure us, drive us to righteous action, provide us with hope. I am not certain that this fiction does any of these things. But it does undo our desire to find salvation in it. It makes us aware of the privilege inherent in the act of reading and removes the easeful comfort in that privilege. In place of comfort it offers us an understanding of our relationship to pain and, in that understanding, a kind of beauty. Only if we relinquish our assumption of hope, do we see these works' defense of survival. The work of Kundera, Coetzee, Paley, Gordimer, Hawkes, and Ibuse cannot make us act as responsible citizens in the world. But if we do act, we will do so with a better understanding of politics because of them.

Notes

CHAPTER ONE: POWER AND WOUNDS

1. Terry Eagleton, *The Function of Criticism: From* The Spectator *to Post-structuralism* (London: Verso Editions, 1984), p. 108.

2. Frank Lentricchia, *Criticism and Social Change* (Chicago: University of Chicago Press, 1983), p. 7.

3. Terry Eagleton, "The Idealism of American Criticism," *New Left Review,* 127 (May–June 1981): 53–65 [65].

4. Edward Said, "Opponents, Audiences, Constituencies, and Community," *Critical Inquiry,* 9 (September 1982): 1–26 [21].

5. Robert Boyers, *Atrocity and Amnesia: The Political Novel Since 1945* (New York: Oxford University Press, 1985), pp. 16 and 232.

6. Paul de Man, "Semiology and Rhetoric," *Allegories of Reading: Figural Language in Rousseau, Nietzsche, Rilke and Proust* (New Haven: Yale University Press, 1979), pp. 3–19 [19].

7. M. H. Abrams, in "The Deconstructive Angel," *Critical Inquiry,* 3 (spring 1977): 425–38 [436], quotes from J. Hillis Miller, "Stevens' Rock and Criticism as Cure, II," *The Georgia Review,* 30 (summer 1976): 330–48 [337].

8. Christopher Norris, in *Contest of Faculties: Philosophy and Theory After Deconstruction* (New York: Methuen, 1985), p. 10, quotes from Paul de Man, "The Resistance to Theory," ed. Barbara Johnson, *The Pedagogical Imperative, Yale French Studies,* 63 (1982): 3–20 [11].

9. Michael Ryan, *Marxism and Deconstruction: A Critical Articulation* (Baltimore: Johns Hopkins University Press, 1982), pp. 1 and 8.

10. Abrams, "The Deconstructive Angel," p. 435.

11. See "Yale Scholar Wrote for Pro-Nazi Newspaper," *The New York Times,* 1 December 1987, pp. B1 and B6. Just what the various schools of literary theory will make of de Man's contributions to *Le Soir* in 1941 and 1942 can be gleaned from *Responses: On Paul de Man's Wartime Journalism,* eds. Werner Hamacher, Neil Hertz, and Tom Keenan (Lincoln: The University of Nebraska Press, 1988). Christopher Norris's *Paul de Man: Deconstruction and the Critique of Aesthetic Ideology* (New York: Routledge, 1988) provides thoughtful consideration of the *Le Soir* pieces. *Newsweek, The Nation, The New Republic,* and *Voice Literary Supplement* (to name a few) have printed responses to the *Le Soir* discoveries, but many of these articles reveal more about the predispositions of the periodicals and their writers than about de Man—let alone about deconstruction. One of the most reasonable analyses of the controversy is Denis Donoghue's "The Strange Case of Paul de Man" in *The New York Review of Books,* 29 June 1989, pp. 32–37. To judge this issue for yourself, see Paul de Man, *Wartime Journalism: 1940–42,* eds. Werner

Hamacher, Neil Hertz, and Tom Keenan (Lincoln: The University of Nebraska Press, 1988).

12. Sander L. Gilman, *Difference and Pathology: Stereotypes of Sexuality, Race, and Madness* (Ithaca, New York: Cornell University Press, 1985).

13. Richard F. Teichgraeber III, "'Cry for the Beloved Country': An Interview with Nadine Gordimer," *Tulanian* (summer 1987): 24–30 [26].

14. Elaine Showalter, "Introduction: The Feminist Critical Revolution," *The New Feminist Criticism: Essays on Women, Literature and Theory* (New York: Pantheon, 1985), p. 10.

15. Elizabeth Abel, ed., *Critical Inquiry*, 8 (winter 1981): 173–78 [174].

16. Eagleton, *The Function of Criticism*, p. 118.

17. See, for example, Seyla Benhabib and Drucilla Cornell, eds., *Feminism as Critique: Essays on the Politics of Gender in Late-Capitalist Societies* (Minneapolis: University of Minnesota Press, 1987); Zillah R. Eisenstein, ed., *Capitalist Patriarchy and the Case for Socialist Feminism* (New York: Monthly Review, 1979); Gayatri Chakravorty Spivak, *In Other Worlds* (New York: Routledge, 1988); or Catharine A. MacKinnon, "Feminism, Marxism, Method, and the State: An Agenda for Theory," *Signs*, 9 (1984): 1–30.

18. Paraphrases and quotations are taken from the pages of Lentricchia, *Criticism and Social Change*, in the order in which they are listed: pp. 1–3, 25, 35, 50, 35, and 12–13.

19. Václav Havel, "The Power of the Powerless," trans. Paul Wilson, *The Power of the Powerless: Citizens against the state in central-eastern Europe*, ed. John Keane (Armonk, New York: M. E. Sharpe, Inc., 1985), pp. 23–96 [92–95].

20. George Konrád, *Antipolitics: An Essay*, trans. Richard E. Allen (New York: Harcourt Brace Jovanovich, 1984), p. 197.

21. Christa Wolf, "A Work Diary, about the Stuff Life and Dreams Are Made Of," *Cassandra: A Novel and Four Essays*, trans. Jan van Heurck (New York: Farrar, Straus and Giroux, 1984), p. 253.

22. Havel, "The Power of the Powerless," p. 37.

23. Peter Uhl, "The Alternative Community as Revolutionary Avant-garde," trans. Paul Wilson, *The Power of the Powerless* [see note 19], pp. 188–97 [194].

24. Konrád, *Antipolitics*, p. 230.

25. Seweryn Bialer, "On the Meanings, Sources, and Carriers of Radicalism in Contemporary Industrialized Societies: Introductory Remarks," *Sources of Contemporary Radicalism*, volume 1 of the series *Radicalism in the Contemporary Age* (Boulder, Colorado: Westview Press, 1977). This volume is the result of workshops on radicalism held at Columbia University in the spring of 1975.

26. Ibid., p. 9.

27. Ibid., p. 12.

28. The limitations of marxian theory are implied throughout Havel's *Power of the Powerless* and Konrád's *Antipolitics*. Bialer makes explicit his reservations about marxian theory on p. 21, for example. The 1989 words of Havel are from his acceptance speech on receipt of the *Freidenpreis des Deutschen Buchandels*, 15 Octo-

ber 1989, translated by A. G. Brain and reprinted as "Words on Words," in *The New York Review of Books*, 18 January 1990, pp. 5–6, 8 [6].

29. Bialer, *Sources of Contemporary Radicalism*, p. 28. In his study Bialer did not include the relationship of intellectuals and working-class radicals in post-totalitarian states, a relationship which changes daily in central-eastern Europe.

30. Seweryn Bialer, *The Soviet Paradox: External Expansion, Internal Decline* (New York: Alfred A. Knopf, 1986), p. 375.

31. In the interview with Richard Teichgraeber, p. 30, Gordimer asserts that the United States civil rights movement and South African antiapartheid movement are fundamentally different because the federal laws in the United States were on the side of the movement. In South Africa, they have not been. As *The Power of the Powerless* explains, the Charter 77 movement in Czechoslovakia has been a civil rights movement similar to the United States movement—and unlike the South African movement—in that its purpose has been to pressure the government into obeying the law.

32. Daniel Berrigan, lecture at Loyola University in New Orleans, November 1984.

33. Helen Caldicott's *Missile Envy* (New York: William Morrow, 1984) provides a scrupulously detailed account of business practices within the so-called military-industrial complex despite her less credible psychological analogies.

34. Terrence Des Pres, "Self/Landscape/Grid," *New England Review and Bread Loaf Quarterly*, 5 (summer 1983): 441–50; and Morty Sklar, ed., *Nuke-Rebuke: Writers and Artists Against Nuclear Energy and Weapons* (Iowa City: The Spirit That Moves Us Press, 1984).

35. I am beholden to John Gery for his reading of Thom Gunn's poem in "How Nothing Has Changed: From Stevens's 'The Snowman' to Gunn's 'The Annihilation of Nothing,'" *Poesis*, 7.1 (1986): 23–34; his reading of John Ashbery's poems in "En Route to Annihilation: John Ashbery's *Shadow Train*," *Concerning Poetry*, 20 (1987): 99–116; and his essay classifying United States poets of the nuclear age, "The Sigh of Our Present: Nuclear Annihilation and Contemporary Poetry," *World, Self, Poem: Essays on Contemporary Poetry from the "Jubilation of Poets"* (Kent, Ohio: Kent State University Press, 1990), pp. 72–93.

36. Robert Jay Lifton with Richard Falk, *Indefensible Weapons: The Political and Psychological Case Against Nuclearism* (New York: Basic Books, Inc., 1982), pp. 13 and 3–4, respectively.

37. Lawrence Freedman, *The Evolution of Nuclear Strategy* (London: The Macmillan Press, 1983), p. 400.

38. Jonathan Schell, *The Fate of the Earth* (New York: Avon Books, 1982).

39. Alan Brinkley, "Dreams of the Sixties," review of Maurice Isserman's *If I Had a Hammer: The Death of the Old Left and the Birth of the New Left* and James Miller's *"Democracy is in the Streets": From Port Huron to the Siege of Chicago*, in *The New York Review of Books*, 22 October 1987, pp. 10–16 [16].

40. Brian Easlea, *Fathering the Unthinkable: Masculinity, Scientists and the Nuclear Arms Race* (London: Pluto Press, 1983).

41. Though both the United States and the Soviet Union are large bureau-

cracies, the ways in which the two are similar and dissimilar are many and complicated. Konrád sees similarities in the United States and the Soviet Union's nuclear politics in Europe, while Havel cautiously avoids drawing any parallels between the two superpower bureaucracies, and Bialer insists on their differences.

42. See, for example, pp. 54–55 in Adrienne Rich, *Of Woman Born,* Tenth Anniversary Edition (New York: W. W. Norton, 1986). The whole of Dorothy Dinnerstein's argument in *The Mermaid and the Minotaur: Sexual Arrangements and Human Malaise* (New York: Harper and Row, 1976) makes evident reasons for revolution quite different from those proposed by marxism, but see especially "Mama and the Mad Megamachine."

43. Michel Foucault, *The History of Sexuality,* trans. Robert Hurley, volume 1 (New York: Vintage Books, 1980).

44. Rich, *Of Woman Born,* pp. 79–80.

45. This appears in a footnote relating a personal communication from Mary Daly to Adrienne Rich on p. 80 in *Of Woman Born.*

46. Abel, *Critical Inquiry,* 8 (winter 1981): 178.

47. Milan Kundera, Afterword to *The Book of Laughter and Forgetting,* trans. Michael Henry Heim (New York: Penguin Books, 1981), pp. 234–35.

48. The quotations from Konrád's *Antipolitics* are taken from the following pages, respectively: pp. 33, 93–94, 113, 230, and 92.

49. Havel, "The Power of the Powerless," p. 27.

50. Konrád, *Antipolitics,* p. 196.

51. Many discussions of feminism, censorship, and pornography are available; see, for example, Fred Berger, "Pornography, Sex, and Censorship," *Social Theory and Practice,* 4 (spring 1977): 183–209; Irene Diamond, "Pornography and Repression: A Reconsideration," *Signs,* 5 (summer 1980): 686–701; Andrea Dworkin, *Pornography: Men Possessing Women* (London: Women's Press, 1981); Joel Feinberg, "Harmless Immoralities and Offensive Nuisances," *Rights, Justice and the Bounds of Liberty* (Princeton: Princeton University Press, 1980); Judith M. Hill, "Pornography and Degradation," *Hypatia,* 2 (summer 1987): 39–54; Annette Kuhn, *The Power of the Image: Essays on Representation and Sexuality* (Boston: Routledge and Kegan Paul, 1985); Howard Poole, "Obscenity and Censorship," *Ethics,* 93 (October 1982): 39–44; Alan Soble, "Pornography: Defamation and the Endorsement of Degradation," *Social Theory and Practice,* 11 (spring 1985): 61–87; and Daniel Wolff, "The Strange and Sexless Marriage of Andrea Dworkin and Edwin Meese," *The Threepenny Review,* 30 (summer 1987): 3–4.

52. Henry Louis Gates, Jr., ed., "Writing 'Race' and the Difference It Makes," *Critical Inquiry,* 12 (autumn 1985): 1–20 [5].

53. Anthony Appiah, "The Uncompleted Argument: Du Bois and the Illusion of Race," *Critical Inquiry,* 12 (autumn 1985): 21–37 [21–22].

54. Gates, "Writing 'Race' and the Difference It Makes," p. 8.

55. Foucault, *The History of Sexuality,* pp. 25–26.

56. Easlea, *Fathering the Unthinkable,* pp. 22–24.

57. Susan Bordo, *The Flight to Objectivity: Essays on Cartesianism and Culture* (Albany, New York: State University of New York Press, 1987), pp. 76–77 and 90–91.

58. Rich documents these accusations in "Hands of Flesh, Hands of Iron," *Of Woman Born,* pp. 128–55.

59. Barbara Johnson, *A World of Difference* (Baltimore: Johns Hopkins University Press, 1987), p. 178.

60. Foucault, *The History of Sexuality,* p. 27.

61. The terms "first world" and "third world" are an inadequate, hierarchical naming of the distinction between the developed and developing nations, but the term "developed nation" is itself static and imperious, and the term "developing nation," is both euphemistic and patronizing. Gayatri Chakravorty Spivak uses the term "subaltern" in reference to an oppressed but assertive other of the "third world" (*In Other Worlds*), but she stipulates a particular subaltern studies with a particular history more specific than I intend in my use of the term "third world." So despite my reservations, I will use the terms "first world" and "third world."

62. Reed Way Dasenbrock, "Intelligibility and Meaningfulness in Multicultural Literature in English," *PMLA,* 102 (January 1987): 10–19 [11].

63. Adrienne Rich, *Blood, Bread, and Poetry: Selected Prose 1979–1985* (New York: W. W. Norton, 1986), p. 208.

64. Abel, *Critical Inquiry,* 8 (winter 1981): 177–78.

65. Elaine Scarry, *The Body in Pain: The Making and Unmaking of the World* (New York: Oxford University Press, 1985), pp. 3–59.

66. Gilman, *Difference and Pathology:* the indented quotation is on pp. 17 and 21; the second quotation, on p. 12.

67. Gayatri Chakravorty Spivak, trans., "Draupadi" by Mahasveta Devi, *Critical Inquiry,* 8 (winter 1981): 381–402 [382].

68. Barbara Johnson, *The Critical Difference: Essays in the Contemporary Rhetoric of Reading* (Baltimore: Johns Hopkins University Press, 1980), pp. xi and x–xi, respectively.

69. Julia Kristeva, "Psychoanalysis and the Polis," trans. Margaret Waller, *Critical Inquiry,* 9 (September 1982): 77–92.

70. Rich, *Of Woman Born,* pp. 64 and 67, respectively.

71. Alan Bass, Introduction to *Writing and Difference* by Jacques Derrida, trans. Alan Bass (Chicago: University of Chicago Press, 1978), p. xv.

72. Lifton, *Indefensible Weapons,* p. 81.

73. Bass, Introduction to *Writing and Difference,* p. xvi.

74. Jacques Derrida, *Writing and Difference* [see note 71], p. 8.

75. Johnson, *A World of Difference,* p. 15.

76. Lionel Trilling, *Sincerity and Authenticity* (New York: Harcourt Brace Jovanovich, 1972), pp. 86 and 87.

77. Ibid., p. 88.

78. Ibid., pp. 122–23.

79. Adrienne Rich, "Power," *The Dream of a Common Language: Poems 1974–1977* (New York: W. W. Norton, 1978), p. 3.

80. Emily Dickinson, #66, *Final Harvest,* selected and introduced by Thomas H. Johnson (Boston: Little, Brown, 1961), pp. 36–37.

81. Rich, *Blood, Bread, and Poetry,* p. 141.

82. Ibid., p. 143.

83. Patrick Brantlinger, "Victorians and Africans: The Genealogy of the Myth of the Dark Continent," *Critical Inquiry,* 12 (autumn 1985): 166–203 [196].

84. These passages are from J. Hillis Miller's "Stevens' Rock and Criticism as Cure, II," [see note 7], pp. 336–37.

85. Jonathan Edwards, "Sinners in the Hands of an Angry God," *The Works of Jonathan Edwards,* ed. Sereno E. Dwight, volume 7 of 10 (New York: C. and G. and H. Carvill, 1829–30).

86. Walt Whitman, "A Noiseless Patient Spider," *Complete Poetry and Selected Prose,* ed. James E. Miller, Jr., Riverside Editions (Boston: Houghton Mifflin, 1959), p. 314. In Miller's deconstructive reading of Wallace Stevens's "The Rock," ("Stevens' Rock and Criticism as Cure," *The Georgia Review,* 30 [spring 1976]: 5–31), he posits a thoroughly Emersonian Whitman whose sense of self is monolithic in contrast to Stevens's deconstructed self. Despite Miller's brilliant reading of "The Rock," I am not convinced by his assumptions about Whitman, whose passion for inclusiveness renders his self a far less stable and enclosed entity than Emerson's, perhaps even than Stevens's. And yet I do not propose that Whitman's was a deconstructive spirit, even if his own methods led him in that direction.

87. Stanley Fish, *Is There a Text in This Class? The Authority of Interpretive Communities* (Cambridge: Harvard University Press, 1980), p. 3.

88. In "On Democracy in Latin America," *The New York Review of Books,* 10 April 1986, pp. 41–42, Albert O. Hirschman quotes first from Adam Przeworski's "Love Uncertainty and You Will Be Democratic," *Novos Estudos* Centro Brasileiro de Analise e Planejamento (July 1984), then from Bernard Manin's "Volanté générale ou délibération? Esquisse d'une théorie de la délibération politique," *Le Débat,* No. 22 (January 1985), translated into English as "On Legitimacy and Political Deliberation" by Elly Stein and Jane Mansbridge for *Political Theory,* 15 (August 1987): 338–68.

89. Jane J. Mansbridge, *Beyond Adversary Democracy* (New York: Basic Books, 1980). In his review of *If I Had a Hammer* by Maurice Isserman and *"Democracy is in the Streets"* by James Miller, Alan Brinkley notes that the New Left defined democracy as "a vehicle through which individuals could feel empowered and enrich their lives." But this enrichment, which was often called "authenticity," became only "personal fulfillment through 'narcissism and erotic exuberance'" (Norman O. Brown's phrase). Brinkley concludes, "The New Left ultimately did not so much betray its commitments to 'participatory democracy' and 'personal authenticity' as succumb to them." [See note 39.] My definition of authenticity differs from that of the sixties counter-culture, and I offer Mansbridge as a warning against the dangers of participatory democracy (i.e., unitary democracy) in hopes of distinguishing my allegiances from those of the Old New Left.

90. Mansbridge, *Beyond Adversary Democracy,* pp. 8 and 9.

91. Ibid., p. 293.

92. "A wild patience has taken me this far" is the first line of Rich's poem "Integrity" in *A Wild Patience Has Taken Me This Far: Poems 1978–1981* (New York: W. W. Norton, 1981), pp. 8–9.

93. Though by economic standards, Japan has every claim to a "first-world"

classification, its unique history as the sole victim of atomic weapons used in wartime raises questions, for many, about the racial relationship between white nation-states and Asian nation-states like Japan. Mrs. Kuti, a character in Wole Soyinka's autobiography, *Aké*, states, without equivocation, what she believes this racial relationship to be. Speaking to a British official immediately after news of the Hiroshima and Nagasaki bombings had reached Nigeria in August 1945, Mrs. Kuti remarks, "I know you, the white mentality: Japanese, Chinese, Africans, we are all subhuman. You would drop an atom bomb on Abeokuta or any of your colonies if it suited you!" ([New York: Aventura/Vintage Books, 1983], p. 224). Because of all the particular conditions which define the relationship of Japan and the white world, I choose to discuss *Black Rain* in the final chapter despite the problems of dealing with a work translated from Japanese.

94. Having begun this chapter with Eagleton's reservations about Fredric Jameson's *The Political Unconscious* (Ithaca: Cornell University Press, 1981), I return to Jameson's text in this closing note to mention that I share his conviction about the "priority of the political interpretation" over any or all texts (p. 17). But while I admire his interfacing of psychoanalysis and marxism, I find his philosophy of history and survey of historicisms, as expressed in *The Political Unconscious,* too certainly marxist ("Only Marxism can give us an adequate account of the essential *mystery* of the cultural past." [p. 19]).

CHAPTER TWO: SEX, MOTHERHOOD, AND THE STATE

1. A. French, *Czech Writers and Politics: 1945–1969,* East European Monographs, Boulder (New York: Columbia University Press, 1982), p. 56.

2. Norman Podhoretz, "An Open Letter to Milan Kundera," *Commentary,* 78 (October 1984): 34–39 [39].

3. David Lodge, "Milan Kundera, and the Idea of the Author in Modern Criticism," *Critical Quarterly,* 26 (spring and summer 1984): 105–26.

4. Terry Eagleton, "Estrangement and Irony," *Salmagundi,* 73 (winter 1987): 25–32.

5. Barbara Johnson, *The Critical Difference* (Baltimore: Johns Hopkins University Press, 1980), p. 18.

6. Robert Boyers, *Atrocity and Amnesia: The Political Novel Since 1945* (New York: Oxford University Press, 1985), p. 25.

7. Ibid., p. ii.

8. Johnson, *The Critical Difference,* pp. 4–5.

9. Ibid., p. 5.

10. Gayatri Chakravorty Spivak, trans., "Draupadi" by Mahasveta Devi, *Critical Inquiry,* 8 (winter 1981): 381–402 [382].

11. Alain Finkielkraut, "Milan Kundera Interview," trans. Susan Huston, *Cross Currents: A Yearbook of Central European Culture,* 20 (1982): 15–29 [27].

12. French, *Czech Writers and Politics,* pp. 252–54.

13. Antonin Liehm, "Some Observations on Czech Culture and Politics in the 1960's," *Czech Literature Since 1956: A Symposium,* eds. William E. Harkins and Paul I. Trensky, Columbia Slavic Studies (New York: Bohemica, 1980), p. 134.

14. Finkielkraut, "Kundera Interview," p. 20.

15. Milan Kundera, "An Introduction to a Variation," trans. Michael Henry Heim, *Cross Currents,* 26 (1986): 469–76 [469]; rpt. fr. *Jacques and His Master* (New York: Harper and Row, 1985). Josef Brodsky refutes Kundera's position on Dostoevsky in the same issue of *Cross Currents.*

16. Normand Biron, "Conversation with Milan Kundera," trans. Andreas Mytze into German for *Europaische Ideen,* 20 (1976), trans. Victoria Nelson into English for *Threepenny Review,* 24 (winter 1986): 11.

17. François Ricard, "Satan's Point of View: Towards a Reading of *Life Is Elsewhere,*" *Salmagundi,* 73 (winter 1987): 58–64 [62].

18. Milan Kundera, "Esch Is Luther," trans. David Rieff, afterword to *Terra Nostra* by Carlos Fuentes, trans. Margaret Sayers Peden (New York: Farrar, Straus and Giroux, 1983), p. 783.

19. Roland Barthes, *S/Z,* trans. Richard Miller (New York: Hill and Wang, 1974), p. 16. Barbara Johnson emphasizes this passage in her introduction of the difference within in *The Critical Difference,* p. 3.

20. Lars Kleberg, "On the Border: Milan Kundera's *The Book of Laughter and Forgetting,*" *Scando-Slavica,* 30 (1984): 57–72 [62].

21. John Berger, "Uses of Photography," *About Looking* (New York: Pantheon Books, 1980), p. 63. For further discussion of what Kundera calls the "polyphonic" form of *The Book,* see his explanation in "Dialogue on the Art of Composition," *The Art of the Novel,* trans. Linda Asher (New York: Grove Press, 1988), pp. 72–77.

22. Berger quotes Walter Benjamin quoting Goethe, ibid., p. 28.

23. Milan Kundera, *The Book of Laughter and Forgetting,* trans. Michael Henry Heim (New York: Penguin Books, 1981), p. 3. All subsequent references to the novel noted parenthetically in the text are from this edition.

24. Peter Kussi, "Milan Kundera: Dialogues with Fiction," *World Literature Today,* 57 (spring 1983): 206–9 [207].

25. Václav Havel, "The Power of the Powerless," trans. Paul Wilson, *The Power of the Powerless: Citizens against the state in central-eastern Europe,* ed. John Keane (Armonk, New York: M. E. Sharpe, Inc., 1985), p. 37.

26. Johnson, *The Critical Difference,* p. 115.

27. Peter Kussi considers the question of paternity in *The Book of Laughter and Forgetting* and in Kundera's earlier fiction in the *World Literature Today* essay (see note 24) but also in his dissertation, "Essays on the Fiction of Milan Kundera," Columbia University, 1978.

28. Dorothy Dinnerstein, *The Mermaid and the Minotaur: Sexual Arrangements and Human Malaise* (New York: Harper and Row, 1976), p. 6.

29. Adrienne Rich makes this observation in the note on p. 119, *Of Woman Born,* Tenth Anniversary Edition (New York: W. W. Norton, 1986).

30. Nancy Chodorow corroborates Dinnerstein's argument in *The Reproduction of Mothering: Psychoanalysis and the Sociology of Gender* (Berkeley: University of California Press, 1978). See, for example, p. 57.

31. Rich discusses the power given to and taken from mothers throughout *Of Woman Born,* but I refer here to pp. 67–68.

32. See, for example, Rich, pp. 188–89, and Dinnerstein, pp. 117–18.

33. Rich, *Of Woman Born*, p. 284.

34. Boyers, *Atrocity and Amnesia*, p. 232.

35. Ibid., p. 231.

36. By thinking through the body, Rich means a self-consciousness that is political and demystifying, not the somatic female mysticism Kundera perceives in Leclerc. In addition, the confusion of sexual liberation with women's liberation (feminism) is one that *The Book* seems to share and one that Rich, Dinnerstein, and others try to clarify.

37. John Ashbery, "The Absence of a Noble Presence," *Shadow Train* (New York: Penguin Books, 1981), p. 11.

CHAPTER THREE: THE BODY, THE WORD, AND THE STATE

1. J. M. Coetzee, *Waiting for the Barbarians* (New York: Penguin Books, 1982). Quotations from this edition are subsequently noted in parentheses in the text.

2. Lance Olsen, "The Presence of Absence: Coetzee's *Waiting for the Barbarians*," *Ariel*, 16 (April 1985): 47–56.

3. I refer especially to Leon Whiteson, *Canadian Forum*, 62 (October 1982): 26, and Irving Howe, *The New York Times Book Review*, 18 April 1983. Olsen provides synopses of the reviews the novel received.

4. Olsen, "The Presence of Absence," p. 53.

5. Ibid., p. 55.

6. Ibid., pp. 55–56.

7. Robert Boyers, *Atrocity and Amnesia: The Political Novel Since 1945* (New York: Oxford University Press, 1985), p. 232.

8. Quoted in Olsen, "The Presence of Absence," p. 48.

9. Rowland Smith, "The Seventies and After: The Inner View in White, English-language Fiction," *Olive Schreiner and After: Essays on South African Literature in Honour of Guy Butler*, eds. Malvern Van Wyk Smith and Dan Maclennan (Cape Town: David Philip, Publishers Ltd., 1983), pp. 196–204.

10. Michel Foucault, *Discipline and Punish: The Birth of the Prison*, trans. Alan Sheridan (New York: Vintage Books, 1979), p. 41.

11. Elaine Scarry, *The Body in Pain: The Making and Unmaking of the World* (New York: Oxford University Press, 1985), p. 4.

12. Peter Singer, "Unspeakable Acts," review of Elaine Scarry's *The Body in Pain* and Edward Peters's *Torture*, *The New York Review of Books*, 27 February 1986, pp. 27–30.

13. Hannah Arendt, "Truth and Politics," *Between Past and Future: Eight Exercises in Political Thought* (New York: Viking, 1968), pp. 237 and 238.

14. Edward Peters, *Torture* (New York: Basil Blackwell Inc., 1985), p. 166.

15. Theodor W. Adorno, *Negative Dialectics*, trans. E. B. Ashton (New York: Continuum Publishing Company, 1973), p. 48.

16. In quoting from the reports of the torture and execution of Damiens the regicide (1757), Foucault provides an excellent example of the individual observing his body as body-for-others. "Despite all his pain, he raised his head from time to time and looked at himself boldly," p. 4. It seems Damiens's self-examination is

noteworthy as a sign of appropriate contrition. Damiens confronts and feels wounds like those he inflicted while he relinquishes his body totally to others: the spectators, the executioner, and especially the sovereign. That he can do this while experiencing intense pain demonstrates his secular dignity and his religious faith.

17. Jean-Paul Sartre, *Being and Nothingness,* trans. Hazel E. Barnes (New York: Washington Square Press, 1966), p. 434.

18. Ibid., p. 438.

19. Ibid., p. 436.

20. Adorno, *Negative Dialectics,* p. 51.

21. See, for example, Adrienne Rich, *Of Woman Born* (New York: W. W. Norton, 1986), and Brian Easlea, *Fathering the Unthinkable* (London: Pluto Press, 1983). For a consideration specifically of Descartes and Coetzee—with conclusions that differ from mine—see W. J. B. Wood, *"Waiting for the Barbarians:* Two Sides of Imperial Rule and Some Related Considerations," *Momentum: On Recent South African Writing* (Pietermaritzburg: University of Natal Press, 1984), pp. 129–40. I do concur with Wood's description of the novel as "exorcism of the ghost of Descartes."

22. Adorno, *Negative Dialectics,* pp. 22, 23, and 43.

23. Susan Bordo, *The Flight to Objectivity: Essays on Cartesianism and Culture* (Albany: SUNY Press, 1987), pp. 76–77.

24. Ibid., p. 76.

25. Ibid., pp. 90–91.

26. Foucault, *Discipline and Punish,* p. 28.

27. See note 21.

28. See especially "The Border" in Milan Kundera's *The Book of Laughter and Forgetting,* trans. Michael Henry Heim (New York: Penguin Books, 1981).

29. Scarry, *The Body in Pain,* p. 20.

30. Peters, *Torture,* pp. 1–2.

31. See, for example, ibid., pp. 177–78.

32. Foucault, *Discipline and Punish,* pp. 35 and 38.

33. Ibid., p. 40.

34. Peters, *Torture,* pp. 163–64.

35. Amnesty International, *Torture in the Eighties* (Oxford and London: Martin Robertson and Co., Ltd. and Amnesty International Publications, 1984), p. 7.

36. Ibid., p. 3.

37. Scarry, *The Body in Pain,* pp. 4, 35, and 27.

38. See Peters, *Torture,* p. 183, and Amnesty International, *Torture in the Eighties,* p. 10.

39. Scarry, *The Body in Pain,* pp. 40–48.

40. Bordo, *The Flight to Objectivity,* pp. 45–46.

41. Robert Jay Lifton, *The Nazi Doctors: Medical Killing and the Psychology of Genocide* (New York: Basic Books, 1986), pp. 15, 17, and 18.

42. Scarry, *The Body in Pain,* p. 49.

43. Ibid., pp. 41–42.

44. Lifton, *The Nazi Doctors,* pp. 14–16.

45. In a section of *Negative Dialectics* entitled "After Auschwitz"—and which might have been called "After Auschwitz and Hiroshima"—Adorno argues that individual consciousness, individual death, can never be thought of in the same way again. "There is no chance any more for death to come into the individual's empirical life as somehow conformable with the course of that life. . . . that in the concentration camps it was no longer an individual who died but a specimen— this is a fact bound to affect the dying of those who escaped the administrative measure," p. 362.

46. Peters, *Torture*, p. 171, and Amnesty International, *Torture in the Eighties*, p. 20.

47. Peters, *Torture*, pp. 175–76.

48. Ibid., p. 176.

49. In arguing for the epistemological value of sympathetic thinking, Bordo finds corroboration in a variety of sources that she describes, pp. 102–3.

50. In *Disease and Representation: Images of Illness from Madness to AIDS* (Ithaca: Cornell University Press, 1988), Sander Gilman offers a contemporary example of this phenomenon. He argues that the West brought AIDS to Africa and not the other way around.

51. Sartre, *Being and Nothingness*, p. 518.

52. Foucault, *Discipline and Punish*, pp. 29–30.

53. Adorno describes this context of guilt not only for camp survivors but for all of us who live "after Auschwitz" (pp. 361–65). Robert Lifton describes survivors' guilt after Hiroshima in *Death in Life* (New York: Basic Books, 1967).

54. Lifton, *The Nazi Doctors*, pp. 459–62.

55. Bordo, *The Flight to Objectivity*, pp. 71–73.

56. Peters, *Torture*, pp. 5–6.

57. Arendt, "Truth and Politics," p. 227.

58. For an example of one language perceived as evil see Gayatri Spivak, who explains that in the Bengali novel "Draupadi" English is used as the language of war because it is understood as the international, heterogeneous, nameless language of domination (*Writing and Sexual Difference: Critical Inquiry*, ed. Elizabeth Abel, 8 [winter 1981]: 390).

59. Olsen, "The Presence of Absence," p. 55.

60. Sartre, *Being and Nothingness*, p. 519.

61. Adorno, *Negative Dialectics*, p. 404.

62. Peters, *Torture*, p. 187.

63. Lifton derives the term "blood cement," used on p. 436, from Leo Alexander's Introduction to Alexander Mitscherlich and Fred Mielke's *Doctors of Infamy: The Story of the Nazi Medical Crimes* (New York: Henry Schumann, 1949 [1947]), p. xxxii. See Lifton, *The Nazi Doctors*, pp. 531–32 and p. 432, note 8.

64. Adorno, *Negative Dialectics*, p. 400.

65. Scarry, *The Body in Pain*, p. 27.

66. Singer, "Unspeakable Acts," p. 27.

67. Peters, *Torture*, p. 7.

68. Amnesty International, *Torture in the Eighties*, p. 4.

69. Lifton, *The Nazi Doctors*, p. 450.

70. Hannah Arendt quotes Valéry and responds to him in *On Violence* (New York: Harcourt, Brace and World, 1970), pp. 86–87.

71. Foucault, *Discipline and Punish*, p. 27.

72. Arendt, "Truth and Politics," p. 241.

73. Ibid., p. 259.

74. Anthony Appiah, "The Uncompleted Argument: Du Bois and the Illusion of Race," *Critical Inquiry*, 12 (autumn 1985): 21–37 [21].

75. Patrick Brantlinger, "Victorians and Africans: The Genealogy of the Myth of the Dark Continent," *Critical Inquiry*, 12 (autumn 1985): 166–203.

76. Ian Buruma, "Japanese Lib," review of *The Issue of War: States, Societies, and the Far Eastern Conflict of 1941–1945* by Christopher Thorne, *New York Review of Books*, 13 March 1986, pp. 3–4 and 6.

77. Appiah, "The Uncompleted Argument," p. 35.

78. Henry Louis Gates, Jr., "Writing, 'Race' and the Difference It Makes," *Critical Inquiry*, 12 (autumn 1985): 1–20 [4, 5, and 6].

79. In *Figures In Black: Words, Signs, and the "Racial" Self* (New York: Oxford University Press, 1987), pp. 19–20, Gates quotes from and analyzes Georg Wilhelm Friedrich Hegel's *Philosophy of History* (New York: Dover, 1956), pp. 91–99.

80. Nadine Gordimer, "Something Out There," *Something Out There* (New York: Penguin Books, 1985), pp. 117–203.

81. William Styron, *The Confessions of Nat Turner* (New York: Random House, 1967).

82. See, for example, Lance Olsen, "The Presence of Absence: Coetzee's *Waiting for the Barbarians*," *Ariel*, 16 (April 1985): 47–56; W. J. B. Wood, "*Waiting for the Barbarians*: Two Sides of Imperial Rule and Some Related Considerations," *Momentum: On Recent South African Writing* (Pietermaritzburg: University of Natal Press, 1984), pp. 129–40; and Joan Gillmer, "The Motif of the Damaged Child in the Work of J. M. Coetzee," *Momentum*, pp. 107–20.

83. Marvin Fisher's *Going Under: Melville's Short Fiction and the American 1850's* (Baton Rouge: Louisiana State University Press, 1977), pp. 179–99, and Scott Donaldson's "The Dark Truth of *The Piazza Tales*," *PMLA*, 85 (October 1970): 1082–86, are two texts about "Bartleby" that do include discussions of "race."

84. Carolyn L. Karcher, *Shadow Over the Promised Land: Slavery, Race, and Violence in Melville's America* (Baton Rouge: Louisiana State University Press, 1980), p. 27.

85. William Faulkner, "Pantaloon in Black," *Go Down, Moses* (New York: Random House, 1942), pp. 135–59.

86. J. M. Coetzee, *Life and Times of Michael K* (New York: Penguin Books, 1985), p. 3. All subsequent references to the novel noted parenthetically in my text refer to this edition.

87. D. J. Enright, "the thing itself," review of *Life and Times of Michael K* by J. M. Coetzee, *Times Literary Supplement*, 30 September 1983, p. 1037.

88. Gates, *Figures in Black*, p. 57.

89. In *Figures in Black*, p. 57, Gates refers to Edward Said, "On Repetition," *The*

World, the Text, and the Critic (Cambridge: Harvard University Press, 1983), pp. 111–25. See Gates's note 35 on p. 279.

90. Herman Melville, "Bartleby," *Piazza Tales,* ed. Egbert S. Oliver (New York: Hendricks House, Inc., 1962), pp. 16–54 [43]. Rpt. from *Putnam's Monthly Magazine,* 2 (November–December 1853): 546–57, 609–15. All subsequent references to the story noted parenthetically in my text refer to the Hendricks House edition.

91. In "Thresholds of Difference: Structures of Address in Zora Neale Hurston," *A World of Difference* (Baltimore: Johns Hopkins University Press, 1987), pp. 172–83 [178], Barbara Johnson paraphrases from Hurston's "What White Publishers Won't Print," *I Love Myself When I Am Laughing and Then Again When I Am Looking Mean and Impressive: A Zora Neale Hurston Reader,* ed. Alice Walker (New York: The Feminist Press, 1979), pp. 169–73 [171].

92. Through the years numerous readers have perceived Bartleby as heroic, inwardly free, or able to transcend humanity. Three recent critics who share this description of Bartleby are Ray B. Browne, *Melville's Drive to Humanism* (Lafayette, Indiana: Purdue University Studies, 1971); William B. Dillingham, *Melville's Short Fiction: 1853–56* (Athens: University of Georgia Press, 1977); and Louise K. Barnett, "Bartleby as Alienated Worker" in *Studies in Short Fiction,* 11 (1974): 379–85. Even the most insightful reviewers of *Michael K,* Nadine Gordimer (*New York Review of Books,* 2 February 1984) and Cynthia Ozick (*New York Times Book Review,* 11 December 1983), use the word "hero" to describe Michael. Also, Ozick perceives Michael as free when he lives in the open. Harriett Gilbert (*New Statesman,* 30 September 1983) believes Michael is free to create meaning in his life.

93. Gates, *Figures in Black,* p. 236.

CHAPTER FOUR: SEPARATION, ASSIMILATION, AND THE STATE

1. Barbara Johnson, "Thresholds of Difference: Structures of Address in Zora Neale Hurston," *A World of Difference* (Baltimore: Johns Hopkins University Press, 1987), p. 178.

2. Elizabeth Bishop, "In the Waiting Room," *The Complete Poems: 1927–1979* (New York: Farrar, Straus and Giroux, 1983), pp. 159–61 [160].

3. Edward W. Said, *The World, the Text, and the Critic* (Cambridge: Harvard University Press, 1983), pp. 24–25.

4. Albert P. Blausten and Gisbert H. Flanz, eds., "South Africa," rev. by Ellison Kahn and Harold G. Rudolph, *Constitutions of the Countries of the World* (Dobbs Ferry, New York: Oceana Publications, Inc., issued June 1984), pp. 1–130 [1–20].

5. Donald L. Wiedner also notes in *A History of Africa: South of the Sahara* (New York: Vintage Books, 1964), p. 522, "One of the characteristics of South Africa under Nationalist rule has been the progressive division of white as well as nonwhite opposition. . . . Ironically enough, the revival of liberal parties, which fragmented the opposition, served only to strengthen the Nationalistic Party position." In "Can South Africa Change?" *The New York Review of Books,* 26 October 1989, pp. 48–55 [55], George M. Fredrickson points to more recent fractures among whites: "The Nationalists emerged from the election on September 6

[1989] with a greatly reduced majority, losing seats in approximately equal numbers to the staunchly pro-apartheid right and the moderately liberal left."

6. Blausten and Flanz, "South Africa," pp. 5, 20, and 66–68. The release of Nelson Mandela and the independence of Namibia early in 1990 may suggest F. W. de Klerk intends to pursue more liberal policies regarding apartheid. Whether or not this is true in 1990, I maintain that the change in voting rights instigated by the 1983 Constitution was not so much a liberal move as it was a logical maneuver.

7. Albert P. Blausten, "South Africa Supplement," *Constitutions of the Countries of the World* (Dobbs Ferry, New York: Oceana Publications, Inc., issued September 1986), pp. 1–18 [17–18].

8. Nadine Gordimer and David Goldblatt, *Lifetimes Under Apartheid* (New York: Alfred A. Knopf, 1986), pp. 62 and 63.

9. Wiedner, *A History of Africa*, p. 521.

10. Stephen Clingman, *The Novels of Nadine Gordimer: History from the Inside* (Boston: Allen and Unwin, 1986), p. 176.

11. Fredrickson, "Can South Africa Change," p. 48. Whether or not President de Klerk's announcements 2 February 1990 will produce changes in grand apartheid remains to be seen. Christopher S. Wren's analysis in *The New York Times* urges caution (reprinted in *The New Orleans Times-Picayune*, 3 February 1990, p. A-5).

12. J. M. Coetzee, *White Writing: On the Culture of Letters in South Africa* (New Haven: Yale University Press, 1988), p. 3.

13. Ibid., pp. 7, 3–4, 19–35, and 88.

14. See Fredrickson's discussion of poverty in "Can South Africa Change," pp. 53–54, where he considers Francis Wilson and Mamphela Ramphele's *Uprooting Poverty: The South African Challenge* (New York: W. W. Norton, 1989). On pp. 49–53 Fredrickson also looks at the troubled relationship of capitalism and apartheid. He cites the analyses of Shula Marks and Stanley Trapido in *South Africa: No Turning Back*, ed. Shaun Johnson (Bloomington: Indiana University Press, 1989), and of Frances Kendall and Leon Louw in *After Apartheid: The Solution for South Africa* (San Francisco: Institute for Contemporary Studies, 1987).

15. Blausten and Flanz, "South Africa," p. 34.

16. Margaret Mead and Rhoda Metraux, "The Egalitarian Error," *A Way of Seeing* (New York: McCall Publishing Co., 1970), pp. 73–76 [73].

17. Adrienne Rich, "Resisting Amnesia: History and Personal Life," *Blood, Bread, and Poetry: Selected Prose 1979–1985* (New York: W. W. Norton, 1986), pp. 136–55 [141].

18. Ibid., pp. 142–43.

19. *Super Chief: Earl Warren*, aired 2 October 1989 on PBS affiliate WYES in New Orleans.

20. Athol Fugard, *Master Harold and the Boys* (New York: Alfred A. Knopf, 1983), p. 20.

21. Gayatri Chakravorty Spivak extends Marx's ideas about workers' alienation to mother's alienation from their labor in *In Other Worlds: Essays in Cultural Politics* (New York: Routledge, 1988), p. 80 et passim.

22. Spivak quotes from Antonio Gramsci on p. 201. The subsequent quotations are, respectively, from pp. 198 and 199.

23. Clingman, *The Novels of Nadine Gordimer,* p. 16 and note 35.

24. Nadine Gordimer, "The Catch," *Selected Stories* (New York: Penguin Books, 1983), p. 36. All the other stories by Gordimer that I will discuss are from this collection except "A City of the Dead, A City of the Living," which is from *Something Out There* (New York: Penguin Books, 1985). Subsequent references to the stories, noted in the text by page numbers in parentheses, are from these editions.

25. Coetzee, *White Writing,* p. 25.

26. Rowland Smith is another South African who admires the historical clarity and political provocation in Gordimer's fiction. See "The Seventies and After: The Inner View in White, English-language Fiction," *Olive Schreiner and After: Essays on South African Literature in Honour of Guy Butler,* eds. Malvern Van Wyk Smith and Dan Maclennan (Cape Town: David Philip, Publishers Ltd., 1983), pp. 196–204.

27. Clingman, *The Novels of Nadine Gordimer,* p. 89 et passim. For an examination of the complex place of liberalism in South African politics, see Fredrickson, "Can South Africa Change?" pp. 51–53, where he discusses Janet Levine's *Inside Apartheid: One Woman's Struggle in South Africa* (Chicago: Contemporary Books, 1988) and the collection of essays, *Democratic Liberalism in South Africa,* eds. Jeffrey Butler, Richard Elphick, and David Welsh (Middletown, Connecticut: Wesleyan University Press, 1987).

28. I choose to write about Gordimer's short stories rather than her novels primarily because I think the stories are more carefully written. Also, the novels have been more written about, recently by Abdul R. JanMohamed, *Manichean Aesthetics: The Politics of Literature in Colonial Africa* (Amherst: University of Massachusetts Press, 1983); John Cooke, *Only Pursue: The Novels of Nadine Gordimer* (Baton Rouge: Louisiana State University Press, 1985); Judie Newman, *Nadine Gordimer* (New York: Routledge, 1988); and Stephen Clingman, *The Novels of Nadine Gordimer* (Boston: Allen and Unwin, 1986). Specifically, I challenge JanMohamed's assumption that there is a "relative absence of those racial and political concerns [evident in the novels] from most of her short stories: the latter [that is, the stories] show that Gordimer can and wants to write about aspects of life that have nothing to do with race," p. 147. What Gordimer's stories show, I argue, is that public and private life are inseparable. Politics is in the home as much as it is in the streets. Whether or not justice can be won in the streets depends upon whether or not it is won in the home, be that home made of tin or brick.

29. See Coetzee's "Farm Novel and Plaasroman" and "The Farm Novels of C. M. van den Heever" in *White Writing,* pp. 63–114.

30. Edward Peters speaks of the paradox of the state's "vast power and infinite vulnerability" in *Torture* (New York: Basil Blackwell, 1985), p. 7.

31. In seeing this story as a precursor of Gordimer's novel *The Conservationist,* Clingman notes that the black body in the story loses its claim to even six feet of

white man's land, but the black body in the novel triumphs over the white weekend farmer, pp. 140–41. Though Coetzee admires the novel as a worthy example of the antipastoral tradition, he questions A. E. Voss's conclusion that Gordimer's novel lays the ghost of the pastoral to rest by bringing the dark side, the black corpse, to light, p. 81. Besides A. E. Voss, "A Generic Approach to the South African Novel in English," *University of Cape Town Studies in English* 7 (1977): 110–19, see also Christopher Hope, "Out of the Picture: The Novels of Nadine Gordimer," *London Magazine* (April/May 1975): 54.

32. Clingman, *The Novels of Nadine Gordimer*, pp. 41–45, 58, 89 et passim.

33. See my essay, "Pleasure and Joy: Political Activism in Nadine Gordimer's Short Stories," *World Literature Today*, 59 (summer 1985): 343–46.

34. JanMohamed, *Manichean Aesthetics*, p. 85.

35. See my essay, "Paley's Community: Gradual Epiphanies in the Meantime," *Politics and the Muse: Studies in the Politics of Recent American Literature*, ed. Adam Sorkin (Bowling Green, Ohio: Bowling Green State University Popular Press, 1989).

36. Adam Mars-Jones, review of *Later the Same Day, Times Literary Supplement*, 22 November 1985, p. 1311.

37. Grace Paley, *The Little Disturbances of Man: Men and Women at Love* (New York: New American Library, 1959), p. 127. I also quote from Paley's other two collections, *Enormous Changes at the Last Minute* (New York: Farrar, Straus and Giroux, 1974) and *Later the Same Day* (New York: Penguin Books, 1986). Subsequent references to Paley's stories, noted in the text by page numbers in parentheses, are from these editions.

38. Like Spivak, I distrust assumptions of essential woman which disregard differences in class, culture, "race," or national laws. See, for example, p. 89 in Spivak's "Feminism and Critical Theory," *In Other Worlds*, pp. 77–92. I argue only that mothers who bear and raise their children in cultures that expect sexual division of labor share certain internal differences. For an examination of critiques of essentialism, see Naomi Schor, "This Essentialism Which Is Not One: Coming to Grips with Irigaray," *Differences*, 1 (spring 1989): 36–58.

39. Blanche Gelfant, "Grace Paley: Fragments for a Portrait in Collage: Settings and Encounters, Real and Imagined," *New England Review* 3 (winter 1980): 276–93 [279].

40. For one discussion of the child-guide, see John W. Crawford, "Archetypal Patterns in Grace Paley's 'Runner,'" *Notes on Contemporary Literature* 11 (September 1981): 10–12.

41. The imagery, broadcast from the moonshot, of the solitary, vulnerable planet elicits hope even in Gordimer's division-worn characters of *The Late Bourgeois World*. The photographs of the Earth from the moon have become emblems of hope for international peace, but a businessman I know observed that he knows people for whom those photographs represent a total market: all of what could be owned or sold captured in a single shot.

42. Susan Sontag, *On Photography* (New York: Farrar, Straus and Giroux, 1977), p. 10.

43. Sontag speaks of photographs as self-consuming, ibid., p. 179.

44. Ibid., p. 19.

45. Sontag writes of Antonioni's *Chung Kuo,* ibid., pp. 168–75.

46. See the argument of José Ortega y Gasset in "The Historical Significance of the Theory of Einstein," *Relativity Theory: Its Origin and Impact on Modern Thought,* ed. L. Pearce Williams (New York: Wiley, 1968), p. 151.

47. John Berger, *Ways of Seeing* (New York: Penguin Books, 1973), p. 33.

48. Sontag paraphrases and quotes from Benjamin in *On Photography,* p. 107.

49. John Berger, *About Looking* (New York: Pantheon Books, 1980), pp. 58–63.

50. Berger, *Ways of Seeing,* p. 153.

51. Edward W. Said, *Orientalism* (New York: Vintage Books, 1978), p. 240.

52. Robert Lowell, "Epilogue," *Day by Day* (New York: Farrar, Straus and Giroux, 1977), p. 127.

CHAPTER FIVE: THEORY, MADNESS, AND THE STATE

1. For an indispensable analysis of Ibuse's career and the place of *Black Rain* in that career, see John Treat, *Pools of Water, Pillars of Fire: The Literature of Ibuse Masuji* (Seattle: University of Washington Press, 1988). Treat points out not only that "Ibuse's standard edition consists of fourteen volumes" and could have been twice as long (ix), but also that the 1980s have produced "a cottage industry of Ibuse studies" in Japan (259). Even a study of those Ibuse works available in English makes evident the fact that *Black Rain* is part of an evolving vision of catastrophe and survival by a prolific and long-lived author and not an isolated phenomenon. In my comparison of *Black Rain* and *Travesty* I cannot consider the complete oeuvre of Ibuse or that of Hawkes, but I am concerned, nevertheless, that my argument not violate those contexts.

I use the Japanese order for Japanese names, family name first. However, in speaking of established artists of earlier centuries and of some especially well-known artists of this one, such as Yoshida Kenkō and Akira Kurasawa, I follow the custom of referring to them by their personal names.

2. Douglas Robinson, *American Apocalypses: The Image of the End of the World in American Literature* (Baltimore: Johns Hopkins University Press, 1985), pp. xi–xii.

3. The differences between, not to mention within, present-day Japan and the United States and how each nation's ideologues choose to present them provoke analyses of all areas of society, areas beyond the scope of my comparison but not my interest. In that spirit I mention two controversial Western analyses—one of politics and the other of economics: Karel van Wolferen's *The Enigma of Japanese Power: People and Politics in a Stateless Nation* (New York: Alfred A. Knopf, 1989) and Clyde V. Prestowitz, Jr.'s *Trading Places: How We Allowed Japan to Take the Lead* (New York: Basic Books, 1988). (Titles like the latter persist whether or not the argument of the book is itself nationalistic.)

4. Treat, *Pools of Water, Pillars of Fire,* p. 212 and note 11 on p. 273.

5. J. Thomas Rimer, *Modern Japanese Fiction and Its Traditions: An Introduction* (Princeton: Princeton University Press, 1978), pp. 68–72.

6. Treat argues throughout his study for the consistency of Ibuse's interest in castaways and survivors.

7. Robert Jay Lifton, *Death in Life: Survivors of Hiroshima* (New York: Basic Books, 1967), p. 553.

8. John T. Dorsey, "The Theme of Survival in John Hersey's *Hiroshima* and Ibuse Masuji's *Black Rain*," *Tamkang Review*, 14 (autumn 1983–summer 1984): 85–100.

9. Rimer, *Modern Japanese Fiction*, p. 250.

10. Brenda Wineapple, "The Travesty of Literalism," *The Journal of Narrative Technique*, 12 (spring 1982): 130–38.

11. Jean-Louis Brunel, "Reading *Travesty*," *Delta*, 22 (February 1986): 149–57 [156].

12. Donald J. Greiner, *Understanding John Hawkes* (Columbia: University of South Carolina Press, 1985), pp. 131 and 135.

13. Patrick O'Donnell, "Self-Alignment: John Hawkes's *Travesty*," *Passionate Doubts: Designs of Interpretation in Contemporary American Fiction* (Iowa City: University of Iowa Press, 1986), p. 39.

14. William F. Van Wert, "Narration in John Hawkes' Trilogy," *The Literary Review*, 24 (fall 1980): 21–39 [38].

15. Thomas LeClair, review of John Hawkes's *Travesty*, *The New Republic*, 8 May 1976, pp. 26–27.

16. Christine Laniel, "The Rhetoric of Excess in John Hawkes's *Travesty*," *The Review of Contemporary Fiction*, 3 (fall 1983): 177–85.

17. Most notable among those who make this argument are Laniel and O'Donnell.

18. Paul Emmett and Richard Vine, "A Conversation with John Hawkes," *Chicago Review*, 28 (1976): 163–71 [169–70]. This passage is quoted by Greiner, *Understanding John Hawkes*, on p. 134.

19. John Hawkes, *Travesty* (New York: New Directions, 1976), p. 128. Subsequent page numbers noted in the text in parentheses refer to this edition.

20. Ibuse Masuji, *Black Rain*, trans. John Bester (New York: Kodansha International, 1969), p. 100. Subsequent page numbers noted in the text in parentheses refer to this edition. John Treat has translated certain passages from *Kuroi Ame*. Where his translation is available and may be critically different from Bester's, I will include it and the page numbers in brackets following Bester's translation.

21. Michel Foucault, *Madness and Civilization: A History of Insanity in the Age of Reason*, trans. Richard Howard (New York: Vintage Books, 1965), p. 78.

22. Charles Baxter, "In the Suicide Seat: Reading John Hawkes's *Travesty*," *The Georgia Review*, 34 (winter 1980): 871–85.

23. Laniel, "The Rhetoric of Excess," p. 178.

24. Foucault, *Madness and Civilization*, pp. 213 and 216.

25. Ibid., p. 27.

26. John Hawkes, *Humors of Blood and Skin: A John Hawkes Reader* (New York: New Directions, 1984), p. 220.

27. Baxter, "In the Suicide Seat," p. 884. My conclusion from Baxter's observa-

tion differs from his own. He asserts that the reader should be more passive in the face of the novel's imagination. I conclude instead that the reader should be less passive, more imaginative herself, and therefore less ignorantly complicit with violence.

28. Foucault, *Madness and Civilization*, pp. 252, 254, and 253.

29. Foucault writes in *Madness and Civilization* that "if . . . we try to assign a value, in and of itself, outside its relation with the dream and with error, to classical unreason, we must understand it not as reason diseased, or as reason lost or alienated, but quite simply as *reason dazzled*. Dazzlement is night in broad daylight, the darkness that rules at the very heart of what is excessive in light's radiance," pp. 107–8.

30. W. S. DiPiero, " 'Design and Debris': John Hawkes's *Travesty*," *The Southern Review*, 13 (winter 1977): 221–23 [222].

31. In Papa's clarity one can hear a parody of Hemingway's. For example, the first sentence of Hemingway's "In Another Country," "In the fall the war was always there, but we did not go to it any more," may be heard in Papa's words, "The war of course. That is another story. Perhaps we shall get to it," p. 26. One can also hear Gertrude Stein's obsessive simplicity *qua* absurdity such as in this echo of Stein's *Ida:* "I am always moving. I am forever transporting myself somewhere else. I am never exactly where I am," p. 75.

32. Foucault, *Madness and Civilization*, pp. 15–16.

33. Ibid., pp. 115–16.

34. Elaine Scarry, *The Body in Pain: The Making and Unmaking of the World* (New York: Oxford University Press, 1985), pp. 35–36.

35. Carol Gluck, *Japan's Modern Myths: Ideology in the Late Meiji Period* (Princeton: Princeton University Press, 1985), p. 101. Contrary to conventional Western opinion, Gluck argues that Meiji ideologies succeeded in making the emperor a ubiquitous human presence whose face all Japanese recognized but not in making him a figure of mystical power. He and the locomotive were very concrete symbols.

36. Lifton, *Death in Life*, pp. 7, 394, 277–78, and 553, respectively.

37. Foucault, *Madness and Civilization*, p. 74.

38. Jacques Derrida, "No Apocalypse, Not Now (full speed ahead, seven missiles, seven missives)," trans. Catherine Porter and Philip Lewis, *Diacritics*, 14 (summer 1984): 20–31.

39. In *Minds at War: Nuclear Reality and the Inner Conflicts of Defense Policymakers* (New York: Basic Books, 1988), Steven Kull interviews defense experts and thus compiles in one book language we are accustomed to seeing and hearing in the media whenever the issue of nuclear weapons is raised. Kull analyzes the arguments and the inner conflicts—internal difference—of those he has interviewed.

40. Robert Jay Lifton with Richard Falk, *Indefensible Weapons: The Political and Psychological Case Against Nuclearism* (New York: Basic Books, 1982), p. 95.

41. Sander L. Gilman, *Difference and Pathology: Stereotypes of Sexuality, Race, and Madness* (Ithaca: Cornell University Press, 1985).

42. Gluck, *Japan's Modern Myths,* p. 39 et passim.

43. Ibuse Masuji, "Lieutenant Lookeast" and "Carp," in *Salamander and Other Stories,* trans. John Bester (New York: Kodansha International, 1981).

44. Gluck, *Japan's Modern Myths,* p. 246, and van Wolferen, *The Enigma of Japanese Power,* throughout. The monolithic and long-standing power of the Liberal Democratic Party, which van Wolferen describes, is being challenged for the first time in decades primarily by the Japan Socialist Party and its woman leader, Takako Doi.

45. On this point Treat and I seem to differ. He argues throughout his book that Ibuse sees in nature, as in history, an inevitability which is to be recorded and survived. However, Treat also notes how much of Ibuse's writing shows the effects of the state's folly on the Japanese common person. Ibuse's castaways are all victims of the state's contradictions, even the lucky John Manjiro.

46. O'Donnell, "Self-Alignment," pp. 23, 35, and 39.

47. Laniel, "The Rhetoric of Excess," p. 184.

48. Greiner, *Understanding John Hawkes,* p. 131.

49. William Gass, Introduction to *Humors of Blood and Skin,* p. xvi.

50. Thomas LeClair, "The Novelists: John Hawkes," *The New Republic,* 10 November 1979, pp. 26–29 [27].

51. Barbara Johnson, "Les Fleurs du Mal Armé: Some Reflections on Intertextuality," *A World of Difference* (Baltimore: Johns Hopkins University Press, 1987), pp. 116–33 [123].

52. Robert Scholes, Introduction to *The Owl* by John Hawkes (1954; New York: New Directions, 1977), p. vii. Greiner quotes this passage in *Understanding John Hawkes,* p. 23.

53. Baxter, "In the Suicide Seat," p. 872.

54. Yoshida Kenkō, "Essays in Idleness," trans. G. B. Sansom, in Donald Keene, ed., *Anthology of Japanese Literature* (New York: Grove Press, 1955), p. 232. Rimer quotes this passage in *Modern Japanese Fiction,* p. 205. Rimer first defines *mono no aware* on p. 14 but throughout his book seeks to explain the rich history and complexity of the concept.

55. Ōe Kenzaburō, "Japan's Dual Identity: A Writer's Dilemma," *World Literature Today,* 62 (summer 1988): 359–69 [365]; reprinted in *Postmodernism and Japan,* eds. Masao Miyoshi and H. D. Harootunian (Durham, North Carolina: Duke University Press, 1989), pp. 189–213. In "The Metaphysics of Translation and the Origins of Symbolist Poetics in Meiji Japan," *PMLA,* 105 (March 1990): 256–72, Earl Jackson, Jr., argues that the ideas of metaphysics and transcendence in Western philosophic and poetic texts were outside the thought and very language of Japan when these texts were introduced in the Meiji period (1868–1912) and the following Taishō years (1912–25). Jackson's meticulous argument seems to me pertinent to Ibuse's nontranscendent theory in *Black Rain* and Ōe's doubts about the relevance of current Western theory for Japanese culture.

56. Theodor Adorno, *Negative Dialectics,* trans. E. B. Ashton (New York: Continuum Publishing Company, 1973), p. 364.

57. In writing of this passage, Treat notes the frequency with which ponds of

death recur in Ibuse's work. Indeed, Treat emphasizes these pools of water in his own title.

58. David Aylward and Anthony Liman, the translators of Ibuse's *Isle-on-the-Billows* in *Waves: Two Short Novels* (New York: Kodansha International, 1986), note this connection to the Japanese flag on p. 113. The passage in the novel describing the image is on pp. 141–42.

59. Treat, *Pools of Water, Pillars of Fire*, pp. 239–40.

60. Adorno, *Negative Dialectics*, pp. 407–8.

61. Thom Gunn, "The Annihilation of Nothing," *Moly and My Sad Captains* (New York: Farrar, Straus and Giroux, 1973), p. 53.

Index

Permissions

This book has been set in Linotron Galliard. Galliard was designed for Merganthaler in 1978 by Matthew Carter. Galliard retains many of the features of a sixteenth century typeface cut by Robert Granjon but has some modifications which give it a more contemporary look.

Printed on acid-free paper.